ECONOMICS

Principles and Applications

Fifth Edition

Rolando A. Santos

Lakeland Community College

Kendall Hunt

publishing company

Cover images © 2016 Corel/Shutterstock.com

Previously titled *Introduction to Economics: Notes and Workbook*

Kendall Hunt
publishing company

www.kendallhunt.com
Send all inquiries to:
4050 Westmark Drive
Dubuque, IA 52004-1840

Copyright © 2008, 2010, 2013, 2016 by Kendall Hunt Publishing Company
Copyright © 2003 by Rolando Santos

PAK ISBN: 978-1-4652-9518-7
Text ISBN: 978-1-4652-9519-4

Printed in the United States of America

CONTENTS

PREFACE AND ACKNOWLEDGEMENTS

The purpose of this book is to give students taking Introductory Economics and Principles of Macroeconomics an insight into the understanding of the basic concepts in economics. As a college professor, I understand the difficulty students have grasping these abstract economic concepts. This book gives basic guidelines to understanding concepts in economics and applies its principles through examination of various current events happening in the global economy. Exercises and conceptual problems at the end of each chapter assess the student's comprehension of the core concepts.

This book is revised from the 2003 edition. As a result of the recent events in the global economy, I have added a few articles relevant to each chapter. I also included articles and notes on the recent financial crisis in the United States and the global markets. In this way, we can connect each economic concept to the real world. I also added a couple of sections related to the "economic way of thinking." The study of economics is relevant to all aspects of our lives. It is the study of human behavior and the consequences of our choices. It is also the study of how the global economic systems are interrelated.

I would like to thank Brian Yager, my research assistant, for his research, editing, and contributions to the different aspects of this book. I would also like to thank my past students, who helped me improve my manuscript. This book is a never-ending project because there is always something that we can improve on. I would also like to thank Lakeland Community College in Kirtland, Ohio, for all the support that the college gave me in this project. I would like to thank the staff of Kendall/Hunt for making this project happen again.

Dr. Rolando A. Santos
Professor of Economics
Lakeland Community College

SUGGESTED WAY OF USING THIS BOOK

For faculty who are interested in teaching this book as a survey course, a brief chapter on cost and production (Chapter 4) and market structure (Chapter 5) is included to look at a brief survey of microeconomics. Faculty should minimize the quantitative aspects of aggregate demand analysis especially on Chapters 10 and 11 (Fiscal Policy). Suggested topics for a survey course:

1. Production Possibility Curves (Chapter 2)
2. Demand and Supply (Chapter 3)
3. Cost and Production (Chapter 4)
4. National Income Accounting (Chapter 7)
5. Inflation (Chapter 8)
6. Unemployment and Business Cycles (Chapter 9)
7. Aggregate Demand/Supply (Chapter 10)
8. Fiscal Policy (Chapter 11)
9. Money and Banking (Chapters 12 and 13)
10. International Trade and Finance (Chapters 14 and 15)

For faculty who are interested in using this book as a macroeconomics course, one can exclude Chapters 4 and 5. The rest of the chapters are classic topics in economics. One of the unique elements of this book is the inclusion of current economic events and policies that are still being tested, such as the Fed's bailout program and ways to get rid of toxic assets from the bank's financial institutions.

Suggested topics and chapters for a Principles in Macroeconomics course are:

1. Production Possibility Curve (Chapter 2)
2. Demand and Supply (Chapter 3)
3. National Income Accounting (Chapter 7)
4. Inflation (Chapter 8)
5. Unemployment and Business Cycles (Chapter 9)
6. Aggregate Demand/Supply/Equilibrium (Chapter 10)
7. Fiscal Policy (Chapter 11)
8. Money and Banking (Chapter 12)
9. Monetary Policy (Chapter 13)
10. International Trade and Finance (Chapters 14 and 15)

ABOUT THE AUTHOR

Rolando A. Santos is a full professor of economics at Lakeland Community College in Mentor, Ohio. He received his PhD in economics from Northeastern University in Boston, Massachusetts, and dual masters' degrees in economics and international studies from Ohio University in Athens, Ohio. His global teaching and academic experience has encompassed the Philippines, France, Slovak Republic, Croatia, Romania, Australia, China, and the United States. He has written numerous academic papers on topics related to international finance particularly on the Asian foreign exchange market and financial crisis. He received various grant awards, including a Title 6B grant in business in an international education program. He also has done various consulting projects in Northeast Ohio region in both academic and business settings. Dr. Santos was also active in the Philippine American Chamber of Commerce in Northeast Ohio and the Ohio Asian American Chamber of Commerce. He is also an adjunct professor at Cleveland State University and John Carroll University.

Chapter 1

Introduction

Anton Prado PHOTO/Shutterstock.com

OBJECTIVES

1. To understand the definition of economics.
2. To explain the difference between microeconomics and macroeconomics.
3. To explain the different ways of analyzing economics.
4. To explain the difference between factor and product market.
5. To explain the concept of model from an economic perspective.
6. To discuss the implication of making an assumption of ceteris paribus.

People continually face important decisions in their everyday lives. For example, as a student you have a choice of reading this textbook or watching a television show like *American Idol*. Or, perhaps, taking this course for a semester or working to make money. No matter what we do in life, there will always be a choice between alternatives that we must decide on. Despite all alternatives, we can choose only one option at a time. We make our choice based on constraints. Our resources are scarce. Therefore, we usually opt for the best alternative given our scarce resources.

Economics is a social science that deals with the allocation of scarce resources given unlimited wants. It is a social science because economics—unlike natural sciences such as biology, physics, and chemistry—deals with human interaction and everyday life. It is not a science in the sense that all experimentation is based on a controlled observation. Because economics focuses on human interaction, there is always a sense of uncertainty when dealing with economic issues. Economics can also be based on unknown shocks that can happen in any or almost any economic phenomena.

There are two basic issues in the study of economics. One is "scarce resources," and the other is "unlimited wants." Scarce resources means that **supply** is fixed, and "unlimited wants" means that **demand** is unlimited. Put simply, economics is the study of demand and supply.

Basic Branches of Economics

1. **Microeconomics**—the study of individual economic activity. Microeconomics pertains to the study of individual economic behavior, the theory of the firm and the industry. Individual economic behavior pertains to decision making in terms of consumption. Your decision to take an economics class rather than to work full time is an example of a microeconomic decision. Microeconomics also includes topics such as cost analysis and production. Issues that deal with output maximization and cost minimization are within the realm of microeconomics.

2. **Macroeconomics**—the study of aggregate economic activity. Macroeconomics deals with the study of gross domestic product (GDP), inflation, unemployment, interest rates and government policies. Macroeconomics looks at the overall economic performance of a country. It also extends its analysis to the microeconomic foundation of macroeconomics and international trade.

Basic Approaches in Economics

There are two ways of analyzing economics:

1. **Positive Economics**—pertains to analyzing factual or "what is" issues of economics. For example, the law of demand states

that as price of a commodity goes up, the quantity demanded decreases. This is a law that no one can refute. Therefore, this is a factual statement. The concept of positive economics can be linked to the study of philosophy. In philosophy, we have a "positive" statement. This, again, pertains to factual statements.

2. **Normative Economics**—pertains to analyzing opinions or "what is ought to be" issues of economics. For example, if former Representative Barney Frank says, "We should increase taxes," then what he is saying is an opinion or value-laden proposition.

Factors of Production

In any economic system, production cannot be attained without factors of production. Factors of production refers to the different elements that are needed to produce final products. The elements that make up the different factors of production are: **land, labor, capital and entrepreneurship.** We designate the price for land as **rent**, the price for labor as **wages**, the price for capital as **interest rate,** and the price for entrepreneurship as **profits.**

We often confuse labor and entrepreneurship in our daily lives. Labor refers to physical skills, and entrepreneurship deals with mental skills. Anyone who works with an employer is considered to be labor. Entrepreneurship, on the other hand, deals with the ability to innovate a business or invent a product. It is a skill that not everyone has innately or can develop. If an entrepreneur becomes successful, then he acquires profits. However, if an entrepreneur fails, she can lose her personal assets because of the venture.

Another important variable studied in economics is the interest rate. By definition, the interest rate represents the cost of capital. In the credit market, the interest rate refers to the cost of borrowing money. When the interest rate increases, it costs more to borrow money, decreasing the demand for capital.

Ceteris Paribus Concept

In economics, the concept of **ceteris paribus** is commonly used to signify "all things being equal." Economic realities are based on the fact that there are numerous factors that can affect an economic variable. For example, an increase in demand for a given commodity can be caused by factors such as an increase in personal income, changes in prices of related commodities, changes in expectations, and much more. When using the concept of ceteris paribus, we allow for a change in only one factor at a time. For example, the statement "an increase in demand for a given commodity can be caused by an increase in personal income and nothing more" is an application of this ceteris paribus concept, in that we assume all other factors that can affect the demand of a commodity remain constant.

Economic Models

Economic models are simplified representations of economic phenomena. Models are used to understand the relationship between economic variables. In most models we try to focus on two variables and their relationships. In these kinds of models we use a linear representation. In cases where we use multiple variables to explain another economic variable, then nonlinear representations are more appropriate.

Econometrics is the methodology in economics that applies statistical methods to the empirical study of economic theories and relationships. It is a combination of mathematical economics, statistics, and economic theory. Where macroeconomics and microeconomics provide general theories, econometrics attempts to quantify and apply those theories. For example, as you progress in your study of economics, you will learn that as the price of a good increases, the supply of that good also increases while demand decreases. Econometrics attempts to answer the "by how much" question that many economics students ponder as they learn the general theory. A more specific example would be to ask, "How much would a $1 tax increase on cigarettes affect a smoker's choice to purchase cigarettes?"

In order to establish a model, we start with establishing a functional relationship between two economic variables. For example:

$$Q = f(L)$$

This is an economic model relating production as a function of labor. Simply put, production of goods depends on labor. In this model, **L,** or **labor,** is a dependent variable and **Q,** or **output,** is an independent variable.

Economists often use graphs to illustrate economic relations. Graphs are like pictures. They are visual aids that communicate valuable information in a small amount of space. A picture may be worth a thousand words, but only to a person who understands the picture and the graph.

It is also important to note here that correlation does not cause causation. Correlation measures the strength of the relationship between two variables. This means that just because there is a correlation between two variables, one variable does not necessarily cause the other one. For example, there is a correlation between the size of a city's police force and the amount of crime it has. An illogical statement would then be that the more police a city hires, the more crime will occur. There are other factors that cause crime, which this statement does not examine. However, it would be logical to say that an increase in crime usually causes a city to hire more police in order to make the city a safer community. Knowing the difference between these statements is important to figuring out problems and how to address them. If a city did not understand the difference between correlation and causation, they could reduce the amount of police in hopes of reducing crime, and as a consequence, the crime rate would increase.

Functional relationships can also be shown graphically to show their linear relationships. For example,

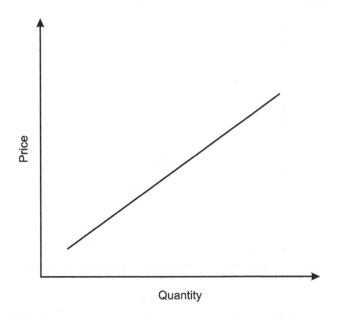

In this model, we see there is a positive relationship between the two economic variables. If X and Y show a positive relationship, then they are directly related. If X increases, then Y increases as well. For example, other things being equal, when price increases, quantity supplied increases.

If the graphical relationship between X and Y is as follows, it means that X and Y are negatively or inversely related.

With an inverse relationship, when X increases, Y decreases. For example, the law of demand shows a negative relationship between prices and quantity demanded. All things being equal, when price of a given product goes up, the quantity demanded decreases.

Economic Theories

A theory is an established explanation that accounts for known facts or phenomena. Specifically, economic theories are statements or propositions about patterns of human behavior that are expected to take place under certain circumstances. These theories help us to sort out and understand the complexities of economic behavior. People ask many things of theories. But most of all, we expect a good theory to explain and predict well. Therefore, a good economic theory should help us to better understand and, ideally, predict human economic behavior.

Economic theories cannot realistically include every event that has ever occurred. This is true for the same reason that a newspaper or history book does not include every world event that has ever happened.

We must abstract. A road map of the United States may not include every creek, ridge, and gully from Los Angeles to Chicago—indeed, such a map would be too large to be of value—but it will provide enough information for a traveler to reach Chicago if traveling by car from Los Angeles.

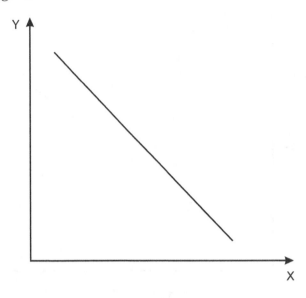

The beginning of any theory is a hypothesis, a testable proposition that makes some type of prediction about behavior in response to changed conditions. A hypothesis in economic theory is a testable prediction about how people will behave or react to a change in economic circumstances.

What Do Economists Do?

Just as there are different branches of economics, there are several different types of economists. Some economists work in the private sector, such as with banks or corporations. Others work in the public sector with government agencies such as the Federal Reserve (also known as "the Fed"), the Bureau of Economic Analysis (BEA), and the Bureau of Labor Statistics (BLS). There are many fields in economics in which economists work, study, and specialize in. Some of these fields include:

1. **Money and Banking**—as you might guess, economists who work in the money and banking system work with banks on different projects. Such projects include analyzing the lending and credit markets, forecasting, monetary policy, inflation, the Federal Reserve System.

2. **Health Care**—economists working in the health care field use economic analysis to understand and evaluate what is happening to the health care profession and current health care policies under consideration. Health care economists may

analyze such topics as Medicare, Medicaid, health care reform, HMOs, and the costs of health care.

3. **Education**—economists in this field analyze current issues with primary, secondary, and higher education from a micro-economic perspective. Economists may analyze topics such as education reform, educational finance (i.e., analysis between private vs. public schools), and efficient production of education.

4. **Industrial Organization**—economists specializing in indus-trial organization examine the structure, operation, and perfor-mance of industrial markets from a theoretical and empirical perspective. Major issues such as antitrust regulation is ana-lyzed in industrial organization.

5. **Public Finance/Public Policy**—economists specializing in the public finance/policy field examine public (government) expenditure and taxation policies, public goods, collective decision making, cost–benefit analysis, equity and efficiency aspects of taxation, and current government policy issues.

6. **International Economics**—those specializing in international economics focus on either international trade (a micro-conomic analysis) or international finance (a macroeconomic analysis). International trade focuses on policy issues such as free trade areas, international trade organizations, current issues in international trade, and the effect of international trade on domestic policy. International finance, on the other hand, focuses on the international monetary relations between nations, including the determination of exchange rates, man-aged exchange rate policies, balance of payment crises, opti-mum currency areas, and international capital flows.

7. **Experimental Economics**—a field that is becoming increas-ingly popular in the realm of economics. It has only recently emerged (in the 1990s) and uses experimental methods to evaluate theoretical predictions of economic behavior. Experi-mental economics seeks to control causative factors in order to provide better *ceteris paribus* (all things equal) comparisons between situations.

8. **Game Theory**—another popular field in economics that stud-ies the strategic interactions among agents, used in economic models where the numbers of interacting agents (such as firms, governments, individuals, etc.) are small enough that each has a perceptible influence on the others. Game theory attempts to mathematically capture behavior in strategic situations, where an individual's success in making choices depends on the choices of others.

9. **Environmental Economics**—concerned with environmental issues, such as regulating and taxing pollution. More specifically, it focuses on market failure and externalities. Environmental economists also focus on environmental sustainability and resource management.

References

Boyes, M., & Melvin, M. *Economics test bank*. Boston: Houghton Mifflin.

Duy, T. *Principles of macroeconomics test bank item file* (5th ed.). Case and Fair Supplement. Upper Saddle River, NJ: Prentice Hall.

Mabry, R., & Ulbrich, H. M. (1994). *Economics test bank and instructors manual* (2nd ed.). Boston: Houghton Mifflin.

How Much Gold Do Investors Need? Zero Should Suffice

Jack Hough

After sliding 6% in May, the price of gold jumped 3.7% on Friday. Skeptics say it is a temporary rise in a longer downturn. Fans of the metal say it is the start of another glorious run.

Picking a side is pointless. Gold defies efforts to calculate its worth—or even to describe how it behaves as an investment. That means there isn't a clear reason to invest in it.

If you must own some gold to sleep better, stick with a multivitamin approach: A little bit won't hurt. A lot can prove toxic.

Gold is prone to long booms and busts. Before its latest dip, it multiplied five times in value over a decade, mocking stocks and other investments. Before that, it lost money for 20 years.

Some investors look to gold as a safe haven. It is one—but only when it wants to be. Just over two years ago, when investors learned that Greece's deficits were much larger than officials there had reported, the metal followed U.S. Treasurys higher while Greek government bonds crashed.

Yet last month, with Greece's fiscal crisis intensifying, Greek government bonds again tumbled while U.S. Treasurys rose, but this time investors dumped gold.

To study how gold behaves, we asked **FactSet Research Systems** to analyze the metal's short-term correlation with two other investments: the 10-year Treasury note, representing safe havens, and the Standard & Poor's 500 stock index, representing risk.

"Correlation" is a measure of how closely two assets track each other. A reading of 1.0 means they trade in lock-step, while zero means they are independent and a reading of minus-1.0 means they act like opposites.

What did FactSet find? Chaos, The correlation between gold and the 10-year Treasury has jumped above 0.6 at some points, over the past five years and has fallen below minus-0.8 during others, changing direction several times. The one between gold and stocks has had similar spasms, with the highs topping 0.9.

In other words, gold might suffer from a multiple personality disorder.

Some investors say gold is a hedge against inflation. That is true of any good or service that consumers can be counted on to want in coming years, such as oil or poultry farms. Gold's wild swings have made it a poor proxy for the consumer-price index, a key inflation measure.

Perhaps that is because only 12% of gold's demand comes from industrial applications, according to the World Gold Council, a trade group. The rest comes from jewelry and investment (and the divide between those two isn't always clear).

Still others view gold as "real money"—the one thing that will hold its value it governments create so much new currency that those currencies lose their value. Taken to its logical conclusion, this means governments would eventually agree to once again use gold as the basis for their currencies, says James Swanson, chief investment strategist at MFS, a mutual-fund company.

That is a fantasy, he argues, because some powerful nations have relatively little gold and some gold-rich nations have little power.

So how much is gold really worth? With stocks, bonds, rental houses and Laundromats, one way to answer that question is to compare the purchase price with expected cash flow. But gold doesn't generate any cash. Indeed, it costs something to store it.

Investors sometimes use the cost of producing the world's next ounce of gold as an approximate floor for its price. That cost is between $1,200 and $1,400 now, depending on the efficiency of the mine, reckons Michael Dudas, a mining-stock analyst at investment bank Sterne Agee. Gold sold for $1,620.50 an ounce on Friday.

There is a catch, however: The cost of mining gold has followed the price of gold higher, as mining firms have bid up machine prices and countries with plenty of gold underground have raised the royalties they charge to miners, Mr. Dudas says. If production costs are a floor for gold's price, the floor is made of straw, not concrete.

Of course, gold's price is ultimately based on supply and demand, and demand has surely soared over the past decade. Exchange-traded funds such as **SPDR Gold Shares** and **iShares Gold Trust** have made gold investing easier than ever. Gold-coin pitchmen have played off the angst and distrust left by a global financial crisis.

But ultimately, as Mr. Swanson puts it, you need a psychology book rather than a calculator to decide how to trade gold, and that means you shouldn't rely on it to do anything specific.

Investors who are determined to stock up on gold following May's dip might wish to give gold stocks a look instead. Year to date, gold's price is up 3.5%, but the **Market Vectors Gold Miners** ETF has fallen 9.4%.

Adrian Day, an Annapolis, Md., money manager overseeing $170 million, says gold miners look unusually cheap relative to the size of their gold reserves. Joseph Foster, manager of the **Van Eck International**

Investors Gold fund, can place fund assets in either gold or mining shares. He says he heavily favors the latter now.

Mr. Foster's top holdings include **Randgold Resources** and **New Gold**. Sterne Agee's Mr. Dudas issued buy recommendations on **Newmont Mining** and **Gold Resource** last month.

For investors who won't feel comfortable without having some physical gold within easy reach, one last piece of advice: Forget about Krugerrands. Buy your spouse something expensive, lovely and high-carat.

That way, even if gold disappoints, at least someone will be happy.

Economics after the crisis
New model army

Efforts are Under Way to Improve Macroeconomic Models

THE models that dismal scientists use to represent the way the economy works are sometimes found wanting. The Depression of the 1930s and the "stagflation" of the 1970s both forced rethinks. The financial crisis has sparked another.

The crisis showed that the standard macroeconomic models used by central bankers and other policymakers, which go by the catchy name of "dynamic stochastic general equilibrium" (DSGE) models, neither represent the financial system accurately nor allow for the booms and busts observed in the real world. A number of academics are trying to fix these failings.

Their first task is to put banks into the models. Today's mainstream macro models contain a small number of "representative agents", such as a household, a non-financial business and the government, but no banks. They were omitted because macroeconomists thought of them as a simple "veil" between savers and borrowers, rather than profit-seeking firms that make loans opportunistically and may themselves affect the economy.

This perspective has changed, to put it mildly. Hyun Song Shin of Princeton University has shown that banks' internal risk models make them take more and more risk as asset prices rise, for instance. Yale's John Geanakopols has long argued that small changes in the willingness of creditors to lend against a given asset can have large effects on that asset's price. Easy lending terms allow speculators with little cash to bid up prices far above their fundamental value. If lenders become more conservative, these marginal buyers are forced out of the market, causing prices to tumble.

Realistically representing the financial sector would help solve the other big problem with mainstream macro models: that they are inherently stable unless disturbed from the outside. This feature is helpful when studying how an economy in "equilibrium" responds to things like a spike in the price of petrol, but it limits economists' understanding of why economies expand and contract in the absence of such external shocks. Highly leveraged financial firms with portfolios of risky assets are bound to upend an economy every so often. Having banks in models would generate shocks from within the system.

The world's big central banks are interested in these new ideas, although staff economists are reluctant to abandon existing "industry-standard" models. If any central bank is likely to experiment, however, it is the European Central Bank, thanks to its "two-pillar approach" to assessing the risks of price stability. The ecb pays as much attention to "monetary analysis", which includes things like bank lending and money creation, as to "economic analysis", which is more concerned with things like inflation and joblessness.

Improving DSGE models is the obvious way to take the lessons of the crisis on board. But others exist too. "Agent-based modelling" tries to depict the transactions that might occur in an actual economy. These models are populated by millions of agents that gradually alter the economy as they interact with each other. The idea was developed in the 1990s when biologists wanted to study the behaviour of ant colonies and the flocking of birds. But modelling an entire economy did not become practical until recently because of the sheet number of calculations needed.

The evolutionary structure of agent-based models allows economists to study how bubbles and crises occur over time. For example, an increase in bank lending means more spending and therefore higher returns on existing investment, which in turn encourages further lending. But too much lending can prompt the central bank to raise rates if inflation starts to accelerate. Higher borrowing costs could lead to a wave of defaults and even to a crisis if too much debt was taken on during the boom.

The EURACE project, an initiative by a consortium of European research bodies, has produced a sophisticated agent-based model of the EU's economy that scholars have used to model everything from labour-market liberalisation to the effects of quantitative easing. In Australia Steve Keen, an economist, and Russell Standish, a computational scientists, are developing a software package that would allow anyone to create and play with models of the economy that incorporate some of these new ideas. Called "Minsky"—after Hyman Minsky, an American economic celebrated for his work on boom-and-bust financial cycles—it places the banking system at the centre of the economy.

A long road lies ahead, however. "Nobody has got something so convincing that the mainstream has to put up its hands and surrender," says Paul Ormerod, a British economist. No model yet produces the frequent small recessions, punctuated by rare depressions, seen in reality. But "ultimately," Mr Shin says, "macro is an empirical subject." It cannot forever remain "impervious to the facts".

Definitions

1. Macroeconomics

2. Economics

3. Microeconomics

4. Positive economics

5. Normative economics

6. Factors of production

7. Ceteris paribus

8. Positive relationship

9. Negative relationship

10. Econometrics

Multiple Choice

1. Economics is best defined as the study of
   a. how to make cash.
   b. how people attempt to maximize their satisfaction.
   c. how prices are set.
   d. how people can allocate scarce resources among unlimited wants.
   e. how firms attempt to maximize their profits, given some production targets.

2. Which of the following is a microeconomic problem or issue?
   a. the growth of GDP per capita
   b. inflation rate
   c. the price of bread
   d. the level of interest rates
   e. none of the above

3. Which of the following is not a resource?
   a. capital
   b. labor
   c. land
   d. the government
   e. entrepreneurial activity

4. Macroeconomics is primarily concerned with
   a. aggregate economic activity.
   b. unemployment in a particular firm or industry caused by mechanization and automation.
   c. how an individual decides when purchasing a particular commodity.
   d. what and how to produce a particular good.
   e. goods a nation should produce in the world economy.

5. Which of the following is a positive statement?
   a. Increased funding for AIDS program is the most important priority for government spending this year.
   b. Inflation is too low.
   c. Women should be paid the same wages as men if they have the same qualifications and responsibilities.
   d. The poverty rate is higher than it was 10 years ago.
   e. The distribution of income in this country is unfair.

6. The *ceteris paribus* assumption means
   a. in the short run.
   b. all things being equal.
   c. people behave like practical economists.
   d. in a market economy.
   e. resources are scarce.

7. Which of the following is a macroeconomic goal?
   a. price stability
   b. efficiency
   c. economic freedom
   d. equity
   e. all of the above

8. Microeconomics is the study of
   a. unemployment rates and GDP growth rates.
   b. decision making by specific individuals.
   c. decision making by the average individual or firm.
   d. how the government affects individuals.
   e. how economic activity is organized differently in different countries.

9. Normative economics pertains to
   a. "what is" or factual statements.
   b. "what is ought to be" or opinions.
   c. laws such as the law of demand.
   d. theories such as the theory of supply.
   e. none of the above.

10. Economic models
    a. are useful simplifications of the real world.
    b. are useless because they are oversimplified.
    c. are too abstract for the average person to understand.
    d. allow economists to make predictions about average behavior.
    e. both a and d are correct.

True/False

Directions: For the following statements, indicate whether the statement is true or false. If the statement is false, make the necessary change(s) in order for it to be a true statement.

1. Economics is a natural science that focuses on the study of human interaction based on limited wants and limited resources.

2. Factors of production refer to different elements required to produce final products and are made up of land, labor, wages, and government.

3. Entrepreneurship refers to manual skills and labor refers to mental skills such as innovation.

4. The interest rate, by definition, is the cost of borrowing money; therefore, when the interest rate increases, it costs more to borrow money.

5. With the concept of ceteris paribus, we are able to study several economic factors or variables at once.

6. Economic models and graphs are simplified representations of different economic phenomena and relations.

7. If you are given a model that has a positive relationship, then the two economic variables X and Y are inversely related.

8. Economic theories are statements or propositions about patterns of human behavior that are expected to take place under all circumstances; they are established explanations that account for known facts.

9. The beginning of any theory is a gathering of data that allows for testing and allows for some type of prediction about behavior in response to changed conditions.

Essay Questions

1. "The government should provide goods such as health care, education, and highways because it can provide them for free." Is this statement true or false? Explain your answer.

2. "Individuals who economize are missing the point of life. Money is not so important that it should rule the way we live." Evaluate this statement.

3. "I examined the statistics for our basketball team's wins last year and found that when the third team played more, the winning margin increased. If the coach played the third team more, we would win by a bigger margin." Evaluate this statement.

4. What is the difference between macroeconomics and microeconomics?

5. How do economists use the ceteris paribus assumption?

6. Discuss the difference between positive and negative relationships between economic variables.

7. From the eight types of specialized fields outlined in "What Do Economists Do," explain one of the fields and why you believe it is relevant or important today.

Chapter 2

Production Possibility Curves

Katrina Brown/Shutterstock.com

OBJECTIVES

1. To define the implications of scarcity in an economic system.
2. To define the meaning of production possibility curves.
3. To understand the economic implication of the production possibility curve model.
4. To discuss the economic importance of the law of increasing opportunity cost.
5. To understand the application of a production possibility curve in the business world.

Because of **scarcity**, certain economic questions must be answered regardless of the level of affluence of a society or its political structure. Some of the basic questions that an economy faces include the following: (1) What and how much should we produce? (2) How will we produce these goods and services? (3) Who will get the goods and services we produce? (4) How can we use our scarce resources efficiently? (5) Will current sacrifices necessary for more rapid economic growth be worth the gains that growth will offer future generations? These questions are unavoidable under the circumstances of scarcity.

In order to decide what to produce and in what quantities, we use a simple model called a **production possibility curve.** This model illustrates an economy's potential for allocating its limited resources to producing various combinations of goods.

Production Possibility Curves (PPC)

A production possibility curve is a curve showing possible combinations of goods that an economy can produce given a fixed amount of resources, fixed technology, and efficient use of these resources.

Let us assume that the United States produces only two goods: food and clothing. This is one way of simplifying, and it shows how an economy can divide the different modes of production. If we classify the modes of production between different countries, we can separate them into two groups. Either they are producing agricultural products or manufacturing products. Third-world countries generally produce agricultural products. One reason for the focus on agricultural products is a more labor-intensive factor of production. On the other hand, first-world countries generally produce manufacturing products. Most first-world countries are abundant with capital resources. Therefore, it is more efficient for first-world countries to produce capital resources.

Assume that the United States is given the following production possibility schedule:

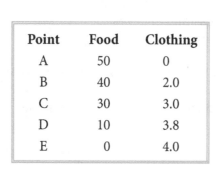

Point	Food	Clothing
A	50	0
B	40	2.0
C	30	3.0
D	10	3.8
E	0	4.0

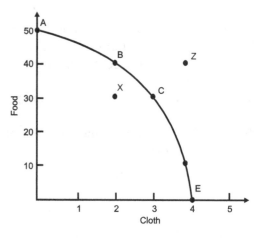

Plotting the points, we have a nonlinear curve called a production possibility curve. The shape of the curve is "concave from the point of origin." As long as the economy is producing along the curve, we consider each production combination to be efficient. By efficient, we mean that the production mix is such that it is maximizing all the resources available in the economy. If we have a point, say point X, which is inside the production possibility curve, then we consider this point as inefficient. One implication of such a point is that the economy is under-employing its resources. For example, if the United States is producing 30 units of food and 2 units of clothing, it can produce an additional unit of food or clothing without losing any production of either good. Points, such as point Z, which are outside of the production possibility curve, are considered unattainable. This point is unattainable because the United States does not have resources to produce both 40 units of food and 4 of clothing.

In summary, as long as the economy produces along the curve, the economy is maximizing its resources. It is important to **maximize resources** because goods are being produced most efficiently. However, as we move along the curve, there is a cost in obtaining more of one commodity relative to another—that is, as we move along the curve, the cost involved is relative to how much we give up of the other good. The cost related to movement along the production possibility curve is what we call an **opportunity cost.** An opportunity cost is the benefits we forgo for the best alternative resource. In our model, it is what we give up in order to gain some other goods that we wanted to acquire. For example, if the United States is currently producing 50 units of food and 0 clothing (point A) and wishes to produce 2 more units of clothing (point B), it must give up 10 units of food. In order to calculate opportunity cost for clothing, we divide the loss of food by the gain of clothing. In our example we will divide 10 (loss of food) by 2 (gain in clothing), which will give us 5. This means for every one clothing we gain, we lose 10 food.

The fact that the production possibility curve is "concave from the point of origin," implies that it follows the law of increasing opportunity cost. The law of increasing opportunity cost states that as we gain more of one commodity, we have to give up more of the other commodity. It also implies that there is always a cost in doing something else.

Simply put, opportunity cost is the cost of gaining one commodity relative to another commodity. The concept of opportunity cost can be applied in many contexts. A good example can be the time spent in studying economics. At this point in time, you could be working or watching TV instead of reading your economics textbook. The cost of reading your economics book can be the time not spent elsewhere. One basic assumption in the concept of opportunity cost is the fact that there is always a trade-off in doing anything.

Opportunity Cost

The concept of opportunity cost is one of the most important topics in economics. As previously defined, it is the benefits we forgo for the best alternative resource. In any decision-making process, there will always be some cost involved. For example, a working person can choose between staying at home with the family or working full time. Given the time constraint, the working person can only do so much, so must choose between time spent with the family and full-time work. If he or she chooses to work, the opportunity cost involved is the foregone time spent with the family. If the working person chooses to stay at home to be with the family, the opportunity cost is the foregone time spent building a successful career.

Some people allocate their resources properly in order to maximize production or choices in life. However, not everyone allocates resources properly given whatever constraints they may face. As an example, if a student spends more time partying instead of studying during a semester, the probability of failing the course is much higher. If the student fails the course, his or her opportunity cost is the wasted time spent in attending this particular course.

How Trade-offs Apply from a Management Point of View

Trade-offs—giving up something in order to get something else—are the mother of all opportunity costs. They lay at the heart of the executive's job. And they are something of a paradox. The more successful you are, the greater the opportunity costs you face. In fact, success is measured by how well executives handle trade-offs, the very thing that haunts and torments them.

Every executive faces two tasks. First up is to work with courage, skill, perseverance, and creativity to create trade-offs where none presently exist. If you face no trade-offs, then your company is poorly managed. If you don't have to settle for less of one thing to get more of another, then it follows that you could have more of everything if you just managed or organized your affairs better. That, in turn, means that there is much fat and slack in the system that needs to be eliminated. Second up is to manage those trade-offs in the best possible way, balancing gain and pain in a manner that leaves your business best off, with the most gain for the least pain.

Managing trade-offs can involve painful decisions about other people's lives, and can require rapid changes in perspectives and ways of thinking. Consider, as an example, the once-vaunted Japanese efficiency. As a matter of management policy Japanese firms have been reluctant to lay off workers during hard times. They have traded the inflexibility of "lifetime" employment for the greater loyalty and motivation it creates. As a result, by one estimate Japanese companies currently harbor a million hidden unemployed—meaning workers who add nothing to company output but nonetheless draw pay. Many of those million workers are in Japan's least-efficient sectors: banking, finance, and real estate. Some are in management jobs and are called *madogiwa-zoku*—those who stare out the window.

Our previous example of the U.S. production possibility schedule illustrates trade-offs. In order to gain more food, the United States must give up clothing and vice versa. This exists because resources are limited. Decisions need to be made for how these resources are allocated. If no trade-offs exist, then the United States is operating below the production possibilities curve, which is considered to be inefficient. As the United States maximizes its resources and produces on the production possibility curve, it then needs to decide how many of each good to produce.

Economic Growth

At any particular point in time, an economy cannot be outside its production possibilities curve. Over time, however, expanding output potential is possible for an economy. This occurs through economic growth, which refers to increased productive capabilities of an economy made possible by either an increasing resource base or technological advances.

We have to remember that the assumption in this model is that all factor resources and technologies are fixed. However, if there is a change in technology, then the production possibilities curve will shift. An improvement in technology will shift the production possibility curve to the right (as seen in the diagram). A recession, on the other hand, can shift the production possibility curve to the left. If the technology helps improve the production for, say, clothing, then the production possibilities curve will pivot to the right. Furthermore, if the technology is only for improving the production for food, then the production possibilities curve will pivot to the left.

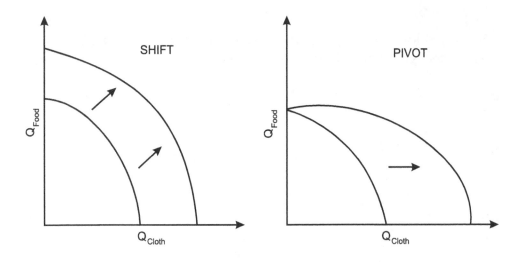

Efficiency in Production

The fact that plants can operate below capacity suggests that it is not just labor resources that should be effectively used. All resources entering into production must be used effectively. For example, an engineering college graduate driving a taxicab may be inefficient because he is not fully utilizing all his resources and capacity. In this example, there is some form of **underemployment of resources**.

The task of creating trade-offs and managing them are related to the economic notion of **efficiency**. Each task involves a different concept of efficiency, focusing on a different sort of management skill. For economists, efficiency is the ratio of what an organization—which could be a group of workers, a production line, a factory, a company division, or a whole firm—actually produces, and what it could feasibly produce with its existing resources, knowledge, and ability.

One reason for inefficiency is when actual output may fall short of full potential output. One is simply waste; resources are wasted when more of something can be produced without making less of anything else. Economists sometimes call this technical inefficiency, or, more often, "X-inefficiency." The late Harvard professor, Harvey Leibenstin, who coined the term "X-inefficiency," wrote a classic article in 1966 in which he made a key observation: Many developing countries hired management consultants at high cost to help them perform better. Most of those consultants' reports gathered dust in a drawer and their recommendations were never implemented. If even some of those reports could have improved performance, then that meant countries who failed to use them were not employing their resources as well as they could. He called this **"X-inefficiency"**—"X" for unknown, as in algebra—because it was not entirely clear what the precise sources of this type of waste were. A generation later, it is apparent that there are a great many causes of X-inefficiency, some of them related to shortcomings in decisions executives make (Maital, 1994).

Reference

Maital, Shlomo. (1994). *Executive economics: Ten essential tools for managers.* New York: Simon and Schuster.

Definitions

1. Production possibility curves

2. Opportunity cost

3. Trade-offs

4. Underemployment of resources

5. Efficiency

6. X-inefficiency

7. Scarcity

8. Maximize resources

9. Law of increasing opportunity cost

10. Concave from the origin

Multiple Choice

1. Which statement concerning opportunity costs is not true?
   a. Every decision involves opportunity costs.
   b. Opportunity costs are the highest-valued alternatives that must be foregone when a choice is made.
   c. The full cost of an item includes the opportunity costs.
   d. Opportunity costs always can be expressed in money.
   e. Economists refer to foregone opportunities and foregone benefits as opportunity costs.

2. The opportunity cost of studying for physics tonight at the library may include
   a. the good time you could be having by going out with your friends.
   b. time that you could be spending studying for your history class.
   c. lost sleep.
   d. time you could be spending listening to music or watching television.
   e. all of the choices are correct.

3. Because of scarcity,
   a. costs are incurred in making choices.
   b. we attempt to utilize our resources as efficiently as possible.
   c. we must make choices between production possibilities.
   d. we are unable to produce all we would like to produce.
   e. all of the choices are applicable.

4. If you have the choice of consuming either two apples, three oranges, or one candy bar, the opportunity cost of the candy bar is
   a. two apples.
   b. three oranges.
   c. two apples and three oranges.
   d. two apples or three oranges, whichever you prefer.
   e. the difference in the prices of the three options.

5. When an economy is operating on its own production possibilities curve, then more production of one good means less production of another because
   a. resources are limited.
   b. resources are not perfectly adaptable to alternative uses.
   c. wants are limited.
   d. wants are unlimited.
   e. some resources are not employed.

6. Which of the following would shift the production possibilities curve to the right?
   a. An increase in capital
   b. International trade
   c. A change in consumer tastes
   d. All of the above
   e. None of the above

7. When a country is on its PPF, (Production Possibility Frontier)
    a. its resources are fully employed.
    b. it is producing the most desirable combination of the two goods.
    c. it can still increase total production by greater efficiency.
    d. all of the above are true.

8. The production possibilities frontier
    a. represents the trade-offs between all possible goods a society can make.
    b. illustrates the law of increasing marginal returns.
    c. shows that society is limited only by the size of its imagination and spirit.
    d. is a graphical representation of opportunity cost for a society with only two goods.

9. An economy exhibits efficiency if
    a. it is operating on its PPF.
    b. it is producing all it can of one good and none of another.
    c. it is producing at the least possible cost.
    d. all of the above are correct.
    e. answers a and c only.

10. If the unemployment rate decreases from 10 to 8 percent, the economy will
    a. move closer to the PPF.
    b. move away from the PPF toward the origin.
    c. remain on the PPF.
    d. remain on the origin.

True/False

Directions: For the following statements, indicate whether the statement is true or false. If the statement is false, make the necessary change(s) in order for it to be a true statement.

1. A production possibility curve shows all possible combinations of goods that an economy can produce given (1) limited number of resources, (2) government intervention, and (3) competitive markets.

2. An opportunity cost is any choice or alternative given up for a different choice.

3. A production possibility curve illustrates an economy's potential for allocating its limited resources to producing various combinations of goods.

4. A change in technology will cause a leftward shift of the production possibility curve for an economy.

5. Even when an economy is operating at 100 percent efficiency, there will be cases of underemployment.

6. As long as the economy is producing along or inside the production possibility curve, then each combination of goods and resources is being used efficiently.

7. Two reasons for inefficiency outlined in the chapter are underemployment and the concept of X-inefficiency.

8. A recession will have no effect on an economy's production possibility curve since the curve is only analyzing two goods, and price is not involved.

Essay Questions

1. What is the difference between a shift in PPC and a pivot in PPC?

2. What is the implication of a production possibility curve that is a straight line and downward sloping?

3. Explain the meaning of why production possibility curves are concave from the point of origin.

4. How are inefficiency and efficiency illustrated with a production possibility curve?

5. Why are we concerned with unemployed or underemployed resources in a society?

6. The table below shows a production possibilities table for steel and automobiles.

Production Alternative	Steel (tons)	Automobiles (by thousands)
A	0	20
B	1	18
C	2	15
D	3	11
E	4	6
F	5	0

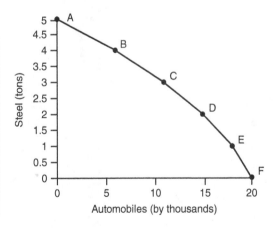

a. Plot these production possibilities on a diagram. Upon what assumption is your production possibilities curve drawn?

b. What is the opportunity cost of the first ton of steel? Between which points is the opportunity cost of a ton of steel the greatest?

c. Explain how this curve reflects the law of increasing opportunity costs.

d. Label a point G inside the curve. Why is this point inefficient? Label a point H outside the curve. Why is this point unattainable? Why might the production possibilities curve shift inward? Why might it shift outward?

7. The production possibilities model describes the limit of what a society can produce. Consider the following possibilities, then plot, label, and connect the points to form a production possibility frontier (PPF) in the figure:

Production	Mangoes	Passion Fruit Possibility
A	500	0
B	400	200
C	300	350
D	200	425
E	100	475
F	0	500

a. Draw a production possibility curve that represents the data above.

b. What shape does the production possibility curve have (linear, concave, or convex)?

c. Draw point (300, 300) on your graph. Label the point *G* in the curve.

d. What can you say about this level of output (obtainable, efficient, or inefficient)?

e. What can you say about the use of resources (unobtainable, efficient, or inefficient)?

f. What is the opportunity cost for passion fruit (in terms of mangoes per passion fruit) for each of the following moves?
    i.   0 to 200?

    ii. 200 to 350?

    iii. 350 to 425?

g. What will happen to the production possibility curve if technology for producing mangoes increases?

8. Explain why the quote "there is no free lunch" illustrates the concept of opportunity cost.

Theory of Demand and Supply

Feverpitch/Shutterstock.com

OBJECTIVES

1. To understand the concept of the law of demand.
2. To explain the difference between a change in quantity demanded versus a change in demand.
3. To explain the different factors affecting demand.
4. To understand the concept of the law of supply.
5. To explain the difference between a change in quantity supplied versus a change in supply.
6. To enumerate the different factors affecting supply.
7. To understand the concept of elasticity.
8. To interpret the meaning of elasticity.

When people buy a given commodity, the first thing they probably think of is the price. How much is Celine Dion's compact disc? If I want to buy a 53-inch flat-screen TV, how much will it cost if you give me a discount? Why are diamonds more expensive than a bottle of Evian water? The purpose of this chapter is to examine a model that determines the market price and quantity for a given commodity. We call this model the **theory of demand and supply.**

This model provides the basic foundation for understanding market economies. There are three basic components of this model: demand, supply, and market equilibrium. Demand pertains to all aspects that a consumer includes in determining his consumption for a particular commodity. Supply refers to all factors pertaining to the supplier's decision to supply or produce a given commodity.

Law of Demand

The law of demand states: Other things being equal, as the price of a certain good goes up, quantity demanded goes down. Similarly, as price of a good goes down, the quantity demanded goes up. There are two intuitive reasons why the law of demand exists. The first reason is the **substitution effect.** This means that as the price of a commodity increases, consumers tend to substitute other commodities because of the change in price. If the price of oranges increases, for example, people might choose to substitute apples for oranges, causing a decline in the demand for oranges. The second reason is the **income effect.** This means that as price goes up, people feel poorer as a result of a decline in the purchasing power of the dollar. This means that the value of the dollar falls as the price of a commodity increases.

Demand Schedule

Below are pairs of numbers showing various possible prices and corresponding quantities demanded at each price.

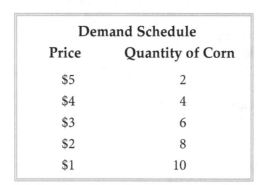

Demand Schedule	
Price	Quantity of Corn
$5	2
$4	4
$3	6
$2	8
$1	10

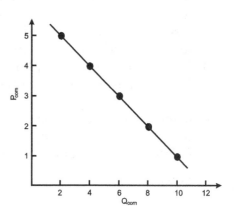

If we plot the points along our X-Y plane, with X as quantity and Y as price, we see a downward sloping demand curve. What this means is that as we move along the demand curve, the quantity demanded increases or decreases because of changes in price. We refer to movement along a demand curve as a **change in quantity demanded.**

However, price is not the only factor that can change the demand for a particular commodity. Suppose that general income increases. In our model, the demand curve will shift to the right.

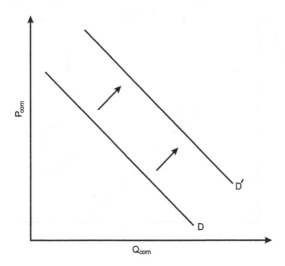

A shift of the demand curve to the right means there is an increase in demand. A shift of the demand curve to the left means there is a decrease in demand. Generally, if there is a leftward or rightward shift of a demand curve, we say that there is a **change in demand.**

External Factors Affecting Demand

Income

A general increase in income causes a shift in the demand curve to the right. This means that an increase in income can cause people to buy more of any given commodity, provided the price of the commodity stays constant.

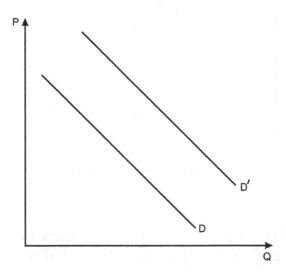

Prices of Related Goods

An increase in price of a related commodity can also shift the demand curve. If the price of oranges increases, then people would tend to substitute apples for oranges. Therefore, from a graphical standpoint, an increase in the price of oranges would shift the demand curve for apples to the right, and the demand curve for oranges to the left.

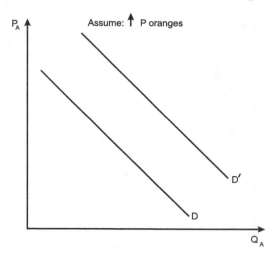

Population

An increase in population means a bigger market. Therefore, an increase in population would shift the demand curve to the right. An example of this concept is China. The main reason American companies invest in China is its population (1.2 billion people). Imagine you are the CEO of McDonald's and you invest your resources in China, which leads to your company selling 1.2 billion hamburgers; this would result in major profits for McDonalds!

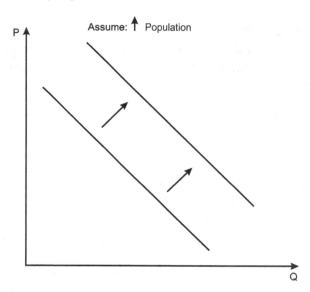

Price Expectation

If we expect that the price for gasoline will increase tomorrow, it is obvious that people will buy more gasoline today in order to take advantage of the current lower price. From a graphical standpoint, an expected increase in future prices for a commodity shifts today's demand curve to the right.

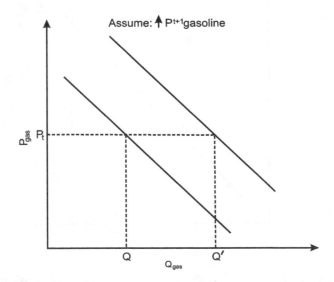

Law of Supply

The law of supply states: Other things being equal, as price of a commodity increases, the quantity supplied increases. Likewise, as the price decreases, the quantity supplied decreases. There are two intuitive reasons why the law of supply exists. One reason is the **production incentive**. This means suppliers have an incentive to produce more if they know that the price of the commodity they sell is increasing. The second reason for the law of supply is **profit incentive**. When price goes up, suppliers make more money on each unit of commodity they produce and sell.

Supply Schedule

Below are pairs of numbers showing various possible prices and corresponding quantities supplied at each price.

Supply Schedule	
Price (per bushel)	Quantity supplied
$1	2
$2	4
$3	6
$4	8
$5	10

If we plot the points along a curve, with X as quantity and Y as price, we see that the supply curve is upward sloping. This means there is a direct relationship between price and quantity supplied. As we move along the curve, quantity supplied increases as price increases. Movement along a supply curve is called a **change in quantity supplied**.

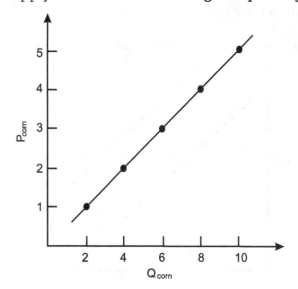

However, price is not the only factor that can change the quantity supplied. For example, an improvement in technology would make production more efficient and less costly. Thus, an improvement in technology would shift the supply curve to the right. Shifting the supply curve to the right or to the left is called a **change in supply**.

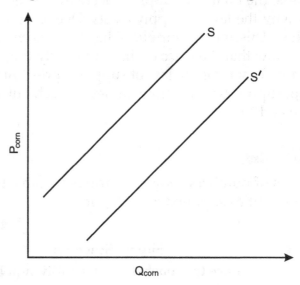

External Factors Affecting Supply

Cost of Inputs

Cost of inputs refers to the different prices of factors of production (e.g., land, labor, capital, and entrepreneurship). For example, an increase in wages would lead to an increase in the cost of production. Eventually this would decrease the supply of the commodity, as resources would have to be diverted in the form of higher wages, shifting the supply curve to the left.

Weather/Natural Disasters

The effects of El Niño destroyed a large portion of crops in the United States. Therefore, droughts or excess flooding can bring about a decline in the production of an agricultural commodity, shifting the supply curve to the left. Good weather, on the other hand, can bring in a bountiful harvest, shifting the supply curve to the right.

Number of Firms

The greater the number of firms, the greater the production from a market standpoint. Therefore, an increase in the number of firms would shift the supply curve to the right. A decrease in the number of the firms, on the other hand, would shift the supply curve to the left.

Price Expectation

An increase in the future price of a commodity can lead to an increase in supply. If the seller anticipates an increase in future price, then there is an incentive for the seller to produce more of that commodity. Therefore, an increase in future prices can lead to a rightward shift in the supply curve.

Market Equilibrium

Market equilibrium is a situation in which quantity demanded is equal to quantity supplied. This is a situation when the market clears.

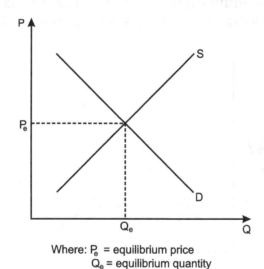

Where: P_e = equilibrium price
Q_e = equilibrium quantity

The price at which the quantity demanded is equal to the quantity supplied is called the **equilibrium price**. The quantity that the buyer and sellers agree upon is called the **equilibrium quantity**. Sometimes, equilibrium price refers to **market clearing price** and equilibrium quantity refers to **market clearing quantity**.

A market cannot always achieve an equilibrium point. Some markets adjust easily and some markets do not. Take the gasoline market, for example. Since the commodity is considered a necessity, it is easier for consumers to accept the market price because they need the commodity to go to work, school, shopping, or wherever they need to go. Consequently, the market adjusts quickly. However, there are markets that take a while to adjust. For example, we can analyze the labor market. In a given year, there will always be a given unemployment rate (usually between 4 and 6 percent). What this means is that the market does not achieve an equilibrium point because there is always a disparity between the demand for labor and the supply for labor.

Price Controls

In a competitive market, the marketplace consists of the buyer and the seller. In reality, the public sector (i.e., the government) intervenes in the market as well. Governments intervene in the market in order to protect the consumer or the producer by changing or distorting the market price.

There are two types of price controls: price ceiling and price floor.

1. **Price ceiling:** the legal maximum price that the seller can set in the market. The reason a price ceiling is imposed by the government is to help the consumer. This is especially true when the market price is higher than what the consumers want to see. Let's say that we start with an initial equilibrium and the government decides to set a price ceiling (P_c) below the equilibrium price. The quantity demanded is then greater than the quantity supplied. Therefore, a price ceiling can lead to excess demand, creating a shortage of a good or service.

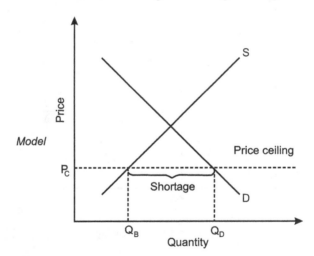

2. **Price floor:** the legal minimum price that the seller can set in the market. One reason why the government might set a price floor is to help the seller augment its revenue. An example is a price support program for farmers (agricultural products). Most farmers raise their revenues through price floors, which can only be done if the government intervenes. Another example is the federal minimum wage. The minimum wage is a price floor imposed by the government that sets the lowest

hourly, daily, or monthly wage that employers may legally pay their employees. Price floor is usually set above the equilibrium price. The result is that quantity supplied exceeds the quantity demanded, leading to a surplus of the commodity.

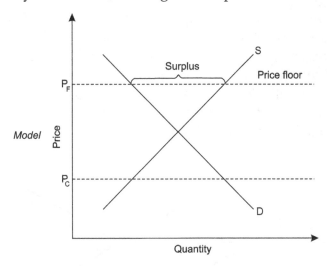

Shifts in Demand and Supply

In a given market scenario, it is not only price restrictions that can distort a market. There can be other factors or shocks that can change not only the price of a commodity but also the market quantity. For example, an increase in disposable income can lead to an increase in the demand for a commodity. From a graphical standpoint, an increase in income can shift the demand curve to the right, causing an increase in both market price and quantity (see graph below).

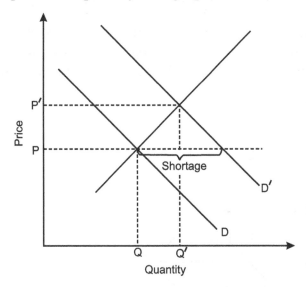

Let us examine carefully how an increase in demand can lead to an increase in both market price and quantity. If we kept the price constant at the original price, the market would experience an excess demand (a shortage). In order for the producers to support the excess demand, other things being equal, they have to increase their production, thus causing prices to increase as additional cost is incurred.

Simultaneously, as prices increase, consumers will react by consuming less. Eventually, they will meet at an agreed price and quantity, which constitutes the market equilibrium. The end result is that both market price and quantity increase.

Next, we examine what will happen to the market of Pepsi if Coca-Cola decides to raise the price of Coke. Both of these related goods are substitutes, meaning that one good can be used in the place of the other. When the price of Coke is increased, more consumers will substitute Coke with Pepsi because Pepsi is less expensive. This will increase the demand for Pepsi causing an increase in both price and quantity sold, as illustrated in the figure below.

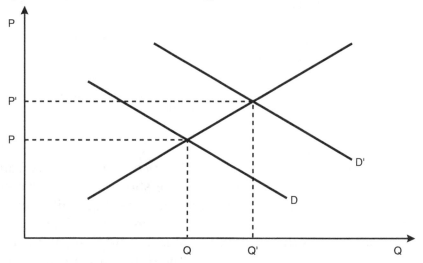

Another good example is the effect of technology on the market. Technology is a supply shock, meaning that an improvement in technology leads to a more efficient way for sellers to produce the commodity. Eventually, the market price will decrease, as production is more cost effective, and market quantity will increase (see graph below).

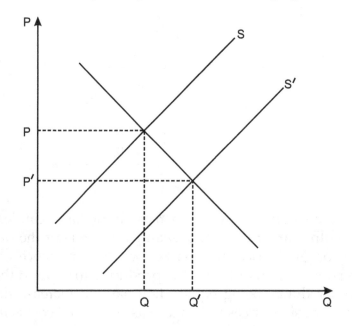

Why is it that the price for personal computers has dropped significantly over the last 10 years? Ten or fifteen years ago, the price of a personal computer was around $5,000 for the best and latest model. Today you can buy the latest model for less than $1,000. We can explain this scenario simply by looking at the demand and supply model. From the initial market equilibrium, a greater demand for a given commodity will shift the demand curve to the right. Initially, this can lead to an increase in the market price of the commodity. However, on the supply side of the market, technology is changing. A change in technology increases the supply (shifting it to the right). In the personal computer marketplace, the change in supply has been greater than the change in demand, leading to a drop in market price and an increase in market quantity:

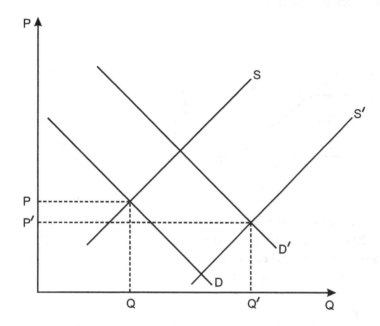

Price Elasticity

Price elasticity refers to the extent to which changes in the price of a product influence demand for that product. Price elasticity is used in determining the effects of changes in prices, especially for sales. If a seller reduces his prices—such as through a sales promotion—it does not necessarily mean that sales or revenue will increase. The same is true for price increases. For example, price increases have little impact on individuals who are addicted to alcohol. Therefore, raising the cost of alcoholic beverages has almost no impact on their consumption. There are situations in which sales will stay constant or even decrease as a result of a price reduction. The key point is that it depends on how sensitive the demand is to changes in price.

The formula for the price elasticity of demand is as follows:

$$e_p = \frac{Percentage\ change\ in\ quantity\ demanded}{Percentage\ change\ in\ price}$$

Criteria:

$$|e_p| = 0 \rightarrow \textbf{Perfectly Inelastic}$$
$$0 < |e_p| < 1 \rightarrow \textit{Relatively Inelastic}$$
$$|e_p| = 1 \rightarrow \textbf{Unitary Elastic}$$
$$1 < |e_p| < \infty \rightarrow \textbf{Relatively Elastic}$$
$$|e_p| = \infty \rightarrow \textbf{Perfectly Elastic}$$

For example: Demand for movie tickets:

At a price of $4 per ticket, 200 tickets will be purchased each day. However, at a price of $3 per ticket, 300 tickets will be purchased each day. Find the price elasticity:

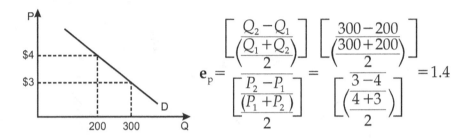

$$e_P = \frac{\left[\dfrac{Q_2 - Q_1}{\left(\dfrac{Q_1 + Q_2}{2}\right)}\right]}{\left[\dfrac{P_2 - P_1}{\left(\dfrac{P_1 + P_2}{2}\right)}\right]} = \frac{\left[\dfrac{300 - 200}{\left(\dfrac{300 + 200}{2}\right)}\right]}{\left[\dfrac{3 - 4}{\left(\dfrac{4 + 3}{2}\right)}\right]} = 1.4$$

Interpretation: Since the coefficient, e_p, is greater than 1, the price elasticity is elastic. It means that movie tickets are very responsive to the changes in price. Small changes in the price of movie tickets will have a greater change in its demand.

Special Cases of Elasticity

If the price elasticity is greater than one, then we call the commodity price elastic, meaning demand is sensitive to price changes. This means that even a slight change in the price of a good results in a dramatic change in the demand for that good. If the price elasticity is equal to one, then the commodity is unitary elastic. If the price elasticity is less than one, then it is price inelastic, meaning demand is not sensitive to price changes. This means that even as price increases, demand will change very little, if at all. An example of this is the market for gasoline. As prices increased from less than $2 per gallon in 2000 to more than $3 per gallon in 2008, the demand curve for gasoline did not shift dramatically to the left (decrease).

In some instances, the demand for a given commodity may not be responsive at all to changes in price. For example, insulin is very important for people who are diabetic, as it is a matter of life and death. In this case, the demand for insulin may not be responsive to the change in price. Since it is a matter of life and death, the buyer will purchase the insulin no matter what the price is.

If the demand for a given commodity is not responsive to the changes in price, then we consider the good as **perfectly inelastic**. This means that it is not responsive to changes in price. Another example of this kind of commodity is illegal drugs such as cocaine. No matter what the price is, cocaine addicts will buy it because of its addictive nature.

On the other hand, small changes in prices can lead to big changes in quantity demanded. In a case when quantity demanded changes even if the price does not change (demand is highly sensitive), we call the commodity **perfectly elastic**. A classic example of this is the demand in competitive markets. The seller is a price taker, meaning that he or she simply accepts the price based on what the market price is. The demand for the seller's commodity can change, but his or her price may not necessarily change because it is determined by the market.

Importance of Price Elasticity

Why do we want to know how much quantity demanded falls when the price is raised? Imagine that you are a movie theater owner, and you know that the demand for popcorn depends on income, tastes, and other products. But you also know that you can use the ceteris paribus assumption for this scenario. Assuming that the price of popcorn is the only immediate influence on the quantity of popcorn demanded, then you must decide whether to increase price. Will an increase in the price of popcorn cause a big drop in sales? How would that affect total receipts?

In 1982, President Ronald Reagan's advisers urged him to raise excise taxes on cigarettes, liquor, and gasoline. The objective of these proposed tax increases was to raise government revenue. In the process, however, the prices of these products would have increased and their sales would have declined. President Reagan concluded that the resulting drop in sales, output, and employment would be too great, and he decided against such tax hikes.

The Relationship between Elasticity and Revenue

Recall:

$$Total\ Revenue\ (TR) = Price\ (P) \times Quantity\ (Q)$$

$$TR = P \times Q$$

When the elasticity of demand with respect to price is elastic, a decrease in price will increase total revenue. Total revenue increases because the increase in quantity demanded is so great that it more than offsets the decrease in price. The opposite effect occurs when demand is elastic and the price is raised. The increase in price is more than offset by the decrease in quantity demanded and total revenue falls.

On the other hand, if demand is inelastic with respect to price, a decrease in price will result in lower total revenue because the increase in quantity demanded will not be large enough to offset the effect of the lower price on revenue. Accordingly, if demand is inelastic and price is increased, total revenue will also increase, because the resulting reduction in quantity sold will not be large enough to offset the effect of a higher price.

In a special case where demand is unitary elastic with respect to price, a change in price will not have an effect on total revenue. This result occurs because if $|e_p| = 1$, a certain percentage change in price produces an equal (in absolute value) decrease in quantity demanded, the two factors offsetting one another exactly.

Do Minimum Wages Cause Lower Wages?

Dwight Lee and Cindy Lee

The standard criticism of the minimum wage is that it reduces employment by artificially elevating the wage for less-productive workers, thereby reducing the number of these workers demanded by employers.

This employment-reducing effect of the minimum wage certainly deserves emphasis. Employment opportunities are foreclosed for those whose skills are worth less than the legal minimum. But there is another employment-reducing effect of the minimum wage that has gone largely unnoticed: The minimum wage, by mandating a wage above the market wage, reduces employment by keeping some wages *below* their market levels.

The minimum wage can thus depress employment both by keeping some wages too high and by keeping some wages too low.

That is as far as the standard analysis of the minimum wage goes. But that analysis ignores the fact that a minimum does not outlaw all wages below the established minimum. While it is against the law for an employer to pay a positive wage that is less than the minimum wage, there is nothing to prevent an employer from paying a wage of zero. And that is precisely what many employers do.

Hospitals, for example, hire students as Candy Stripers to perform simple nursing tasks in return for a zero wage. The Candy Stripers receive useful work experience and information about a nursing career, but they also provide hospitals with valuable services. In the absence of minimum wage legislation, it is likely that hospitals would be willing to pay Candy Stripers a small, but positive, wage.

A positive wage, even though small, would increase the number of students willing to work a few hours a week as Candy Stripers, and it would be an attractive opportunity for hospitals to obtain more help in the performance of routine tasks. The minimum wage in this case reduces not only employment, but wages as well.

Think of the enormous quantity of volunteer work that is now performed in the economy. The availability of a wage greater than zero would surely increase this quantity. Some volunteers, of course, would prefer to remain volunteers—they could still work for a zero wage, or contribute their wage to charity. The point is that a minimum wage reduces the quantity of this labor available to the firms and agencies that use it, and it reduces the wage received by the people who do this work.

In an unregulated market, workers who are willing to make only an occasional commitment to the workplace are likely to receive lower wages than workers who are willing to make a more definite commitment to an employer. The likely response to a minimum wage, then, is that only "committed" workers will be hired at the minimum wage; workers who are not willing to make such commitments get jobs only if they are willing to work for nothing. Their wages, once again, are reduced by a minimum wage.

Minimum wages clearly reduce employment opportunities for unskilled workers; no economist doubts that. Some economists are willing to accept that result because a minimum wage increases the wage of those workers who keep their jobs.

Our analysis suggests that a minimum wage increases the wage of only some workers. For others, it results in a wage of zero. That raises the possibility that a minimum wage may reduce the average wage paid to those individuals who continue to work after it is imposed.

What's Really Happening in Housing Markets?

Morris A. Davis, Francois Ortalo-Magne, and Peter Rupert

Recent trends in house prices have induced a certain amount of hand-wringing among leading economists, policymakers, and bloggers of some repute. In the eight-year boom ending sometime last summer, they warned that house prices were rising much faster than ever before, and that such appreciation was unwarranted. As a consequence, these commentators are predicting that prices will fall, perhaps disastrously so.

According to the most widely cited historical data on house prices (compiled by Robert J. Shiller for the 2005 edition of his book, *Irrational Exuberance)*, house prices were roughly flat from 1890 to 1997 (after adjusting for inflation), but since 1998, they have climbed 6 percent per year in the aggregate. Adding to analysts' sense of trouble is that the rate of house-price appreciation over the boom has varied widely across the United States. The more populated coastal states, such as California and Florida, have experienced nominal gains on the order of 10 percent per year, whereas prices in midwestern and interior states, like Michigan and Nebraska, appreciated approximately 4 percent per year. The acceleration of prices in the aggregate reflects the fast growth of house prices in the coastal states, so the argument goes, but because growth in house prices has outpaced the growth of residents' income in these states, analysts argue that the rise in house prices is not supported by economic "fundamentals." Their observations imply that house prices on the coasts, and therefore in the aggregate, should fall to be more in line with income and fundamentals.

But there is a problem with the data on which these projections rest. They are inaccurate in a particularly important period—the 1970s, a decade that, as it turns out, does offer a precedent for the current situation. A different source of data on housing prices suggests that a housing boom similar to the 1998–2006 boom occurred sometime between 1970 and 1980.

As for what might be behind the latest housing boom, two reasonable explanations spring to mind. One has to do with the price of land, and the other with relaxed credit constraints.

The value of the land on which a house sits contributes a part of the total price of a home. While housing structures are reproducible with little additional cost, land is in fixed supply. To understand changes in

Source: Federal Reserve Bank of Cleveland.

house prices, it is necessary to study the price of residential land. Data indicate that the real price of land has been marching steadily upward since 1950. If the 1998–2006 boom for house prices reflects demand for housing-related amenities, then the data on land prices argue that this boom is a continuation of earlier trends.

Relaxed credit constraints could explain the outpacing of house-price appreciation to incomes. House prices can and should be expected to surge if credit constraints are unexpectedly relaxed for first-time home-buyers who are credit or down-payment constrained. This surge can occur even when incomes remain constant; when credit constraints change over time, incomes and house prices should not be expected to increase at the same rate.

Historical Housing Prices

Until recently, the only long time series of house prices for the United States had been compiled by Shiller (2005). Shiller constructed this series by splining together available house-price data from 1890–1934 from Grebler, Blank, and Winnick (1956), the home-purchase component of the CPI-U from 1953–1975, the OFHEO from 1975–1987, and the Case-Shiller-Weiss index from 1987–2005. To fill in the gap, Shiller constructs an index of house prices from 1934 to 1953 by compiling data on the sales price of houses from five major cities based on newspaper advertisements. These data, after adjusting for consumer price inflation, show almost no trend increase in house prices until about 1997, leading Shiller and others to conclude that the boom for house prices from 1998–2006 is historically anomalous.

But there are reasons to believe the Shiller series is inaccurate for the late 1960s and early 1970s—a period for which his data source was the CPI-U. John Greenlees (1982) first reported that the home purchase component of the CPI-U is significantly biased down—a result of the methodology used to extract the housing data. But Shiller does not correct for the bias when he incorporates the CPI-U housing prices into his series.

Davis and Heathcote (2006) have compiled a long time series of constant-quality house prices by reconciling decade-by-decade changes in the aggregate market value of housing (based on micro data from the Decennial Census of Housing) with year-by-year data on residential investment, as published in the National Income and Product Accounts (NIPA). Although the Shiller series and Davis and Heathcote series differ in every decade, the most pronounced difference between the two series occurs in the 1970s (see Table 3.1). The Davis and Heathcote data show a real average annual rate of appreciation just shy of 41/2 percent per year, whereas the rate of growth of the CPI-U in that decade is less than 2 percent per year. If the Davis and Heathcote data are to be believed, the boom for house prices in 1998–2006 in the aggregate has a close historical precedent in 1970–1980.

Decade	Shiller 2005	Davis and Healthcote 2006
1950–1960	0.23	0.10
1960–1970	0.11	0.62
1970–1980	1.79	4.35
1980–1990	0.63	1.32
1990–2000	0.81	1.01
2000–2006	X	6.60

Land Prices

Housing prices are based on two components of the house, land and structure. Because increasing the quantity of structures is less costly than increasing the quantity of "good" residential land, any change in the price of housing will largely come from an increase in the demand for land. By "good" we mean land with short commutes, low crime, or other desirable amenities.

On average in the United States, the price of land used for residential purposes has been rising rather steadily since the 1950s.[1]

Because the price of land has been rising faster than the cost of structures, land has become a larger proportion of the housing price. This proportion is quite different in different cities across the United States, however. If land's share of house prices is high in a location, then an increase in the demand for land will have a large effect on the price of the house (land plus structure). Conversely, if land is a small component of the overall price, then an increase in the demand for land will have only a small effect on housing prices. What this means is that observing housing prices alone can mask the increase in demand for certain locations.

Changes in the price of land have been large not only in the coastal cities, but in many of the interior cities as well (see Table 3.2). Indeed, the growth in land prices in St. Louis has far outpaced that in New York, Boston, and San Francisco. The increase in land prices in Minneapolis is roughly the same as that seen in New York City. Of course, the price of land did not appreciate this rapidly for every city in the United States.

Four cities located in the Fourth Federal Reserve District were included in the study from which Table 3.3 is taken, and three of these did not see a pronounced change in the price of developed residential land, the exception being Pittsburgh.

The evidence suggests that for the price of land—the component of housing that is in fixed supply—the 1998–2004 period was not a time of unprecedented growth. In addition, although the growth of housing

Table 3.2 Land's Share in 1998 and Real Growth in House and Land Prices from 1999–2004

| | Land's share, 1998 | Real cumulative percent increase, 1999–2004 | |
		Home values	Land values
Coastal cities			
Boston	0.60	81.2	128.6
Los Angeles	0.65	96.9	139.0
New York City	0.44	92.4	192.3
San Francisco	0.81	73.5	89.4
Other interior cities			
Houston	0.19	25.4	107.2
Milwaukee	0.33	35.5	90.7
Minneapolis/St.Paul	0.25	59.6	190.8
St.Louis	0.12	34.4	233.1
Fourth District cities			
Cincinnati	0.34	20.8	41.0
Cleveland	0.36	17.1	33.0
Columbus	0.39	18.9	29.6
Pittsburgh	0.13	22.8	153.0

Source: Davis and Palumbo (2006).

prices took place mainly on the coasts, this is largely because land is a much more scarce resource on the coasts, land is a larger share of the house price, and house prices on the coasts more closely track the price of land. The price of land, in contrast, rose in most of the 46 cities studied. We see, then, that the boom was widespread across the United States (not just on the coasts), and probably reflects a continuation of demand-side pressure for housing that may have origins as early as 1950.

Credit Constraints and Prices

Any change in the ability to purchase a home, such as from innovations in the lending environment, can have a large impact on the level and volatility of housing prices. In a world where first-time homebuyers face binding constraints and housing is in fixed supply, prices can vary without any changes in income. Two common constraints faced by homebuyers are that a mortgage payment cannot be any larger than a given fraction of income and that a homebuyer must put down equity in the house of no less than a certain percentage.

The best way to see the impact of a change in constraints on house prices is through a simple example using a change in the down payment requirement. Consider the case where starter homes cost $100 and the down-payment requirement is 10 percent. Households need to save $10 in order to purchase a home. At any point in time, there are a number of households that are working toward this objective and that will have accumulated savings ranging between $0 and $10. If the down-payment requirement is suddenly reduced to 5 percent, then all households with savings between $5 and $10 can afford a starter home, assuming the price remains fixed at $100. However, if more starter homes cannot be built instantaneously, and the price remains fixed at $100, then more people will be able to purchase starter homes than the number of starter homes that are available to be purchased. Given no new starter homes are built, a requirement for the market for starter homes to clear—that is, the number of sellers of starter homes equals the number of households that can afford to buy—is that only households with savings of $10 are able to buy a home of their own. With the required down payment set at 5 percent, the price of starter homes must rise to $200—because 5 percent of $200 is $10.

As Ortalo-Magne and Rady (2006) noticed, the effects on the housing market do not end with the increase in the price of starter homes. This is because many of those who own starter homes would have bought more expensive homes if they had not been constrained by their ability to obtain credit. As the price of their starter home increases, they enjoy capital gains; in the previous example, the capital gains would be $200 − $100 = $100. These capital gains enable them to trade up to a more expensive house. The fact that all owners of starter homes enjoy significant capital gains, by the same reasoning as before, pushes up the demand for, and price of, more expensive homes.

The key take-away from this reasoning is that changes to credit constraints directly map to changes in house prices when housing is in relatively fixed supply. If housing is not in relatively fixed supply, then a change in credit constraints might lead to more new housing and relatively small changes in house prices. The fact that house prices outpaced income in the coastal areas and not in the interior could very well reflect a combination of two factors: the relaxation in credit constraints that may have occurred everywhere, and the fact that new housing is relatively hard to build in many places on the coasts and is more easy to build in the so-called "fly-over" states.

What's Next?

House prices may still fall in the future, but for a different reason than most analysts seem to realize. To start, the change in credit constraints discussed above will cause house prices first to rise but then to fall. The process centers around the fact that, assuming credit constraints do not change again, the price of starter homes will remain flat. New starter-home owners will therefore have little or no capital gains to use to finance the purchase of a more expensive trade-up home. The fact that these homeowners have no capital gains implies that, relative to the previous cohort of expensive-home buyers, they have relatively low down payments to apply to the purchase of their more expensive trade-up homes. Since the equilibrium price of expensive homes is directly linked to the down payment, low down payments (relative to the previous set of expensive-home buyers) will drive down the price of these homes. Second, private mortgage originators have announced substantial changes to their subprime variable-rate mortgage programs, which are likely to result in the sharply curtailed availability of this type of credit. Using exactly the same reasoning as before, tightening credit standards will cause the price of starter homes to fall, thus reducing the wealth of the current owners of starter homes, which will itself trigger a chain-reaction decline in the price of trade-up homes.

Endnotes

[1]The price of farm land, on average in the United States, has also been increasing since 1950 at an average annual real rate of 1.9 percent per year. However, unlike the price of land used for residential purposes, the price of farm land peaked in 1982, declined sharply until 1994, and then increased again from 1994–2006, such that the inflation-adjusted price of farm land did not return to its 1982 level until 2005. See the USDA web site http://www.ers.iisda.gov/Briefing/LandUse/aglandvaluchapter.htm for details.

Multiple Choice

1. Demand describes the amount of a good or service that
   a. consumers are willing and able to buy at all possible prices.
   b. consumers think they might buy at some prices.
   c. consumers will buy at a particular market price.
   d. consumers might buy when they like certain advertising campaigns.
   e. both a and b are correct.

2. Mathematically speaking, the law of demand says
   a. quantity demanded of a good is positively related to its price.
   b. quantity demanded of a good is inversely related to its price.
   c. quantity demanded increases as the prices of related goods fall.
   d. quantity demanded at each price is represented by an upward-sloping curve.
   e. both a and d are correct.

3. The market prices of goods reflect the
   a. relative costs of resources used to make the goods.
   b. value consumers place on each good relative to all other goods.
   c. costs producers incur when producing the goods.
   d. relative scarcity of each good.
   e. all of the above are correct.

4. The law of supply tells us that as price falls,
   a. quantity supplied of the good increases.
   b. quantity supplied of the good decreases.
   c. quantity supplied of the good remains unchanged.
   d. quantity supplied of the good may or may not change, depending on resource prices.
   e. consumer purchases from firms increase.

5. The equilibrium price occurs where the
   a. quantity demanded is the amount suppliers forecasted.
   b. quantity demanded is equal to the quantity supplied in a market.
   c. quantity demanded is an amount that does not exhaust resources.
   d. quantity supplied is enough to satisfy everyone's demand for the good.
   e. quantity supplied is just the right amount for sustained production over time.

6. At the equilibrium price
   a. there is a tendency for the price to rise.
   b. there is no pressure upon price to rise or fall.
   c. quantity demanded exceeds quantity supplied.
   d. quantity supplied exceeds quantity demanded.
   e. there is a tendency for the price to fall.

7. Price elasticity of demand measures the
   a. slope of the demand curve.
   b. size of the shift in demand in relation to a change in one of the determinants of demand.
   c. responsiveness of firms to changes in their markets.
   d. responsiveness of quantity demanded of a good to changes in its price.
   e. relative shift in demand given an initial shift in supply.

8. If the price of a hardback novel increases from $25 to $30 and quantity demanded falls from 60,000 to 30,000 in response, what is the coefficient of price elasticity of demand using the simplest definition of price elasticity?
   a. 0.25
   b. 1
   c. 1.25
   d. 2.50
   e. 3

9. Which of the following is a determinant of supply?
   a. incomes
   b. tastes
   c. prices of complements
   d. prices of resources
   e. number of buyers

10. Elasticity depends on
    a. the number of close substitutes available.
    b. the amount of time consumers have to adjust to price changes.
    c. the total amount of spending on the good relative to the consumer's whole budget.
    d. all of the above.
    e. none of the above.

True/False

Directions: For the following statements, indicate whether the statement is true or false. If the statement is false, make the necessary change(s) in order for it to be a true statement.

1. An increase in disposable income will lead to a change in the quantity demanded for a particular good.

2. A change in demand occurs when you move up or down along the demand curve.

3. As prices of music CDs increase, the number of people downloading music has increased. This is an example of the substitution effect.

4. According to the law of supply, price and quantity are inversely related.

5. Market equilibrium occurs when quantity supplied equals quantity demanded.

6. An increase in population will lead to a change in quantity demanded and a change in quantity supplied.

7. Price is the only variable that can change the quantity supplied of a particular good.

8. An example of a price ceiling is the minimum wage, which requires employers to pay employees at least a specific amount of money per hour, week, or month.

9. Price ceilings and price floors are just two examples of how government can intervene in the economy.

10. When a good is considered to be perfectly elastic, demand is very sensitive to price.

11. An example of a good that is inelastic is gasoline.

Chapter 4

Theory of Production and Cost

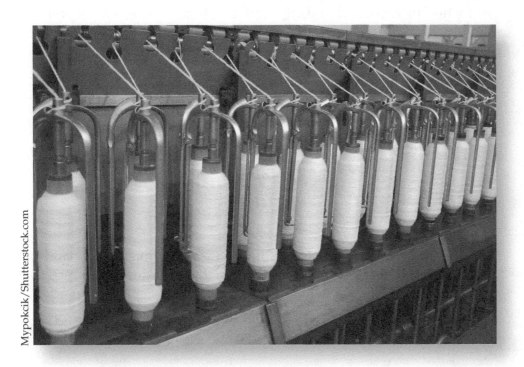

Mypokcik/Shutterstock.com

OBJECTIVES

1. To define the different concepts relating to a production function.
2. To explain the link between marginal and average product.
3. To define the concept of the law of diminishing marginal returns.
4. To understand the different stages of production.
5. To discuss the difference between explicit and implicit cost.
6. To define the different types of cost.
7. To explain the meaning of economies of scale.

With the theory of production and cost, we make a transition from the sector of the economy that consumes goods and services to the sector that produces them. To economists, production is the transformation of inputs into outputs. The output of one productive process might become the input of another. For example, the U.S. steel industry views sheet steel as an output, while General Motors uses it as an input. The ultimate object of production is to transform inputs into outputs that yield "utility," or satisfaction, directly to consumers.

Relationship between Outputs and Inputs

A firm takes numerous inputs, combines them using a technological production process, and ends up with an output. There are, of course, many factors of production or inputs. We classify production inputs into two broad categories (ignoring land): labor and capital.

1. **Production Function**—a function that establishes the relationship between inputs and outputs. For example:

$$Q = f(L, K)$$

Where:

$$Q = \textbf{output}$$

$$L = \textbf{labor}$$

$$K = \textbf{capital}$$

The way to read this is: output (Q) is a function of labor and capital. This function simply states that in order to produce a good, both labor and capital are required.

2. **Production Schedule**—shows various levels of inputs and their corresponding outputs.

Q_i (Input)	Q_o (Output)	AP	MP
0	0	0	0
1	10	10	10
2	26	13	16
3	36	12	10
4	44	11	8
5	50	10	6
6	54	9	4
7	56	8	2
8	55	6.8	−1

3. **Average Product (AP)**—output divided by input

$$AP = \frac{Q_o}{Q_i}$$

Average product is the ratio of output and input based on levels of their values and not on an increment. A good example of the use of average product is the average productivity of labor. Using our previous steel example, the average product of labor in steel production is the total output of steel divided by the number of hours of labor used to produce steel.

4. **Marginal Product**—change in Output divided by the Change in Input.

   Marginal productivity is an important concept because it is used to define a strategic decision in given firm. The formula for marginal productivity is as follows:

$$MP = \frac{\Delta Q_o}{\Delta Q_i} - \frac{Q_{o2} - Q_{o1}}{Q_{i2} - Q_{i1}}$$

A note about mathematical notation: The Greek letter Δ (delta) represents "a change in." Graphically, it would be the same as defining the slope of a straight line.

Marginal product is the specific application of cost-value logic in the context of primary resources such as labor and capital. Applied to labor and capital, cost-value logic asks:

- What does one more hour of labor or capital cost?

- What does one more hour of labor or one more machine hour contribute to the firm's output of goods or services?

This is marginal product. Its use is in quantifying the value of an added amount of labor or machinery in a way that permits comparison with their cost. The notion of marginal cost is not limited solely to labor and capital; it is applicable to other resources, even information, though the marginal product of other resources is often much harder to pin down.

Of all executive decisions, the most crucial involve the creative combination and allocation of labor, capital, and knowledge to create value for customers. How productive are our workers and our capital, compared to those of our competitors? Should we hire new workers, or fire old ones? Should workers be replaced by machines? Are existing machines (particularly computers) being used efficiently? Are workers being overpaid or underpaid? How can we increase productivity? These questions and other similar questions involving the use and allocation of resources have always had a prominent place on managers' dockets, but in the 1990s, their importance has grown. Growing numbers of large and small firms, both profitable and unprofitable ones, are undertaking "restructuring" or "downsizing," euphemisms for the radical shedding of excess debt and excess workers acquired during the 1980s. Now confronted with shrinking sales, burdensome debt, and growing competition, many executives are calling for help.

When they do, this means bad times for business but good times for business consultants. In Europe, consultants' fees approached $10 billion in 1994—25 percent greater than in 1990—40 percent of which was spent in Germany alone. Much of Europe's consulting services were not in traditional long-term strategies, but in short-term services such as crisis management. Business consultants in the United States are also doing very well (Maital, 1994).

Even with the wisest, most experienced consultants at their side, executives ultimately bear responsibility for hard decisions. The cost–value logic of economics can be a powerful tool for executives either already grappling with restructuring or executives who fear they might need to restructure.

The Law of Diminishing Marginal Returns

The law of **diminishing marginal returns** is defined as the tendency, beyond a certain point, for the marginal product of an input to fall as additional amounts of that input are used, holding constant production technologies and the quantities of other inputs into production. Furthermore, beyond a certain point, the average product also falls. The concept of diminishing marginal returns applies to many different situations. For example, let's assume that you like to eat pizza. Eating one pizza will make you happy; eating two pizzas might increase your overall happiness, but you will not have that same level of happiness or satisfaction after eating the second one as you did after the first. As you continue to eat more and more pizza, your satisfaction begins to decrease with every new slice of pizza that you eat.

As successive equal increases in a variable factor of production—such as labor—are added to other fixed factors of production—such as capital—there will be a point in which the extra or marginal product that can be attributed to each additional unit of the variable factor of production will decline.

Stages of Production

Stage I corresponds to usage of the variable input to the left of point 5, where MP achieves its maximum. Stage II corresponds to usage of the variable input between points 5 and 6, up to where the MP of the variable input is zero. Stage III corresponds to usage of the variable input to the right of point 6, where the input (MP) is negative.

The producer would never produce in Stage III, since when she is in stage III she can get more output by using less of the variable input. Such inefficiencies in the use of scarce production factors will always be avoided. If the firm is in a competitive industry, it would never produce outside of Stage I because, in Stage I, by expanding output it can reduce unit costs while receiving the same price for each additional

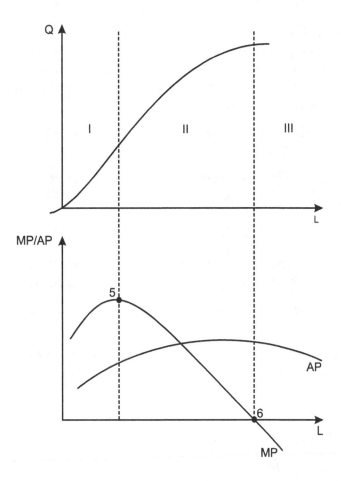

unit sold, and this means an increase in total profit. Thus we see that inefficient production begins in Stage II, and worsens in Stage III.

Theory of Cost

Resource Costs

The law of diminishing returns has important implications for the costs of production. The economic cost of a product is measured by the value of the resources needed to produce it. What we have seen here is that at some point those resource requirements increase. Each additional seamstress produces fewer and fewer jeans. In effect, each additional pair of jeans produced uses more and more labor.

Definitions

1. **Firm**—an organization that brings together different factors of production, such as labor, land, and capital, to produce a product or a service that can be sold for a profit.

2. **Profit**—also called *accounting profit*, it is the difference of total revenue (TR) minus cost (C).

3. **Opportunity Cost of Capital**—the normal rate of return or the amount that must be paid to an investor to induce him or her

to invest in a business. This simply expands our earlier definition of opportunity cost—the benefits foregone for the next alternative resource. For example, a grocer who runs his own business might take into account what he might make as a salary worker at a similar job.

4. **Economic Profit** = Total Revenue − Total Opportunity Cost of All Inputs Used

5. **Economic Cost** = Accounting Cost + Opportunity Cost of Capital

Time Periods

Understanding time periods is essential in microeconomics, especially in making decisions. Time periods are classified into two parts:

1. **Short Run**—that time period in which a firm cannot alter the current size of its plant.

2. **Long Run**—that time period in which all factors of production can be varied.

Types of Costs

1. Total Costs (TC) = Total Fixed Cost + Total Variable Cost

   Total cost refers to all costs of a firm combined, including rent, payment to workers, interest on borrowed money, and so on.

2. Total Fixed Cost (TFC)—refers to cost that does not vary with output (e.g., rent on building, price of machinery). Fixed cost in the long run becomes a variable cost. Another term for total fixed cost is **sunk cost.**

3. Total Variable Cost (TVC)—costs that vary with the rate of production (e, wages paid to workers, costs of materials, and more.

4. **Average Fixed Cost (AFC)** = $\dfrac{\text{TFC}}{\text{Total Output}}$. Another common term for averaging fixed cost is "spreading the overhead." This kind of cost is only relevant in the short run, and not in the long run.

5. **Average Variable Cost (AVC)** = $\dfrac{\text{TVC}}{\text{Total Output}}$

6. **Average Total Cost (ATC)** = $\dfrac{\text{TC}}{\text{Total Output}}$

7. **Marginal Cost (MC)** = $\dfrac{\Delta \text{TC}}{\Delta \text{Output}}$

Rattan Chair Factory Cost Schedule

Q	TFC	TVC	TC	AFC	AVC	ATC	MC
0	400	0	400				
1	400	800	1200	400.0	800	1200	800
2	400	1250	1650	200.0	625	825	450
3	400	1550	1950	133.3	516.6	650	300
4	400	1800	2200	100.0	450	550	250
5	400	2100	2500	80.0	420	500	300
6	400	2600	3000	66.7	433.3	500	500
7	400	3350	3750	57.1	478.5	535.7	750
8	400	4450	4850	50.0	556.2	606.2	1100
9	400	6050	6450	44.4	672.2	716.6	1600

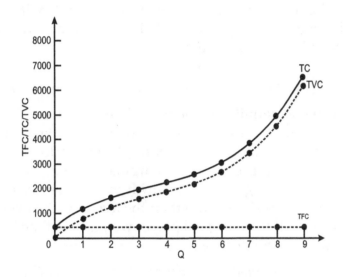

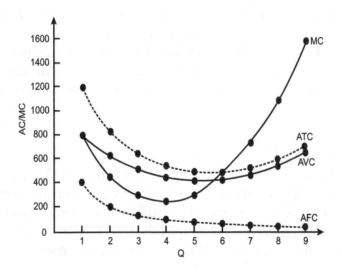

Theory of Sunk Cost

Sunk cost is a cost incurred in the past that cannot be changed by current decisions and therefore cannot be recovered. For example, a firm must purchase a $10,000 government license before it can legally produce and sell lamp poles. Furthermore, suppose the government will not buy back the license or allow the firm to sell it to another firm. This is an example of a sunk cost. It cannot be changed by current decisions and cannot be recovered.

Another good example of sunk cost is a student choosing his or her final major in college. Let's say that Mary is a junior majoring in accounting. Suddenly, she changes her mind and decides that she really would like to major in music and art appreciation. Would an economist recommend that Mary change her major based on the fact that she spent three years of her life in the business program? An economist would recommend that Mary not base her current decision to change major on what has happened in the past. If a person lets what she has done influence her present decisions, she runs the risk of compounding her problems.

The theory of sunk cost is similar to the teaching of Zen. It is related in the sense that we "don't cry over spilled milk." Things that happened in the past should not influence future decisions.

Relationship between Average and Marginal Cost

There is always a definite relationship between average and marginal cost. Consider the example of 10 football players with an average weight of 200 pounds. An eleventh player is added. His weight is 250 pounds. This represents the marginal weight. What happens now to the average weight of the team? It must increase. Thus, when the marginal player weighs more than the average, the average must increase. Likewise, if the marginal player weighs less than 200 pounds the average weight will decrease.

To minimize cost, *marginal cost must equal average cost (MC = AC)*. At this point, average cost is the lowest. Using the same analogy as the football example, if the marginal cost is equal to average cost, then the average costs will never go down. Thus, average cost is said to be at its minimum point. This condition is used to explain efficiency of production. However, this condition does not apply for profit maximization. The criterion for profit maximization assumes that revenue is factored in our analysis.

Long-Run Theory of Costs

All of our discussion thus far has been confined to short-run production costs. The short run is characterized by a commitment to plant and equipment. A factory, an office building, or some other plant and equipment have been leased or purchased. We are stuck with fixed costs. In the long run, note that fixed costs are not relevant.

1. Long-run average total cost (LRAC)

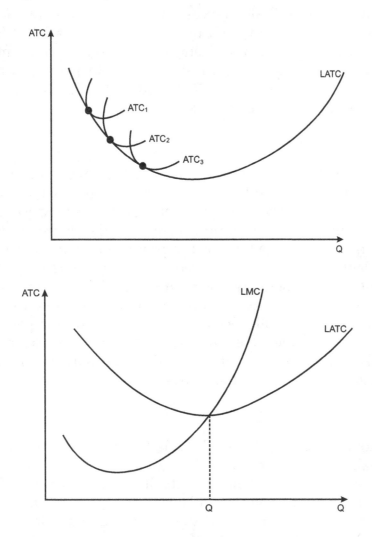

Long-run cost possibilities are determined by all possible short-run options. In this case, there are three options of varying size (ATC1; ATC2; ATC3). In the long run, we would choose the option that yielded the lowest average cost for any desired rate of output. The solid portion of the curves (LRAC) represents these choices. The smallest factory (ATC1) is the best for output levels below a, the largest (ATC3) for output rates in excess of b.

2. Long-run costs with unlimited options

If plants of all sizes can be built, short run options are infinite. In this case, the LRAC curve becomes a smooth U-shaped curve. Each point on the curve represents lower-cost production for a plant size best suited to one rate of output. The long run ATC curve has its own MC curve.

3. Economies and diseconomies of scale

Economies of scale are the reductions in minimum average costs that come about through increase in the size (scale) of plant and equipment.

Types of Economies of Scale

Constant Returns to Scale: Increases in plant size do not affect minimum average costs; minimum per unit costs are identical for small plants and large plants. The average total costs are constant, so the percentage in the output level causes total cost to increase by the same percentage, which keeps the LRAC constant. That is, the long-run average cost curve first reaches its lowest levels.

Economies of Scale

An economy of scale is a decrease in costs as plant size increases. This implies that a jeans producer who wants to minimize costs should build one medium-size factory rather than try to produce the same quantity with two small factories. Economies of scale are the decreases in the long-run average total cost of production that occur when the firm's plant size is increased, as represented by the falling portion of the LRAC curve. There are several reasons why a larger firm might have lower unit costs. Specialization or division of labor can contribute to economies of scale. Second, as the firm grows larger and produces more, valuable experience in production processes can lower cost. Finally, large firms can also take advantage of research and development and lower the cost that way.

Diseconomies of Scale

Even though large plants may be able to achieve greater efficiencies than smaller plants, there is no assurance that they will. In fact, increasing the size or scale of a plant may actually reduce operating efficiency. Workers may feel alienated in a plant of massive proportions and feel little commitment to productivity. Moreover, a large plant may offer greater opportunities to slack off without getting caught. For these and other reasons, a large plant may require more intensive managerial supervision, which raises production cost.

Economies of Scope

The cost of a particular product can be affected by the interactions between product-specific and plant-specific economies. For example, the merger of Germany's Deutsche and Dresdner banks (*The Economist*, March 11, 2000) led to lowering costs of operating their e-commerce business. Branches were closed or sold and jobs were cut. Deutsche Bank was planning to spend €1 billion a year on e-commerce, and Dresdner was to spend half as much over two years. The new merged retail bank did not need to spend as much as the combined amount.

Economies of scope refers to the reduction in unit cost resulting from a firm's production of two or more products. Economies of scope occur whenever inputs—such as labor and capital equipment—can be shared in the production of different products. One commonly cited example of economies of scope is the airline industry, where the cost of transporting both passengers and freight on a single airplane is less than the cost of using two airplanes to transport passengers and freight separately (McGuigan, Moyer, and Harris, 1993).

References

The Economist, March 11, 2000.

Maital, 1994.

McGuigan, Moyer, and Harris, 1993.

Economies of scale made steel

The economics of very big ships

ABOARD one of the world's largest container ships, moving almost imperceptibly through the seas off Vietnam, it's easy to appreciate the economies of scale that allow a T-shirt made in China to be sent to the Netherlands for just 2.5 cents.

The *Eleonora Maersk* and the other seven ships in her class are among the biggest ever built: almost 400m long, or the length of four football pitches, and another half-pitch across. The ship can carry 7,500 or so 40-foot containers, each of which can hold 70,000 T-shirts. On the voyage your correspondent took, the *Eleonora* was carrying Europe's New Year celebrations: 1,850 tonnes of fireworks, including 30 tonnes of gunpowder.

To move all this cargo from China to Europe in just over three weeks, the *Eleonora* boasts the largest internal-combustion engine ever built, as powerful as 1,000 family cars. This engine turns the longest propeller shaft (130m) ever made, at the end of which is the largest propeller, at 130 tonnes. Yet the ship is so automated that it requires a mere 13 people to crew it. Reassuringly, most captains prefer to take a few more.

Maersk Lines, the world's biggest container-shipping company and owner of the *Eleonora*, is betting that, given the current economies of world trade, the only way to go is yet bigger. In February it announced an order for 20 even larger ships with a capacity of 18,000 twenty-foot-equivalent units (TEUs), the standard measure of container size. (The *Eleonora* can carry a mere 15,000.) The new ships will cost $200m each. And judging by this year's order books, Maersk's example will be followed by others. Singapore's Nepture Orient Lines has ordered ten vessels of 14,000 TEUs; Orient Overseas Container Line has ordered ten of 13,000 TEUs. This is excellent news for South Korean shipyards (see article (http://www.economist.com/node/21538104)).

Most of these vessels will be designed for the Europe-Asia run—now the world's busiest trade route. Given the rising price of fuel, many shippers think they need huge ships to turn a profit. Fears of a renewed slowdown in global trade accelerate the rush to find economies of scale.

Freight rates have plummeted in recent months, thanks to weakening demand and an oversupply of container ships, many of them ordered in the optimistic years before 2008. Freight rates on the Europe-Asia run are now below $700 per TEU, less than half the peak a year ago. At this price, says Janet Lewis, an analyst at Macquarie, a bank, "It's hard for any container company to be making any cash."

Recent financial results bear this out. On November 9th Maersk said its container business had lost $297m in the latest quarter. Neptune posted a third-quarter loss of $91m, having made a profit of $282m a year earlier. Japan's "K" Line reported a loss of $239m on its container-shipping unit in the fiscal first half. And things could get a lot worse.

Companies are searching for new strategies to differentiate themselves from rivals, or merely to survive. Maersk has launched what it calls the "Daily Maersk" service on the China-Europe run, deploying 70 vessels to promise daily deliveries to Felixstowe, Bremerhaven and Rotterdam, the three main European container ports. The firm is hoping to deliver 95% of these containers on time, up from 80% for its own service on that route. This would be far higher than the industry average of about 65%. If a container arrives more than a day late, Maersk pledges to compensate the customer. Orient Overseas, by contrast, is focusing on the quality of its cargo-handling. It charges more, for example, to ship perishable items, such as blood plasma.

Given the stormy waters that may well be ahead, it seems likely that shippers will seek economies of scale not only from bigger ships but also from mergers. The industry is too crowded, many analysts believe. Smaller firms may soon be swallowed like containers vanishing into the hold of the *Eleonora Maersk*.

Definitions

1. Production function

2. Average product

3. Marginal product

4. Diminishing marginal returns

5. Firm

6. Profit

7. Opportunity cost of capital

8. Economic profit

9. Economic cost

10. Short-run period

11. Long-run period

12. Total cost

13. Total fixed cost

14. Total variable cost

15. Average fixed cost

16. Average variable cost

17. Average total cost

18. Marginal cost

19. Sunk cost

20. Marginal cost must equal average cost

21. Constant returns of scale

22. Economies of scale

23. Diseconomies of scale

24. Economies of scope

Multiple Choice

1. In economics, production efficiency means a firm should
   a. not waste resources.
   b. not use any expensive resources.
   c. choose that combination of inputs that will produce a given level of output at the lowest possible cost.
   d. choose to use as much of the least capital as possible.
   e. all of the above.

2. In the long run, the amounts and types of productive inputs used to produce a good
   a. are fixed.
   b. are variable.
   c. always increase as firms produce more.
   d. always decrease as firms use resources more efficiently.
   e. are not influenced by their market prices.

3. In the short run, the productive inputs used by a firm
   a. are all fixed.
   b. are all variable.
   c. may be variable or fixed, but at least one input is fixed.
   d. can all be changed as input prices and technology change.
   e. both b and d are correct.

4. Economic profit is
   a. the difference between total revenue and total cost.
   b. always positive in the short run.
   c. always equal to the full opportunity cost of producing a given level of output.
   d. something evil that is never earned.
   e. both a and c are correct.

5. Economic profits provide
   a. payment to entrepreneurs for their entrepreneurial talent.
   b. an incentive for entrepreneurs to take risks.
   c. an incentive to organize firms for production.
   d. a powerful incentive for new firms to enter economically profitable markets.
   e. all of the above.

6. The choice of inputs used in the production of a good depends on
   a. the firm's production function for that good.
   b. the level of technology available.
   c. the relative prices of the inputs.
   d. the least costly combination of inputs.
   e. all of the above.

7. Accounting profit is
    a. always equal to economic profit.
    b. equal to total revenue minus explicit costs.
    c. equal to total revenue minus implicit costs.
    d. equal to total revenue minus economic costs.
    e. always a positive number.

8. Sunk costs are
    a. costs that have already been incurred, making them unavoidable in the short run.
    b. costs like property taxes.
    c. costs like rent required during a contact period.
    d. costs like insurance premiums on the property required by the mortgage company.
    e. all of the above.

9. Fixed costs
    a. vary as output increases.
    b. do not vary as the level of output varies even if output is zero.
    c. include raw material costs.
    d. can be avoided if the firm shuts down.
    e. can be avoided if the firm merges with another firm.

10. A baseball player is hitting .400 (getting a hit 40 percent of the time). In his last game, he had three hits in four at-bats. As a result
    a. his batting average will fall.
    b. his marginal batting performance is below his average batting performance.
    c. his marginal batting performance is above his average batting performance, and his batting average will rise.
    d. he will be taken out of the lineup.

True/False

Directions: For the following statements, indicate whether the statement is true or false. If the statement is false, make the necessary change(s) in order for it to be a true statement.

1. The ultimate object of production is to transform inputs into outputs that yield profits to firms who produce them (called utility).

2. The production function $Q = f(L, K)$ basically states that output can be produced with either labor or capital.

3. Using the average product formula as given in the chapter, it is possible to compare workers across countries; for example, output per Japanese worker versus output per American worker.

4. Marginal productivity is not as important in economics as average productivity.

5. The law of diminishing marginal returns basically states that a person's satisfaction for a good decreases as that person's income decreases.

6. According to its definition, a firm is an organization that uses factors of production to produce goods or services for a profit.

7. The difference between economic profits and accounting profits is that economic profits do not factor in variables found on the balance sheets as accounting profits do.

8. Fixed costs remain constant both in the short run and the long run.

9. Wages and cost of materials or inputs are examples of fixed costs.

10. Average variable cost (AVC) is also called "spreading the overhead" and is only relevant in the short run, not the long run.

11. A sunk cost is a cost that can only be recovered in the short run.

12. To minimize cost, fixed costs must equal variable costs.

Short Answer/Essay Questions

1. Explain why the following reasoning is incorrect: "Now that I have paid off my van, it won't cost me anything except for running expenses, such as gas, oil, and tune-ups when I actually go somewhere with it."

2. Complete the following table and then graph the marginal cost (MC) and average cost (AC) curves. Identify the lowest per-unit cost.

Rate of Output	Total Cost	MC	AFC	AVC	ATC
0	100	_____	_____	_____	_____
1	110	_____	_____	_____	_____
2	130	_____	_____	_____	_____
3	165	_____	_____	_____	_____
4	220	_____	_____	_____	_____
5	300	_____	_____	_____	_____

3. How does the economist's definition of cost differ from the accountant's?

4. What distinguishes the long run from the short run?

5. Why is the average total cost curve U-shaped?

Chapter 5

Market Structure and the Nature of Industries

Alin Popescu/Shutterstock.com

Perfectly **competitive markets** is an economic model with the following characteristics: (a) economic agents act as a price taker; (b) homogeneous product (meaning products are assumed to be identical); (c) free mobility of all resources; (d) free entry/exit of business; (e) no government intervention; and (f) complete and perfect information.

In a perfect world, these are the assumptions with which we wish to operate. However, in reality, some of these assumptions are unrealistic. For example, we assume the firms have no form of government intervention, but we know that even the nearest form of a perfectly competitive market, like the stock market, is still governed by the Securities and Exchange Commission (SEC).

In analyzing competitive markets, we also have to introduce the concepts of total revenue, average revenue, and marginal revenue.

$$\textbf{Total Revenue} = \textbf{Price} \times \textbf{Quantity } (P \times Q)$$

$$\textbf{Average Revenue} = \textbf{Total Revenue / Quantity}$$

If the market is competitive, we can define marginal revenue as follows:

$$\textbf{MR} = \textbf{Change in TR / Change in } Q \textbf{ or } P$$

Given that marginal revenue is the same thing as price, we assume that the seller is considered as a **price taker.** This means that the seller accepts the price based on the market price.

Short-Run versus Long-Run Competitive Markets

Short-run analysis of competitive markets can be done based on the profits earned by a particular firm given the market. **Economic profit** is defined as the difference between total revenue and total cost. If total revenue exceeds total cost, the firm is making pure economic profit. However, if total cost exceeds total revenue, the firm is experiencing an economic loss. There are two kinds of loss that we have to consider. When the price per unit is less than the average variable cost, then we assume that the firm is operating at a **shutdown profit.** However, if the price is between the average total cost and average variable cost, then the firm is indifferent about staying in business. If the case is that the price is between ATC and AVC, then we assume that the firm is recouping its variable cost and losing some of its fixed cost.

The table below shows the cost of production and revenues from the sale of output:

Q	TC	P	TR	Profit	ATC	AVC	MC	MR
0	10	5	0	−10				
1	15	5	5	−10	15	5	5	5
2	18	5	10	−8	9	4	3	5
3	20	5	15	−5	6.67	3.33	2	5
4	21	5	20	−1	5.25	2.75	1	5
5	23	5	25	2	4.6	2.6	2	5
6	26	5	30	4	4.33	2.67	3	5
7	30	5	35	5	4.28	2.86	4	5
8	35	5	40	5	4.38	3.12	5	5
9	41	5	45	4	4.56	3.44	6	5
10	48	5	50	2	4.8	3.8	7	5

The model can be plotted as follows:

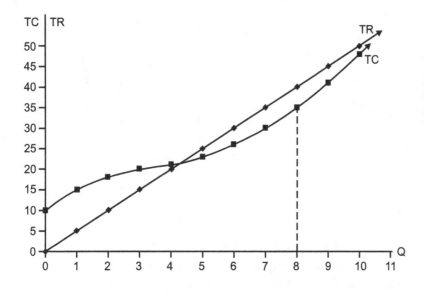

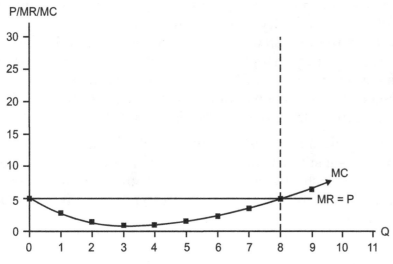

Clearly, profit maximization can be determined as the point when marginal revenue equals marginal cost. At that point, it gives the largest distance between marginal cost and marginal revenue. Marginal revenue is represented by the individual firm demand, DD, which is a horizontal line at $5. It intersects the marginal revenue curve at a rate of output and sales of somewhere between seven and eight handbags per day.

In the long run, however, economic profit is assumed to be zero or normal profit. Because of the assumption of free entry, the firm will stay in business only as long as it can pay all its cost. It is normal profit in economics because total cost includes opportunity or implicit cost.

Equilibrium Model for a Long-Run Competitive Firm and Industry

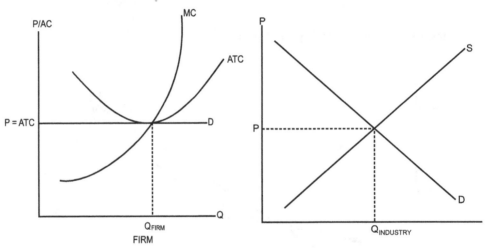

Monopoly

In a purely competitive market, each firm's production is such a small proportion of industry output that a single firm has no influence on the market price. As we have seen, the competitive firm is a price taker. The opposite of a purely competitive market is a pure **monopoly**, a single seller in an industry. The pure monopoly, in fact, is an industry. It alone faces the industry demand curve for its output, and it can affect market price by changing the amount of output that it produces. For this reason, we refer to the pure monopoly firm as a price maker. It must seek the price that maximizes its profits. The ability of the pure monopoly firm to affect market price is not absolute, however.

A pure monopoly is an industry composed of a single seller of a product with no close substitutes and with high barriers to entry. Examples of pure monopoly include eighteenth-century European monarchs granting monopoly to individuals for a variety of production undertakings.

For example, the tobacco monopoly in the Philippines was granted by the Spaniard monarchy in the fifteenth century. One of the main reasons monopolies exist is **barriers to entry.**

Typically, barriers to entry are government actions that prohibit other firms or individuals from producing particular products or from entering particular occupations or industries; such barriers take the form of legal franchises, licenses, and patents. A patent grants an inventor a monopoly over a product or process for 20 years in the United States. The patent prohibits others from producing the patented product and thereby confers a limited-term monopoly on the inventor. The purpose of a patent is to encourage innovation by allowing inventors to reap the exclusive fruits of their inventions for a period of time. A patent establishes a legal monopoly right. In effect, the social benefit of innovation is traded off against the possible social costs of monopoly.

In some industries, low unit costs may be achieved only through large-scale production. Such economies of scale put potential entrants at a disadvantage. To be able to compete effectively in the industry, a new firm has to enter on a large scale, which can be costly and risky. The effect is to deter entry. In a natural monopoly, economies of scale are so pronounced that only a single firm can survive in the industry. In such a case, government enacts some sort of regulatory scheme to control the natural monopoly. Public utilities such as natural gas, water, and electricity distribution are examples of natural monopolies that are regulated (Ekelund, 2000).

Market Model for a Monopoly

Let's say that a monopoly's demand and total revenue is given as follows:

Price ($)	Quantity	Total Revenue	Marginal Revenue
10	0	0	
9	1	9	9
8	2	16	7
7	3	21	5
6	4	24	3
5	5	25	1
4	6	24	−1
3	7	21	−3
2	8	16	−5
1	9	9	−7

Plotting the demand and marginal revenue curves:

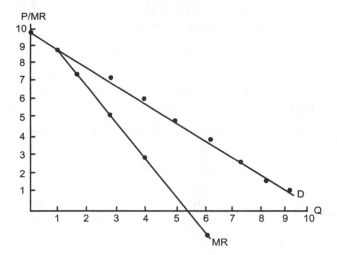

The demand curve faced by a monopolist is downward sloping. As opposed to a competitive firm, the monopolist's demand curve is the same as the industry's demand curve. The relationship between demand and marginal revenue depends on the elasticity of demand. The relationship can be derived as follows:

$$MR = \frac{\Delta TR}{\Delta Q}$$

$$MR = \frac{dTR}{dQ}$$

$$MR = \frac{d(PxQ)}{dQ}$$

$$MR = Px\frac{dQ}{dQ} + Qx\frac{dP}{dQ}$$

$$MR = P\left[1 + \frac{Q}{P}\frac{dP}{dQ}\right]$$

$$MR = P\left[1 + \frac{1}{e_p}\right]$$

Therefore, marginal revenue is a function of price and the inverse of its price elasticity.

Price Discrimination in Monopoly

Price discrimination is charging different prices for the same commodity given two or more different markets. In a monopoly, the seller can charge different prices for different markets depending on how the markets respond to the changes in prices. Looking at the relationship between marginal revenue and prices, it also depends on the price elasticity of demand.

There are four elements of prices discrimination:

1. The seller must be able to separate the markets.

2. Goods that are being sold must be identical for each market.

3. Different markets have different price elasticities.

4. Marginal cost is insignificant in separating the markets.

There are three types of price discrimination: first-degree price discrimination, second-degree price discrimination, and third-degree price discrimination.

First-Degree Price Discrimination

Firms usually do not know the reservation price of every consumer. But sometimes reservation price can be roughly identified. For example, doctors' fees, lawyers' fees, and accountants' fees all depend on the willingness of the clients to pay. There are no exact set prices for a given market. Doctors may offer a reduced fee to a low-income patient whose willingness to pay is low, and charge a higher price to an upper-income patient.

The model can be viewed as follows:

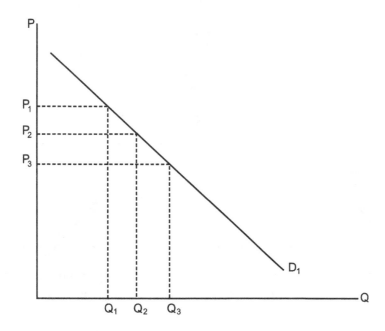

Second-Degree Price Discrimination

Firms can discriminate according to the quantity consumed. In other words, firms can charge different prices for different quantities, or "blocks," of the same goods or services. Examples include water, heating fuel, and electricity. If there are scale economies, then the average cost and marginal cost are declining. In the case of electricity, the state agency that controls the company's note may encourage block pricing. By expanding output and achieving greater scale economies, consumer welfare can be increased, even allowing for greater profit for the company.

Third-Degree Price Discrimination

This is a form of price discrimination in which market separation depends on the price elasticity of each market. An example of this kind of price discrimination can be seen in airline ticket pricing. The service that is being sold is the actual flight. However, airline companies can separate the market into first class and economy class. They can change quality of service for each class. For example, in the first-class section, each passenger can be served caviar, fresh salad, and wine with fine china and linen, and the ratio of flight attendants to the number of passengers is better for the first-class section. When you fly in the economy section you end up with a smaller seat, lousy food or no food at all, and busy flight attendants. There are some differences in cost for separating the markets, but the cost difference is insignificant for the company as a whole.

The model can be viewed as follows:

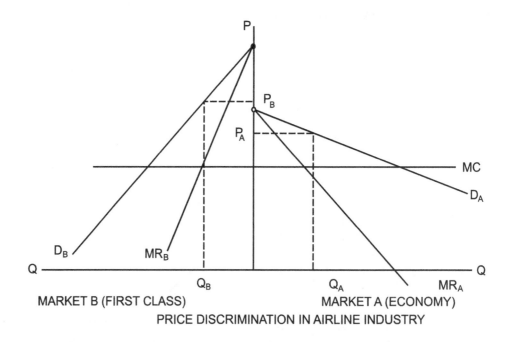

PRICE DISCRIMINATION IN AIRLINE INDUSTRY

One implication of price discrimination is that it may not always be worthwhile for the firm to try to sell to more than one group of consumers. In particular, if demand is small for a group of consumers and marginal cost is rising, the increase in cost of producing and selling to this group may outweigh the increase in revenue. The firm is better off charging a single price, P*.

Monopolistic Competition

All models of firms and markets other than the extremes of pure competition and pure monopoly are called theories of imperfect competition. The word *imperfect* means that not all the conditions for pure competition are met. Some imperfectly competitive markets contain large numbers of sellers (as in pure competition) selling slightly different products (unlike pure competition). These are monopolistically competitive markets.

The general characteristic of a monopolistically competitive market is that there are many sellers in the market. However, the products that they are selling are slightly differentiated. This means that their products are distinct, in the consumer's eyes, from close substitutes. Products may be distinguished by brand names, location, services, even differences merely perceived by the consumer. Product differentiation is an example of *nonprice competition,* a term commonly used to refer to any action other than price cuts taken by a competitor to increase demand for its product.

Entry in monopolistic competition is relatively unrestricted in the sense that new firms may easily start the production of close substitutes for existing products. This occurs with restaurants, styling salons, barber shops, and many forms of retail activity. Because of relatively free entry, economic profits tend to be eliminated in the long run, as was the case in perfect competition (Sexton, 1999).

Equilibrium Model for a Monopolistic Competitive Market

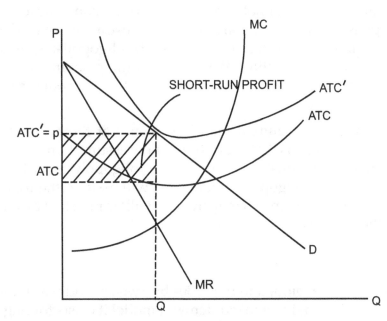

Note: In the short run, a typical firm is making a profit as a result of excessive advertising. It gives this firm the edge over other firms that can make the firm act as if it is operating in a monopolistic market. However, as more firms enter the market, a typical firm in this kind of market will produce normal profits.

Oligopoly

Oligopoly is a market where there are few sellers controlling all or most of the production and sale of a product. The product being sold can be homogenous or differentiated, as long as the barriers to entry are high enough to discourage new firms from entering the market. Examples of oligopoly markets include commercial airlines, oil, automobiles, tobacco, steel, and breakfast cereals.

Economies of scale make operation on a small scale during the early years of a new firm extremely unprofitable. A firm cannot build up a large market overnight; in the interim, average total cost is so high that losses are heavy. Recognition of this fact discourages new firms from entering the market. Oligopoly is also characterized by **mutual interdependence,** where firms react to what other firms are doing in a given industry. For example, in the airline industry if one airline lowers the price, the rest of the industry follows.

Oligopoly is a result of the relationship between technological conditions of production and potential sales volumes. For many products, a reasonably low cost of production cannot be obtained unless a firm is producing a large fraction of the market output.

The Oligopolist's Demand Curve

Now we are faced with the difficult task of drawing the demand curve for an oligopolist. We cannot use the industry demand curve because the oligopolist is not a monopolist. We cannot use a horizontal demand curve at the market clearing price because the oligopolist is, by definition, not a perfect competitor. We can say nothing about the demand curve of an oligopolist until we make an assumption about the interaction among oligopolists.

The fact that there is mutual interdependence at the heart of every oligopoly model means that every time a new assumption about interaction among oligopolists is made, a new oligopoly model is born. For the simplest of oligopoly models, we will assume the following: Each firm expects that any change in price will be matched by all other firms in the industry.

The Kinked Demand Curve

This model was developed in the 1930s by Sweezy and was known as the Sweezy solution. In a kinked demand model it exists for oligopoly firms that believe rivals will follow a price decrease but not a price increase.

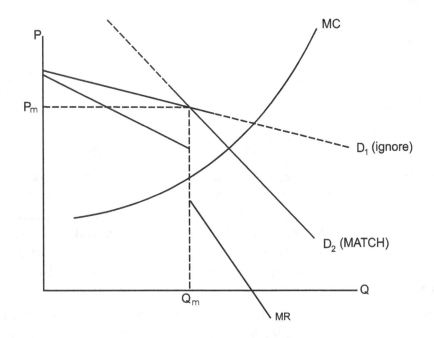

Profit Maximization with a Kinked Demand Curve

D_1 is the demand curve that would apply if other firms in the industry did not follow a single firm when it changed price. On the other hand, demand curve D_2 applies when all other firms will follow a price change made by one firm. P_m is the going market price. The kinked demand curve theory states that firms will not follow a price increase above P_m but will follow a price decrease below P_m whereas D_2 applies at lower prices. As a result, the demand curve for the firm has a kink in it at P_m and Q_m. Also, the marginal revenue curve is discontinuous (has a gap) at Q_m. As long as its marginal cost curve passes through the gap in the marginal revenue curve, the firm will maximize profit by producing Q_m units of output and charging a price equal to P_m.

References

Ekelund, 2000.

Sexton, 1999.

Opening a business in Brazil

Why make it simple?

São Paulo

Setting up shop has just got easier. But not much

Brazil is not an easy place to start a business. The World Bank ranks it 120th our of 183 countries–worse than Burkina Faso or Nigeria. Take one small example. Until recently, you needed at least two partners to form a limited-liability company. Sole traders had to find a "1% socio" – an employee, friend or family member willing to lend his name to the articles of association, or a shell company set up solely to hold a tiny share.

Things may have just got a little easier. A new law, which supposedly came into effect on January 9th, allows a lone business-owner to set up an *Empresa Individual de Responsabilidade Limitada* (Eireli for short): a single-holder limited-liability firm. The main requirement is capital of 62,200 reais ($35,250).

This is a big deal. Alas, it may not happen as planned. In December the federal body that oversees state business registries told them to turn away firm trying to register Eirelis, as well as foreigners without permanent right of residence. No reason was given. Later, lawyer were briefed that the law's aim was to let Brazilian sole traders protect their personal goods against lawsuits or bankrutcy—not to make life easier for big business or foreigners.

Since the restrictions have no basis in the law, challenges are inevitable. Hosam Abboud of Establish Brazil, a company formation specialist, is thinking of Brazilian style direct action: simply trying to register an Eireli for a firm or a foreigner, and seeing what happens. "We won't be trying just once, but many times," he says cheerfully. "In Brazil, it always depends who's on the desk on the day."

A few speedy locals have already set up Eirelis. "It was quick and easy, because I didn't have to hunt for a partner," says Taise Litholdo, an architect. Sebastião Lino da Silva, an accountant in São Paulo, is helping a medical research firm, which recently lost a partner, to convert into an Eireli. The remaining owner would otherwise have to find a new partner or close. João Marcelo Pacheco of Pinheiro Neto Advogados, one of Brazil's largest law firms, says that some wealthy clients will use Eirelis to make their lives simpler.

All this amounts to a tweak, not a revolution. By January 18th only 14 Eirelis had been registered with São Paulo's board of trade, Brazil's biggest. "The truth is Eirelis are not really suitable for most small businesses," says Mr. Abboud. Few hot-dog vendors and hair-dressers have enough spare cash to satisfy the capital requirement, he points out.

That is an argument for scrapping the capital requirement. The Social-ist People's Party, an opposition group, has asked the Supreme Court to rule it unconstitutional for discriminating against micro-traders.

Even if foreigners are allowed to set up Eirelis, breaking into Brazil will remain though. The biggest hurdle—finding a permanent resident willing to hold power of attorney for foreign owners—will remain. Establish Brazil and its rivals will do this for foreign clients, but only until a local manager has been appointed, or an expatriate has arrived on a permanent business visa.

The snag is that acting for a foreign firm leaves agents vulnerable to Brazil's capricious tax authorities and labour courts, which tend to ignore limited liability and pursue individual owners. "They want to be able to freeze someone's bank account if problems arise," explains Stephen O'Sullivan of Mattos Filho Advogados, another big São Paulo law firm. "And if they're the only people in the country, they'll go after the local managers, or even the lawyers." Unsurprisingly, Mattos Filho is willing to fulfil this role for old and valued clients. Eirelis may even-tually make it easier to set up shop in Brazil. But only a little.

Appendix 5

Economics and Art of Business and Making Money

OBJECTIVES

1. To discuss the different types of businesses and their impact on the whole economy.
2. To explain the advantages and disadvantages of the different types of businesses.
3. To explain the difference between a stock and a bond.
4. To explain the meaning of capital markets.
5. To discuss the importance of capital markets in the economy.

Different Types of Businesses

To explain the different components of business and their economic implications, it is important to list the different types of businesses. There are basically three types of businesses: (a) single proprietorship;(b) partnership; and (c) corporation.

A *single proprietorship* is a form of business that is owned by one individual who makes all business decisions, receives profits, and is legally responsible for the debts of the firm. One of the advantages of a single proprietor is that the proprietor owns 100 percent of the profits. The owner is responsible for all strategic decisions for the business. These strategic decisions can make or break a business. Thus, a single proprietor is responsible for all consequences of any strategic decisions he or she makes for the business. A single proprietor is legally responsible for any damages or costs related to the business. If the business goes bankrupt, the proprietor is personally responsible for any debts or loans. Single proprietorships are often businesses started from the ground up.

The second type of business is a *partnership*. A partnership is a business that is owned by two or more co-owners who share any profits the business earns. In a partnership, there are general partners who are personally responsible for any liability related to the business. However, there also may be limited partners who are responsible only for a limited amount depending on their initial investment. Most businesses formed as partnerships are professional services such as medical, accounting, legal, or dental offices. For example, a tax lawyer can partner with a tax accountant because they complement each other.

The third type of business is a *corporation*. A corporation is a legal entity that can conduct business in its own name the way an individual does. The owners of the corporation are *stockholders*. A stock is a certificate of ownership stating that the person owns some share of the company. Because a corporation is its own legal entity, owners of the corporation are not personally liable. Corporations continue to exist even if one or more owners of a corporation sell their shares or die. The corporation's life is independent of the lives of any of the owners. One disadvantage of a corporation is double taxation. Since the entity of the stockholder is separate from the entity of the corporation, both the stockholder and the corporation pay taxes. Another disadvantage of a corporation is the problem of ownership and control. It is more difficult to control a corporation because control depends on the opinion of the majority of the stockholders.

The dominant form of business in the United States in terms of numbers is the single or sole proprietorship. This is because it is easier to start a business as a sole proprietor. However, corporate firms account for 90 percent of sales revenues of all business firms in the United States. In 1986, total revenue of sole proprietorships was approximately $559 billion, or 6.1 percent of the total revenue of all the firms. Partnerships accounted for $378.7 billion, or 4.1 percent of the total. Corporations accounted for $8,281.1 billion, or 89.8 percent of the total (Irwin, 1992).

Reading a Stock and Bond Quotation

It is important to understand how to read a stock or a bond quotation. In the *Wall Street Journal* or any business section of a newspaper, a reader can see the listing of different stock and bond quotations. There are two different types of stock market quotations. The first is the New York Stock Exchange, and the second is the NASDAQ. Most of the companies listed in the New York Stock Exchange are solid companies like blue-chip stock and income stocks. NASDAQ stocks are stocks that are mostly new, including initial public offerings (IPOs) and technology stocks.

In reading a stock quotation, the following components are listed for each company: (a) high and low prices for the previous year; (b) stock exchange symbol; (c) yearly dividend; (d) dividend as a percent of price; (e) price–earnings ratio (PE); (f) number of shares traded (in hundreds); (g) high and low for the day; (h) closing price of the stock; and (i) change in price from previous day. Dividends are profits that are distributed to the stockholders after the company announces that profits were realized. Price–earnings ratio measures how highly a stock is valued.

HI	LO		SYM	Div	Yld (%)	PE	VOL (100s)	Hi	Lo	Cls	Net Chg
42	29	PepsiCo	PEP	0.721	2.4	15	12333	30¾	30³/₈	30½	−0.5

Legend:

HI and LO	High and Low price for previous year	Hi and Lo	High and Low for the day
SYM	Stock symbol	Cls	Closing price of stock
Div	Yearly Dividend	Net Chg	Change in price from previous day
Yld (%)	Dividend as a percent of price		
PE	Price-earnings ratio		
Vol	Number of shares traded (in hundreds)		

Sample Bond Quotation for PepsiCo (PEP)

	Rate	Maturity	Yld	Vol	Close	Net Chg
PEP	6½	12	7	40	100	0

Legend:

Rate	Coupon Rate
Maturity	Year bond matures
Yld	Yield to Maturity
Vol	Number of bonds traded
Close	Closing Price
Net Change	Change in price from previous day

In a bond quotation, the following variables are listed for each company: (a) coupon rate; (b) maturity of the bond; (c) yield to maturity; (d) number of bonds traded; (e) closing price; and (f) change in price from previous day. The coupon rate is the interest rate on the bond, and the yield to maturity is the interest rate based on the current price of the bond.

The volatility of the stock prices in the recent years has challenged those who claimed that the "new era" economic paradigm of rising productivity, low inflation, and global capitalism justified the high level of stock prices. Such paradigms are critical for estimating earnings far in the future—and such estimates dominate the valuation of any long-term asset such as stocks. Thus, if the paradigm changes, it has a critical impact on equity prices.

It is important to understand the relation between the valuation investors place on earnings and the return to shareholders. Since 1871 the average price of a stock on Standard and Poor's 500 has been about 14 times annual earnings. This implies that the earnings yield, which is the inverse of the price–earnings ratio, has averaged about 7 percent. The earnings yield measures the rate of return firms have earned on the market value of their stock and almost exactly matches the 7 percent average real return (return after inflation) that investors have earned on stocks over the past two centuries.

Interest Rates, Bond Prices, and Present Values

A bond is a loan or IOU. We can classify five characteristics of a bond:

1. They are issued for a certain number of years (n).

2. They have a face value or par value (F).

3. The issuer agrees to make equal, periodic interest payments.

4. The issuer agrees to repay the face value at maturity.

5. The periodic payments are called coupon payments, and are equal to the coupon rate on the bond multiplied by the face value of the bond.

A bond represents a stream of future payments that can be defined as follows:

$$P = \frac{C_1}{(1+i)^n} + \frac{C_2}{(1+i)^2} + \cdots + \frac{C_n}{(1+i)^n} + \frac{F}{(1+i)^n}$$

where:

$P =$ **price of the bond (present value)**

$C =$ **coupon payment on the bond**

$F =$ **face or par value of the bond**

$I =$ **interest rate**

$N =$ **number of years**

Suppose Jane is about to buy a bond that will mature in 1 year, has a face value of $1,000, carries a coupon payment of $60, and the prevailing interest rate is 6 percent. What is Jane willing to pay for the bond?

Using the formula above:

$$P = 60/(1+ .06) + 1000/(1+.06)$$

$$= 56.60 + 943.40$$

$$= \$1,000.00$$

This is what Jane will pay for the bond. If Jane keeps the bond for $1,000 and the next day the prevailing interest rate is 8 percent, what effect does this have on the value of Jane's bond? Remember, Jane's bond will pay her $1,060.

Fluctuations in Interest Rates and Managing a Bond Portfolio

In a financial crisis, one often hears conversation about the interest rate. People will ask, for example, "Do you think interest rates will fall or rise?" In such a discussion, reference to interest rates is, in fact, a reference to maturity or yields. The question that one should ask is,

"Why would a manager of a bond portfolio for a large pension fund be concerned with the likely direction of the interest rate?"

Simply put, if rates rise sharply the value of the manager's portfolio, which contains previously purchased bonds goes right out of the window. Conversely, if rates fall, the prices of previously purchased bonds increase and capital gains are in the offing. Such possibilities are what motivate managers and their advisers to pay so much attention to the factors that determine interest rates. More specifically, a portfolio manager who believes the Fed is about to engage in actions that will raise interest rates is likely to sell a considerable number of bonds now to avoid capital losses on bonds held. Conversely, the expectation of a fall in interest rates would encourage the purchase of bonds in anticipation of the capital gains that will accompany a fall in market rates. www.citizensbanking.com/

The Emergence of the Limited Liability Company

An LLC is an entity formed under state law with both tax and legal advantages. It separates business assets from personal assets and thus can generally limit business-related claims on personal assets. It has relatively simple and favorable income tax attributes because it is generally taxed as a partnership if there is one member. This means income

Table 5.1 Standard and Poor's Bond Ratings

Grade	Description
Investment Grade	
AAA	Highest quality. Ability to pay interest and principal is very strong.
AA	High quality. Ability to pay interest and principal strong.
A	Medium to high quality. Ability to pay interest and principal, but more susceptible to changes in circumstances and the economy.
BBB	Medium quality. Adequate ability to pay, but highly susceptible to adverse circumstances.
Speculative or Junk Rating	
BB	Speculative. Less near-term likelihood of default relative to other speculative issues.
B	Current capacity to pay interest and principal, but highly susceptible.
CCC	Likely to default, where payment of interest and principal is dependent.
CC	Debt subordinate to senior debt rated CCC.
C	Debt subordinate to senior debt rated CCC-D
D	Currently in default, where interest or principal has not been made as promised.

is taxed to the members, not the entity. If there is only one member of the LLC, the income tax situation is even simpler; it is ignored. Most importantly, you can choose the intended income tax result. An LLC is a hybrid between a corporation and a partnership. The tax and legal advantages that the LLC form offers may make it the preferred choice for new transactions (Shenkman and Taback, 2003).

Although LLCs have been in use for a number of years, they are still quite new compared with other forms of ownership for businesses and investments. Thus, some caution must be exercised. There are likely to be changes in state laws. Court cases interpreting both the tax and legal rules will take years to develop into a thorough and consistent resource. LLCs are formed and exist solely in accordance with the specific state law under which they were formed. Hence, to properly understand any LLC that is in existence, you must examine the state statute under which that particular LLC was organized. There can be important differences from state to state.

Money Markets versus Capital Markets

The flow of funds around the world may be divided into different segments, depending on the characteristics of financial claims being traded and the needs of different investors. One of the most important divisions in the financial system is between the money market and the capital markets.

The money market is designed for the making of short-term loans. It is the institution through which individuals and institutions with temporary surpluses of funds meet the needs of borrowers who have temporary funds shortages (deficits). Thus, the money market enables economic units to manage their liquidity positions. By convention, a security or loan maturing in one year or less is considered to be a money market instrument. One of the principal functions of the money market is to finance the working capital needs of corporations and to provide governments with short-term funds in lieu of tax collections. The money market also supplies funds for speculative buying of securities and commodities.

In contrast, the capital market is designed to finance long-term investments by businesses, governments, and households. Trading of funds in the capital market makes possible the construction of factories, highways, schools, and homes. Financial instruments in the capital market have original maturities of more than one year and range in size from small loans to multimillion-dollar credits.

Who are the principal suppliers and demanders of funds in the money market and the capital market? In the money market, commercial banks are the most important institutional supplier of funds to both business firms and governments. Nonfinancial business corporations with temporary cash surpluses also provide substantial short-term funds to the money markets. On the demand-for-funds side, the largest borrower in the U.S. money market is the Treasury Department, which borrows billions of dollars weekly. Other governments around the world are often among the leading borrowers in their own domestic money markets (Rose and Marquis, Money and Capital Markets, 2006).

The Role of the Financial System and Markets

The financial system is one of the most important component of modern society. Its primary task is to move scarce loanable funds from those who save to those who borrow to buy goods and services and to make investment in new equipment and facilities so that the global economy can grow and increase the standard of living enjoyed by its citizenry. Without the global financial system and the loanable funds it supplies, each of us would lead a much less enjoyable existence. The financial system determines both the cost and the quantity of funds available in the economy to pay for the thousands of goods and services we purchase daily. Equally important, what happens in the system has a powerful impact on the health of the global economy. When funds become more costly and less available, spending for goods and services falls. As a result, unemployment rises and the economy's growth slows as businesses cut back production and lay off workers. In contrast, when the cost of funds declines and loanable funds become more readily available, spending in the economy often increases, more jobs are created, and the economy's growth accelerates (Rose and Marquis, 2006).

The financial markets were assumed to be an efficient market. In an efficient market, both buyer and sellers have perfect information about the market. In the efficient market hypothesis, an example that can be shown to explain the theory is the stock market. All the relevant information about the market is reflected in the current price of the stock. According to this theory, no one can beat the market and all the relevant information is reflected in the current price of the stock. However, because of issues that deal with inside information, the stock market has some asymmetric information between the buyers and the sellers. By asymmetric information, the buyer and the seller possess different information about a market transaction. Recently, scandals such as the Madoff Ponzi scheme, the derivatives market, and the mortgage meltdown are examples of asymmetric information. Investors and managers have imperfect information about the financial instrument being marketed. These factors can influence the volatility of prices that can lead to distortions in the market.

References

Irwin, 1992.

Rose and Marquis, *Money and Capital Markets,* 2006.

Shenkman and Taback, 2003.

U.S. NEWS

Interesting Situation: When Rates Turn Negative

David Wessel

It has been five years since the onset of the global financial crisis. The first cracks in financial markets appeared in August 2007. That is so long ago, it's easy to overlook just how unusual these tunes are.

Here's one signpost: Investors are so skittish that instead of demanding interest when they lend to governments, they are actually paying to put money into the coffers of the financially sturdiest governments. We have blown past zero interest rates. Investors lend 100 euros (or Danish kroner or Swiss francs) and get back 99 and change.

Wow.

The European Financial Stability Facility, backed by the stronger governments of Europe, this week borrowed €1.43 billion ($1.77 billion) for three months at a yield of minus 0.0217%. Denmark recently raised 420 million kroner ($70 million) at minus 0.59%. Even more remarkable, Germany borrowed €4.17 billion for *two years* at an average yield of minus 0.06%. Markets have pushed two-year yields on Swiss government debt below zero regularly, and Belgium, Finland and the Netherlands occasionally.

Interest rates below zero used to be more economists' fantasy than reality. Few thought central banks would ever need, let alone be able, to cut rates below zero. When the U.S. was struggling in 2009, Harvard University's Greg Mankiw observed that minus 3% rates would help. "You could borrow and spend $100 and repay $97 next year," he wrote. That would give spending a boost. The problem, he added, is "nobody would lend on those terms. . . . It would be better to stick the cash in your mattress."

Then Mr. Mankiw joked that the Fed could say that one year hence it would pick a digit between zero and nine and cancel all currency with a serial number ending in that digit. "Suddenly, the expected return to holding currency would become negative 10%," he wrote. "People would be delighted to lend money at negative 3% since losing 3% is better than losing 10%." He wasn't serious. (Though some readers thought so.) His point was to illuminate the difficulties central banks have when they take short-term interest rates to zero—and still can't get the economy moving. Which is pretty much where we are today.

(One alternative is more inflation. The sticker price on money remains at zero, but rates adjusted for inflation go negative, giving people a reason to borrow and spend. But that's for another column.) So why would anybody put their money in a security that is guaranteed to pay less than they put in?

One, they are scared. With so much anxiety about the ability of some governments to pay their debts and the viability of some banks, investors are paying for safety. In Europe, if they hold euros, they want to be sure they get euros back; they are avoiding countries that might abandon the common currency.

Two, new rules on banks are stepping up demand for government securities, deemed safer and more liquid than alternative investments.

Three, central banks are pushing already-low benchmark rates lower. Denmark is charging banks a fee for parking money at the central bank; it wants to keep its rate below the European Central Batik's to keep its currency from rising against the euro. The ECB last month cut the rate it pays banks on overnight deposits to zero. The next obvious step is to charge a fee. ("On the negative deposit rates, I will say only that for us these are largely unchartered waters," ECB President Mario Draghi said the other day.)

The Federal Reserve is still paying 0.25% on bank reserves, but cutting that rate is on its things-to-think-about list.

The notion is that cutting that rate would give banks an incentive to lend more and store less money at the Fed. The U.S. Treasury, meanwhile, is pondering tweaks to its debt auctions so that it could borrow at negative rates as Germany does.

Negative rates are just the latest wrinkle in today's low-interest-rate world. "The average person on the street is beginning to feel the collateral dance age," says Mohamed El-Erian or bond giant Pimco. "Not getting paid much on your money-market fund, or, if you're European not being able to access money-market funds. Underfunded pension funds. Less attractive life insurance products. The bet that's being made by central banks is that the overall benefits of very low or negative yield is compensate by keeping the economy going."

Several European money-market actual funds have stopped taking new money: They can't invest it at a rate high enough to cover their costs. Few banks are actually charging to take deposits, but a move by the Few to push down the interest it pays on reserves could prompt that. Last year, Bank of New York Mellon drew headlines when it told large clients it would charge them a fee for deposits; the bank couldn't invest the big sums profitably.

Negative rates on overnight or other short-term money are difficult enough. When rates on two-year and longer-term debt securities go negative and stay there, then banks and insurance companies start to run into trouble. They make much of their money by borrowing at short-term rates and lending at higher long-term rates or, effectively, guaranteeing higher rates to their customers. That doesn't work so well when yields on two- or three-year securities are negative. The global financial crisis is five years old. It isn't over yet.

Definitions

1. Competitive markets

2. Total revenue

3. Economic profits

4. Price taker

5. Economic growth

6. Shutdown profit

7. Monopoly

8. Barriers to entry

9. Oligopoly

10. Mutual interdependence

Multiple Choice

1. Characteristics of a market with pure competition include
   a. a large number of buyers and sellers.
   b. homogeneous products.
   c. free entry and exit of firms into and from the market.
   d. all of the above.

2. Barriers to entry in a market include
   a. licensing requirements for lawyers and engineers.
   b. patents on certain kinds of production technology.
   c. the large advertising budgets needed to promote a new breakfast cereal line.
   d. all of the above.

3. Examples of producers in markets that fit the pure competition model fairly closely are
   a. automobile makers (Ford, GM, Honda).
   b. computer equipment design and manufacturing firms (IBM, Digital Equipment).
   c. farmers, home construction companies, and consumer loan and financial service firms.
   d. utilities (Southwestern Bell, Con Edison, Duke Power).
   e. none of the above come close to operating in purely competitive markets.

4. A price taker is a
   a. producer or consumer that lacks market power and takes the current price as a given.
   b. firm like an electrical utility.
   c. purchaser of labor like General Motors.
   d. computer firm like IBM.
   e. a city board that hires teachers.

5. When a firm's marginal revenue exceeds marginal cost
   a. a competitive firm will maximize profits.
   b. a rational firm manager will cut output.
   c. consumers will boycott the firm.
   d. the firm should increase its output.
   e. the firm does not need to do anything except enjoy the profits rolling in.

6. In pure competition, when prices are below average variable cost
   a. firms increase output.
   b. firms raise price.
   c. firms enter the market.
   d. firms shut down.
   e. none of the above are true.

7. Which of the following is not a benefit of pure competition?
   a. allocative efficiency
   b. production efficiency
   c. below marginal cost pricing
   d. no advertising
   e. all of the above

8. The additional revenue a firm receives from hiring an additional worker is called the
   a. marginal cost of labor.
   b. marginal social value of labor.
   c. resource revenue of labor.
   d. marginal revenue product of labor.
   e. none of the above are correct.

9. Monopoly describes a market in which
   a. there is one seller.
   b. there is one buyer.
   c. there are few large sellers.
   d. domestic firms dominate the market.
   e. both c and d are correct.

10. Which of the following is not an example of a barrier to entry?
    a. inelastic demand
    b. control over raw materials
    c. patents and trademarks
    d. licenses and franchises
    e. economies of scale

RESOURCES

Economics Mabry

Externalities and Market Failure

Kodda/Shutterstock.com

OBJECTIVES

1. Explain the difference between public and private goods.
2. Define the method for determining an optimal public good.
3. Learn the meaning of "externalities" and understand their implications for markets.
4. Understand the concept of "Coase Theorem."
5. Explain the meaning of "market failure."

Recently, the financial industry saw its worst crisis in many decades. The financial industry was operating in a competitive market where it did a good job in allocating scarce resources efficiently. However, some markets may have been at a disadvantage, courtesy of deregulation, which caused distortions in the financial markets that eventually led to the current economic crisis. Today, the government plays a major role in making sure that the financial industry returns to its normal efficiencies. When private markets fail, there is an economic role for the public sector. In this chapter, we will examine that role as it relates to public goods, and also its effects, such as externalities. We will also see the negative effects of too much government, fear of which can hinder the role of government in its economic recovery efforts.

Private versus Public Goods

Most goods produced and sold in competitive markets are considered to be private goods. Private goods include all goods offered and sold in the malls and stores near you, including cars, clothing, TVs, shoes, food, and so on. Private goods are defined as goods that have two characteristics: rivalry and excludability. Rivalry means that one person purchasing and consuming a given commodity precludes another person from buying and consuming that same commodity. For example, if Steve buys a whole pizza, then it will not be available for purchase and consumption by John. Excludability means that sellers can keep people who do not pay for a commodity from benefiting from it. Thus, only people who can afford to pay for a certain product can obtain that commodity.

Public goods, on the other hand, are commodities that are non-rival and non-excludable. Non-rivalry means that one person's consumption of a good does not preclude consumption of the good by others. Everyone can simultaneously obtain the benefit from public goods such as roads, bridges, street lighting, and national parks. Non-excludability means that there is no effective way of excluding individuals from the benefit of the good once it becomes available. One problem with public goods is the creation of a "free-rider" problem. Once the product is available as a public good, nobody can be excluded from enjoying the product, even people who could not otherwise afford it. Thus, people have no incentive to pay for these products since they are available and are free.

Free-ridership is a big issue, especially in terms of health care. There are proponents for offering a universal health care policy. Basically this means that the government would be responsible for providing health care services to everyone in the country. This would make health care a public good: a non-rival good because one person's consumption of health care services would not preclude the consumption of health care services by another person; and non-excludable because health care services could not denied to anyone. The problem with providing health care services as a public good is the free-ridership problem. Not everyone can pay the fees demanded by health care services, so the government could only finance these services through expanded taxation policies.

Optimal Public Good

In the case of public goods, consumers need not reveal the true demand in the marketplace. But the question that the government sector is faced with is the issue of how much quantity of a public good is needed in order to avoid any surplus or shortage. The government has to estimate the demand for a public good through primary data (i.e., public surveys or questionnaires). The criterion for the optimal demand for public good is to compare the marginal benefit of an incremental unit of commodity against the marginal cost incurred in providing it. Thus, the criterion can be summarized as follows:

Marginal Benefit = Marginal Cost

Another way of interpreting this criterion is the **cost-benefit analysis**. A cost-benefit analysis is simply a comparison of marginal costs and marginal benefits of a given proposed project, in this case by the government.

A good example of this analysis can be applied to the recent fiscal stimulus package implemented by the Obama administration. The purpose of this fiscal stimulus package is to revive the economy through infrastructure and public works. Because the economy's resources are limited, any decision to use more resources in the public sector means fewer resources for the private sector. For a government project to be optimal, we compare the marginal benefit and the marginal cost of providing that project. Cost-benefit analysis can indicate more than whether a public project is worth doing. It can also help the government decide on the extent to which a project should be pursued, in other words, how big or small the project should be.

Externalities

In a competitive market, we assume that the benefits and costs of a commodity are fully reflected in the market. There are some markets, however, where the benefits or costs may be implicit to the buyer or the seller. The costs and/or the benefits of a good that are passed on to a third party in a given market are called **externalities**. An externality is an external benefit or cost that accrues to a party that is not directly related to the buyer or seller in a market transaction.

Negative Externalities

Negative externalities are costs inflicted on a third party without compensation. The most common example of a negative externality is pollution. When a manufacturing firm dumps its waste in a lake or

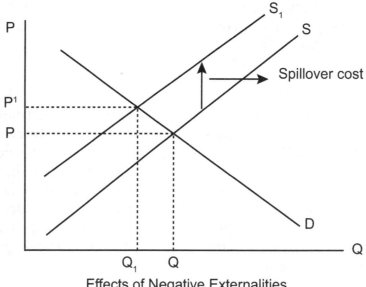

Effects of Negative Externalities

an oil company pollutes the air with smoke, people who live in and around the area suffer negative externalities. Community residents who live around the lake or around the factory may suffer health problems related to the externality, but the company that polluted the lake or air does not compensate the residents of the area. Therefore, the cost of health care services due to the environmental pollution is borne by the community residents.

The figure above illustrates the implications of negative externalities. When a producer shifts some of its spillover cost onto the resident community, the marginal cost is lower. This is showed by the supply curve S. However, this supply curve does not reflect all of the cost incurred in the production. Factoring the effects of the spillover costs or negative externalities, the supply curve should be at S_1. Thus, the optimal output should be at Q_1.

Positive Externalities

Spillover effects can also be positive in nature. The production or consumption of a commodity may have positive spillover, or external benefits, on a third party not involved in the given market transaction. Education is a classic example of a **positive externality**. Education benefits individual people. Higher education means that people are better informed and can allocate resources more efficiently. Better-educated people can also mean higher income for the community. Furthermore, education reduces other social costs such as crime, regulations, and welfare programs.

The figure on next page shows the effects of positive externalities on resource allocation. When positive externalities occur, the demand curve lies to the left of the optimal demand curve. The initial demand,

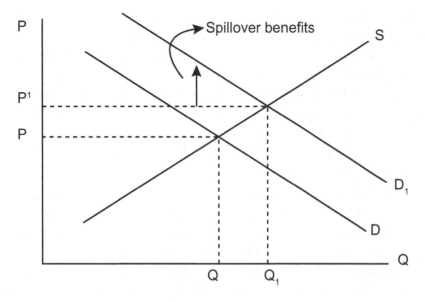

Effects of Positive Externalities

D, does not include the spillover benefits or positive externalities. With positive externalities, the full-benefits demand curve is D_1. With education, the positive externalities increase the full-benefits demand to a higher level. More educated people means that people are well informed about the market and have a higher income. Therefore, the demand increases to D_1.

Coase Theorem

Economists have suggested several solutions to the problems of negative and positive externalities. In some instances, market solutions can still occur as a result of these externalities. However, when markets fail, only some form of government intervention can solve these problems.

One form of market solution is the Coase Theorem. This was formulated by the great Nobel Prize–winning economist Ronald Coase at the University of Chicago. According to his theory, government is not needed to provide a solution for externalities where: (a) property ownership is clearly defined; (b) the number of people involved is small; and (c) bargaining costs are insignificant. Under this situation, the government should limit its role to making sure that the bargaining process is still efficient between the parties involved. Property rights place a tag on an externality, creating opportunity costs for all parties. The bargaining process can be a mutually beneficial solution to the externality problem, especially if the economic interests of the parties are at stake.

Property rights can often affect the incentive to produce or to reduce pollution. One way of thinking about the problem of pollution and property rights is that in unregulated markets, no one has a property right to clean air. If nobody has a property right to clean air, then nobody needs to compensate you for infringing on your property right to clean air. If you have a property right to your land, somebody cannot come onto your front yard and dump garbage because you own that property. But you do not own the air over your property in the same sense. If you had property rights that were clear and enforceable, then one party or another would have the appropriate incentives to avoid creating the negative externality of pollution. So, let us think about how you might have property rights that could be used in a way to avoid getting the dirty air.

Coase said that what you want to do is to think about a train that goes past a farmer's field, and that train is emitting sparks. Sometimes, the parks start a fire in the farmer's field. So, we want to think about this as an example of pollution. The train is emitting sparks; the farmer's field is burning. How do we figure out a way to deal with this through property rights? We can approach this in two different ways. First we could say, "Look, a train has a property right to emit sparks, in which case, farmer, it is up to you to figure out how to reduce the chance of fire starting in your field." Alternatively, we could say, "Look, farmers, you have a property right not to have your field set on fire by sparks from the train, in which case the railroad has to find a way to reduce the chance of fire or else pay the farmer when fires break out." Whether you give the property right to the railroad and let it emit sparks or you give the property right to the farmer and say he or she is protected from the emission of sparks determines who has to pay. But, either way, if the property right is clear, then one party has a reason to find a way to reduce the chance of fire, preferably a low-cost method.

When the property rights are clear, often there will be some reason to try to prevent pollution from happening. A classic example is the ownership of federal lands. Oftentimes no one really owns federal lands, so they end up being abused for recreational, logging, hunting, or other purposes. No one has a reason, in terms of property rights, to protect them.

Market Failure and Government Intervention

Market failure occurs when the competitive market system does not allocate any resources whatsoever to the production of certain goods, or either under-allocates or over-allocates resources to the production of certain goods. When a market fails, an economic role for the government sector arises.

The role of the government is not an easy task, especially in performing its economic function. Governments should set the rules and regulations, redistributing income when desirable and stabilizing the economy, especially if there are shocks in the market, as there were in the recent financial crisis. The economic role of the government is defined in the context of its leadership's political perspective.

A good example of market failure is the health care industry in the United States. The U.S. health care market can be characterized by rising prices of health care services in general. If we look closely in terms of the demand and supply for health care, there are a lot of factors that can be attributed to causing these rising prices. From the supply side, resources are fixed and do not adjust to the market efficiently because these resources are heavily regulated. For example, doctors need to get training for a minimum of ten years before they can even practice as a medical resident intern. The cost of training is prohibitive, and licensure is based on the rigorous American Medical Association criteria. From the demand side, the demand for health care services is ever increasing thanks to an aging baby boomer population and an increase in the general population. Because of these distortions, market prices for health care services are increasing and are sometimes unaffordable for a typical middle-income person. One governmental policy suggestion to remedy this is the call for a universal health care system. This means that the government would be responsible for offering the service to the public. This is an example in which government can intervene in order to allocate the resources more efficiently than the private market does.

From a political perspective, public goods such as health care services are sometimes produced not because their benefits exceed their costs, but because their benefits accrue to firms located in states served by powerful elected officials. The result of such situations is market inefficiencies because of the lack of an incentive to hold down costs. The failure of programs to achieve their goals may lead to huge costs. Furthermore, policies to correct negative externalities such as these can be blocked politically by the very parties whose decisions produced the externalities.

References

Council of Economic Advisers, "Chapter 9: Protecting the Environment," in *Economic Report of the President*, February 2004.

"The Global Environment: The Great Race," *The Economist*, July 4, 2002.

Asch, Peter, and Gary A. Gigliotti, "The Free-Rider Paradox – Theory, Evidence and Teaching," *Journal of Economic Education*, Winter 1991, pp. 33–38.

Coase, R. H., "The Lighthouse of Economics," *Journal of Law and Economics*, October 1974, pp. 374–376.

Carbon Offsets: A Small Price to Pay for Efficiency

Robert H. Frank

Are carbon offsets a good thing? They are intended to reduce the environmental impact of consumption. Traveling by plane, for example, causes carbon dioxide to be emitted into the atmosphere, so travelers can pay a specialist to offset those emissions some other way—perhaps by planting vegetation or installing renewable-energy technologies. It all sounds reasonable.

Yet carbon offsets have drawn sharp criticism, even ridicule. A British Web site called Cheat Neutral (www.cheatneutral.com) parodies the concept—by offering a service under which someone who wants to cheat on his partner can pay someone else who will refrain from committing an act of infidelity. The site's founders say they wanted to use humor to demonstrate why the market for carbon offsets is a moral travesty.

But the criticism is misguided. If our goal is to reduce carbon emissions as efficiently as possible, offsets make perfect economic sense.

Consider the decision of whether to buy a hybrid car. Because of the expensive batteries and other complex equipment in such cars, they can cost much more than similar vehicles powered by standard combustion engines. Many people drive so little that they wouldn't save enough on gasoline to recoup the higher cost. Yet many such people buy hybrids anyway, because they think they are helping the environment. Well and good, but they could help even more by buying a standard car and using the savings to buy carbon offsets.

The same goes for someone who wonders whether it's O.K. to eat foods grown far from home. A New Yorker may worry, for example, that the diesel fuel burned to ship California grown tomatoes to him in winter will accelerate global warming. But suppose he would be happy to pay $10 more than the cost of shipping those tomatoes rather than eat locally grown root vegetables nine months a year. That would buy more than enough carbon offsets to neutralize the greenhouse gases emitted by shipping the tomatoes. So it would be much better, for him and the planet, if he bought offsets and ate winter tomatoes.

Of course, carbon offsets alone won't eliminate global warming. People also need stronger incentives to take into account the environmental consequences of their actions.

President Obama has proposed attacking the problem with a carbon cap-and-trade system. The government would first set a limit. on annual carbon emissions, then auction emissions permits to the highest bidders. Companies could still use processes or sell products that emit carbon, but only by first buying a permit for each unit of carbon released, if the government wanted to limit carbon emissions to five billion tons a year, for example, it would auction that many tons of annual carbon permits.

This approach was first used in the United States to address acid rain, when the Clean Air Act established a market for permits to emit sulfur dioxide. Compared with more traditional regulatory measures, the auction method substantially reduced the cost of achieving the law's air-quality target.

As people learn more about such an approach, they seem less likely to oppose it. Although several environmental groups once bitterly opposed pollution permit auctions, they now endorse them enthusiastically.

A carbon cap-and-trade system is functionally similar to a carbon tax. Both approaches would raise the cost of activities that generate carbon dioxide emissions, giving people a powerful incentive to reduce their carbon foot-prints. Carbon offsets are no substitute for the stronger incentives inherent in carbon taxes or cap-and-trade, but they can reinforce their effects. Both carbon taxes and permit auctions would also generate revenue that could be used to buy additional carbon offsets.

Dozens of companies, nonprofit and for-profit, sell carbon offsets, and some critics question how their work can be verified. But with various certification programs now in place—including the Gold Standard and Green-e Climate, to name two—there is no reason that fraud should be harder to curb in carbon-offset markets than in other domains.

At last count, Cheat Neutral, the British infidelity neutralization Web site, said it had offset 65,968 cheats, and had recruited a roster of "9,002 faithful people ready to neutralize your misdemeanors." The Web site draws out the parallel this way: "When you cheat on your partner you add to the heartbreak, pain, and jealousy in the atmosphere." Cheat Neutral claims that its plan "neutralizes the pain and unhappy emotion and leaves you with a clear conscience."

Actually, no. Only you will know whether your conscience is clear, but it is certain that higher rates of marital fidelity in London do nothing to eliminate the anguish caused by straying spouses in Manchester. In contrast, one person's reduction in carbon dioxide emissions anywhere on the planet fully offsets anyone else's contribution to the total. Carbon offsets, though much maligned, are an excellent idea. If you want to help reduce carbon emissions, consider buying some.

CHAPTER 6

Name _____

Definitions

1. Market failure

2. Private goods

3. Public goods

4. Coase Theorem

5. Negative externalities

6. Positive externalities

7. Externalities

8. Cost-benefit analysis

9. Non-rival goods

10. Non-excludable goods

Multiple Choice

1. An externality is
   a. an overall cost to a society of producing an additional output of goods and services.
   b. the amount of dollars that a consumer pays to consume a given commodity.
   c. a cost or benefit borne by a third party not involved in a given market transaction.
   d. a problem intrinsic in private goods.

2. Air pollution is an example of
   a. a negative externality.
   b. a moral hazard.
   c. adverse selection.
   d. a positive externality.

3. Education is an example of
   a. a positive externality.
   b. a negative externality.
   c. a moral hazard.
   d. adverse selection.

4. A firm that is overproducing or under producing in a given market is an example of a(n)
   a. externality.
   b. public good.
   c. market failure.
   d. moral hazard.

5. The Coase Theorem states that
   a. under some conditions, private parties can agree on a solution without government intervention.
   b. the public sector will fail to produce an efficient amount of public goods.
   c. if there are external costs in production, government must intervene in the market.
   d. the public good should be produced when marginal costequals marginal benefit.

6. The Coase Theorem will only apply if
   a. the courts can be used to determine the amount of damages given to a party.
   b. the amount of compensation is small enough.
   c. the number of people involved is small enough.
   d. an individual who is not affected by the externality can negotiate a settlement.

7. If the production of a good generates external benefits, the government could increase efficiency by
   a. regulating the sale of the product.
   b. mandating licensing for the production of the commodity.
   c. subsidizing production of the good to increase the amount produced.
   d. taxing the production of the commodity.

8. Public goods are
   a. rival in production and their benefits are non-excludable.
   b. non-rival in consumption and non-excludable in benefits.
   c. rival in consumption and their benefits are non-excludable.
   d. rival in consumption and benefits.

9. If one person's enjoyment of the benefits of a commodity does not interfere with another's consumption of it, the good is said to be
   a. non-rival.
   b. non-excludable.
   c. rival.
   d. excludable.

10. The free-rider problem arises when
    a. government produces a good.
    b. there is a shortage of the product.
    c. people realize they will still receive the benefits of a good whether they pay or not.
    d. there is a surplus of the product.

Chapter 7

National Income Accounting

emin kuliyev /Shutterstock.com

OBJECTIVES

1. To define the concept of gross domestic product.
2. To explain the two approaches in measuring GDP.
3. To explain the different problems faced in measuring GDP.
4. To describe the concept of economic growth.

National Income Accounting

National income accounting refers to the bookkeeping system that a national government uses to measure the level of the country's economic activity in a given time period. National income accounting records the level of activity in accounts such as total revenues earned by domestic corporations, wages paid to foreign and domestic workers, and the amount spent on sales and income taxes by corporations and individuals residing in the country.

National income accounting provides economists and statisticians with detailed information that can be used to track the health of an economy and to forecast future growth and development. Although national income accounting is not an exact science, it provides useful insight into how well an economy is functioning, and where monies are being generated and spent.

Some of the metrics calculated by using national income accounting that we will cover in this chapter include **gross domestic product (GDP)**, gross national product (GNP), and gross national income (GNI).

Gross Domestic Product

Gross domestic product measures the final goods and services produced by an economy within a given period of time. In the study of gross domestic product, we have two classifications of goods: **final goods**, and **intermediate goods**. By final goods, we mean goods used for final consumption or in the economy. Intermediate goods are goods used to produce final goods. For example, steel in the automobile industry is an intermediate good. However, steel in the steel industry is a final good. The problem that can arise from this distinction is the fact that some goods can be counted twice. This problem is known as **double counting**.

Time Period

Understanding the time period is essential in measuring GDP. GDP is an example of a **flow variable**. This means that the variable is measured from one point in time to another. Other examples of flow variables include the inflation rate and income statement. The opposite of a flow variable is a **stock variable**. A stock variable is a variable that is measured at one point in time. An example of a stock variable is the amount of money in your savings account on January 1, 2008. The interest rate, stock prices, and the unemployment rate are other examples of a stock variable.

Approaches in Measuring GDP

There are two approaches in measuring GDP: the expenditure approach and the income approach. The expenditure approach takes into account

[Billions of chained (2009) dollars]

| | Line | 2013 | 2014 | Seasonally adjusted at annual rates | | | | |
| | | | | 2014 | | | 2015 | |
				II	III	IV	I	II
Gross domestic product	1	15,583.3	15,961.7	15,901.5	16,068.8	16,151.4	16,177.3	16,333.6
Personal consumption expenditures	2	10,590.4	10,875.7	10,826.3	10,918.6	11,033.3	11,081.2	11,178.9
Goods	3	3,612.8	3,731.2	3,718.0	3,755.2	3,793.2	3,803.7	3,855.0
Durable goods	4	1,307.6	1,384.1	1,377.2	1,402.5	1,423.5	1,430.4	1,458.3
Nondurable goods	5	2,319.8	2,367.8	2,361.0	2,375.2	2,393.7	2,397.8	2,423.0
Services	6	6,977.0	7,144.6	7,108.5	7,163.8	7,240.4	7,277.4	7,325.3
Gross private domestic investment	7	2,577.3	2,717.7	2,709.5	2,758.1	2,772.5	2,830.2	2,864.8
Fixed investment	8	2,501.9	2,633.8	2,613.4	2,663.5	2,679.7	2,701.4	2,735.5
Nonresidential	9	2,023.7	2,148.3	2,129.8	2,176.3	2,180.0	2,188.6	2,210.6
Structures	10	429.7	464.6	464.4	462.3	467.1	458.2	465.2
Equipment	11	969.5	1,026.2	1,013.7	1,053.1	1,040.0	1,046.0	1,046.9
Intellectual property products	12	626.9	659.5	653.4	663.8	675.0	687.1	701.0
Residential	13	478.0	486.4	484.4	488.5	500.2	512.4	524.0
Change in private inventories	14	61.4	68.0	77.1	79.9	78.2	112.8	113.5
Net exports of goods and services	15	−417.5	−442.5	−443.5	−429.1	−463.6	−541.2	−534.6
Exports	16	2,018.1	2,086.4	2,086.8	2,096.0	2,123.9	2,091.4	2,117.5
Goods	17	1,382.3	1,443.0	1,439.1	1,460.1	1,474.3	1,429.3	1,452.0
Services	18	635.5	642.9	647.3	635.4	649.1	660.6	664.4
Imports	19	2,435.6	2,528.9	2,530.1	2,525.1	2,587.5	2,632.5	2,652.1
Goods	20	1,991.3	2,076.5	2,078.4	2,074.1	2,123.8	2,161.1	2,178.4
Services	21	443.5	450.8	450.1	449.4	462.2	469.8	472.1
Government consumption expenditures and gross investment	22	2,854.9	2,838.3	2,836.5	2,849.2	2,839.0	2,838.5	2,856.9
Federal	23	1,144.1	1,116.3	1,114.5	1,124.7	1,108.3	1,111.3	1,111.3
National defense	24	716.6	689.1	689.8	697.3	678.6	680.3	680.8
Nondefense	25	427.5	427.0	424.6	427.1	429.4	430.7	430.2
State and local	26	1,710.2	1,720.8	1,720.8	1,723.5	1,729.3	1,725.9	1,744.1
Residual	27	−23.9	−35.1	−31.5	−40.3	−41.5	−40.8	−44.6

Legend / Footnotes:

Legend / Footnotes: Note: Chained (2009) dollar series are calculated as the product of the chain-type quantity index and the 2009 current-dollar value of the corresponding series, divided by 100. Because the formula for the chain-type quantity indexes uses weights of more than one period, the corresponding chained-dollar estimates are usually not additive. The residual line is the difference between the first line and the sum of the most detailed lines.

all variables included in the demand expenditure, such as consumption or investment expenditures. The income approach, on the other hand, includes all income received by the economy. Why do we need to have two methods for calculating GDP? The simple answer is based on the principle that whatever we received as income should reflect our expenses. For purposes of cross-checking accuracy in measurements, it is important to look at both income and expenditure approaches.

Expenditure Approach

$$GDP = C + I + G + (X - M)$$

where

C = personal consumption

I = gross private domestic investment

G = government expenditure

X = exports

M = imports

(X – M) is considered an economy's net exports

C, I, G, X, and M are all expenditures from the different sectors of the economy. Personal consumption is the expenditure incurred by the household sector. Gross private domestic investment is the expenditure from the business sector. Government expenditure is the expenditure from the public sector. Net exports (X – M) is expenditure from the foreign sector.

Theory to Application

What Is Investment?

Newcomers to macroeconomics are sometimes confused by how macroeconomists use familiar words in new and specific ways. One example is the term *investment*. The confusion arises because what looks like investment for an individual may not be investment for the economy as a whole. The general rule is that the economy's investment does not include purchases that merely reallocate existing assets among different individuals. *Investment*, as macroeconomists use the term, creates new capital.

Let's consider some examples. Suppose we observe these two events:

1. Smith buys a 100-year-old Victorian house.

2. Jones builds a brand-new contemporary house.

What is total investment here? Two houses, one house, or zero?

A macroeconomist seeing these two transactions counts only Jones's house as investment. Smith's transaction has not created new housing for the economy; it has merely reallocated existing housing. Smith's purchase is investment for Smith, but it is disinvestment for the person selling the house. By contrast, Jones has added new housing to the economy; her house is counted as investment.

Similarly, consider these two events:

1. Bill Gates buys $5 million in IBM stock from Warren Buffett on the New York Stock Exchange.

2. General Motors sells $10 million in stock to the public and uses the proceeds to build a new car factory.

Here, investment is $10 million. In the first transaction, Gates is investing in IBM stock, and Buffett is disinvesting; there is no investment for the economy. By contrast, General Motors is using some of the economy's output of goods and services to add to its stock of capital; hence, its new factory is counted as investment.

Since investments are measured as a flow variable, the value of capital changes over time because of depreciation or the wear and tear of such capital goods. The wear and tear of such capital goods are also called capital consumption allowances. Another way of measuring investment is called "net investment." The formula for net investment can be expressed as follows:

Net Investment = Gross Investment − Capital Consumption Allowances

$$50 = 100 - x \qquad x = 100 - 50 = \$50$$

Income Approach

Gross domestic product can also be derived using the income approach. The government will sum up all sources of income from the different factors of production. We derive income from the factors of production: land, labor, capital, and entrepreneurship. Therefore, under the income approach:

$$GDP = rent + wages + interest\ income + profits + CCA + IBT$$

where:

CCA = capital consumption allowance (also called depreciation)

IBT = indirect business taxes

If we sum up the first four items in this formula, we derive national income (NY).

It is obvious that there will always be a difference between the income and expenditure approach. There are many reasons why there will be some disparity between these methods. Income approach will always be understated since people will not always report their precise income (for tax purposes or for any other reason). Thus, for accuracy, the expenditure approach will always be a superior approach in measuring our national output.

Profits under Income Approach

Profits can be divided into two components: (a) unincorporated profits; and (b) total corporate profits before taxes. Unincorporated profits are profits earned from single proprietorship and partnerships. Total corporate profits before taxes is obviously profits earned by corporations before taxes. In income approach, there are three components of total corporate profits before taxes: (a) corporate income taxes; (b) dividends; and (c) undistributed corporate profits or retained earnings.

Recently, much has been written about corporate dividends and retained earnings. Corporate dividends are earnings given to shareholders after announcing profits by the corporation. In the past, most investors would shy away from companies that pay out dividends because this can be a sign that the company has no room for growth or expansion. Thus, stock prices may not necessarily increase as a result of this. Most investors would like to see companies keeping this money for future growth. However, this may be changing because of the recent corporate scandals such as the Enron case. In this case, Enron tried to inflate their profits by adding unrealized future profits from their investments. As a result of the news, the market panicked and led to the demise of the company. Today, investors would look at companies who are giving out dividends as this is a sign that the company is realizing profit and shareholders are benefitting from them.

Other National Income Accounts

Net Domestic Product

$$NDP = \textbf{\textit{Gross Domestic Product}} - \textbf{\textit{Depreciation (CCA)}}$$

Net domestic product is an output variable because it measures national output minus depreciation. **Depreciation** is the wear and tear of capital goods. Since GDP is measured within a given period of time, the value of the national output should be adjusted based on the wear and tear of capital goods or depreciation.

National Income (NY)

$$NY = GDP - CCA - \textbf{\textit{Indirect Business Tax (IBT)}}$$

Another measure for national output is national income. The difference between GDP and national income is depreciation and indirect business tax (IBT). Indirect business tax refers to the tax that is imposed indirectly to businesses' income. For example, a sales tax is a tax that is imposed on revenues as opposed to profits or net income.

Table 7.2 Personal Income and Its Disposition

| | Line | Billions of dollars | | Seasonally adjusted at annual rates | | | | |
| | | 2010 | 2011 | 2010 | 2011 | | | |
				IV	I	II	III	IV
Personal Income	1	**12373.53**	**3276.425**	**12577.6**	**12846.9**	**12955.3**	**13056.8**	**13105.7**
Compansation of employees, received	2	7971.375	2093.95	8050.8	8172.5	8219.7	8338.3	8375.8
Wage and salary disbursements	3	6408.225	1688.3	6477	6578.2	6617.1	6724.3	6753.2
Private industries	4	5217.4	1391.05	5288.4	5387.1	5425.2	5535	5564.2
Government	5	1190.85	297.2S	1188.6	1191.1	1191.9	1189.3	1189
Supplement to wages and salaries	6	1563.125	405.65	1573.7	1594.4	1602.7	1614	1622.6
Employer contributions for employee pension and insurance fund:	7	1089.95	279.9	1096.8	1103	1108.7	1112.6	1119.6
Employer contributions for government social insurance	8	473.175	125.75	476.9	491.4	494	501.3	503
Proprietors' income with inventory valuation and capital consumption adjustments	9	1036.45	279.925	1081.5	1095.6	1106.5	1113.7	1119.7
Farm	10	52.2	15.675	60.1	66.1	67.3	67.5	62.7
Nonfarm	11	984.225	264.25	1021.4	1029.5	1039.2	1046.2	1057
Rental income of persons with capital consumption adjustment	12	350.2	106.8	354.8	385	396.9	406.3	427.2
Personal income receipts on assets	13	1721.175	446.575	1743.5	1777.2	1802.3	1794.2	1786.3
Personal interest income	14	1003.425	244.2	989.6	1004.7	1015.9	994.8	976.8
Personal dividend income	15	717.725	202.375	753.9	772.5	786.4	799.4	809.5
Personal current transfer receipts	16	2281.2	583.275	2341.2	2328.1	2347.3	2336.6	2333.1
Government social benefits to persons	17	2242.875	573.375	2301.9	2288.6	2307.9	2297.2	2293.5
Social security	18	690.175	180.575	699.9	703.1	712.2	716.3	722.3
Medicare	19	518.45	138.825	535.3	547.8	553.9	557.8	555.3
Medicaid	20	405.35	102.875	439.8	432.1	437.4	416.4	411.5
Unemployment insurance	21	138.675	25.025	128.7	117.5	108.8	103	100.1
Veterans' benefits	22	57.875	16.075	59.4	61.3	62.8	65	64.3

(Continues)

Table 7.2 Personal Income and Its Disposition (Continued)

Other	23	432.375	110	438.7	426.9	432.7	438.6	440
Other current transfer receipts, from business (net)	24	38.3	9.9	39.3	39.5	39.4	39.4	39.6
Less: Contributions for government social insurance, domestic	25	986.825	234.075	994.1	911.5	917.4	932.4	936.3
Less Personal currant taxes	26	1198.879	354.85	1240.9	1365.9	1896.2	1409.1	1419.4
Equals: Disposable personal income	27	11179.65	2921.575	11336.7	11481	11559.2	11647.7	11686.3
Leer Personal outlays	28	10586.9	2800.29	10748.6	10902.1	11002.6	11114.6	11201
Personal consumption expenditures	29	10245.55	2717.9	10417.1	10571.7	10676	10784.5	10871.6
Personal interest payments	30	173.375	39.175	162.7	160.3	155.9	158.4	156.7
Parsonal currrent transfer payments	31	168	43.2	168.9	170.1	170.7	171.6	172.8
To government	32	95.125	24.8	96.5	96.6	97.1	97.8	99.2
Equals: Personal saving	34	592.779	121.325	988.1	578.9	556.5	533.1	485.3
Personal saving as a percentage of disposable personal income	35	5.325	1.05	5.2	5	4.8	4.6	4.2
Addenda:								
Personal income excluding current transfer receipts. billions of chained (2005) dollars	36	9083.075	2348.95	9166.7	9329.8	9332.9	9377.3	9395.8
Disposable personal income								
Total, billions of chained (2005) dollars	37	10061.68	2548.175	10152	10183.2	10169.7	10188.6	10192.7
Per capita:								
Current dollars	38	36089	9336.25	36491	36895	37082	37293	37345
Chained (2005) dollars	39	52480.25	8143	32678	32724	32625	32621	32572
Population (midperiod, thousands)	40	309774	78232.25	310670	311184	311717	312330	312929
Percent change from preceding period:								
Disposable personal income, current dollars	41	4.875	0.325	3.5	5.2	2.8	3.1	1.3
Disposable personal income, chained (2005) dollars	42	3.575	0.05	1.5	1.2	−0.5	0.7	0.2

Source: Bureau of economic Analysis (beau.gov)

**Personal Disposable Income (PDY) = Personal Income (PY)
− Personal Income Tax
(PYT)**

In an aggregative sense, this is similar to one's personal take-home pay. Personal disposable income is the amount that households have to spend or save. The amount of disposable income left after personal spending is called *personal savings*. If your monthly disposable income is $1,000 and you spend $800, you have $200 left at the end of the month. Your personal savings is $200. In some instances, when you have to spend more than what you earn, you may use credit cards to pay bills. In this case, your personal savings can be negative or dissavings.

In 2005, U.S. consumers spent more than they earned resulting in a negative rate of savings for the first time since the Great Depression. Savings, as a percentage of income fell to −0.5 percent in 2005 down from 1.8 percent in 2004 (Kirchoff and Hagenbaugh, 2006). However, other economists said that the measure can be misleading gauge of Americans balance sheets. Savings have decline in the past two decades as the value of such assets as stocks and homes has risen, numbers not counted in the government estimate of personal savings (Kirchoff and Hagenbaugh, 2006)[i].

Sample Problem on National Income Accounting

Assume that a given economy has the following data:

GDP	$1000
PDY (Personal Disposable Income)	$800
GI (Gross Investment)	$350
IBT (Indirect Business Tax)	$150
PS (Personal Savings)	$400
NE (Net Exports)	−$100
NI(Net Investment)	$200

Compute for the following variables:

    A. National Income (NY)

    B. Consumption (C)

    C. Government Expenditure (G)

Solution

    1. To solve for NY, we use the expenditure approach:

        $NY = GDP − CCA − IBT$

        $NY = 1000 − CCA − 150$

Since CCA is unknown, we find another formula to solve for CCA. We can use the net investment formula:

$NI = GI - CCA$

Net investment = gross investment $-$ CCA

$200 = 350 - CCA$

$CCA = 150$

We then plug this number into the previous equation:

$1000 = NY + 150 + 150$

$NY = 700$

2. Personal Disposable Income (PDY)

$PDY = PC + PS$

$800 = PC + 400$

$400 = PC$

3. Government Expenditure (G)

Using the GDP formula:

$GDP = C + I + G + (X - M)$

$1000 = 400 + 350 + G + (-100)$

$350 = G$

Mismeasurement Problems in GDP

As we stated earlier, there are many reasons why the income approach will always be understated. In this section, we examine some of the reasons there will also always be some mismeasurement problems in calculating the national output.

1. **Underground Economy:** This refers to any kind of economic transaction that results in unreported or undocumented income. Examples include the informal sector, or cash transactions from street vendors, drug dealers, or any kind of under-the-table cash transaction. Some waiters are paid in cash (such as tips) and most of these waiters do not report their tips when it comes to taxes. By law, these people should report 10 percent of their tips. But since this is a cash transaction, there is no way for the government to determine how much income is derived.

2. **Household Activities:** Activities such as cleaning the house, cooking for the family, and taking care of children are considered productive activities. Household duties should be included as part of our national income because they add up to the final production of goods and services. Unfortunately,

there is no way for the government to quantify these services, and therefore the value of GDP is understated.

3. **Value Added**: In the first part of this chapter we mentioned the difference between intermediate and final goods. Recall that intermediate goods are goods and services purchased for resale or further processing or manufacturing, for example, the purchase and use of chocolate chips in baking chocolate chip cookies. Chocolate chips are the intermediate good. Final goods are goods and services purchased for final use by the consumer, not for resale or for further processing or manufacturing. In our example, the finished chocolate chip cookie is the final product of intermediate goods. However, there are some goods that can be both intermediate and final goods. For example, steel in the steel industry is a final good, but steel in the automobile industry is an intermediate good. We can avoid multiple counting by measuring and adding only the **value added**—the market value of a firm's output excluding the value of the inputs the firm has bought from others. This concept of value added overstates the value of GDP.

Rate of Economic Growth

The rate of economic growth is the percentage change in the level of economic activity from one year to the next. Typically, analysts look at the rate of growth in an economy's real GDP.

The rate of economic growth is simply the change in real GDP (RGDP) between two periods divided by real GDP in the first period (denoted $RGDP_1$).

$$Growth\ Rate = \frac{\Delta RGDP}{RGDP_1} = \frac{RGDP_2 - RGDP_1}{RGDP_1}$$

To illustrate, suppose that in Year 1 real GDP is $1,000 and in Year 2, real GDP is $1,200. Hence, the rate of growth between Year 1 and Year 2 is:

$$Growth\ Rate = \frac{1,200 - 1,000}{1000} = \frac{200}{1000} = 0.2$$

Therefore, the rate of growth for the economy between Year 1 and Year 2 in our example is 20 percent.

The output level of an economy is determined by the level of inputs (land, labor, capital, and entrepreneurship) used, and the production methods used to convert the inputs into goods and services. Output can only be increased through additional inputs or more efficient use of the available inputs. How fast we can increase inputs is limited, since land is essentially fixed and population growth and participation rates determine the size of the labor force.

In less-developed economies such as Mexico or China, a large fraction of inputs are underutilized and the level of capital is usually low. These economies can grow rapidly by increasing inputs and/or increasing production efficiency—for example, by moving toward state-of-the-art technology and raising the level of education. More developed economies, like the United States or Germany, which are starting from a higher level of input use and efficiency, have more difficulty sustaining high rates of economic growth. Innovation and improvements in existing technology are the keys to increased growth rates in developed economies (Carbaugh, 2000)[ii].

References

Carbaugh, Robert. *Introduction to Economics* (Atlanta: Thompson Publishing, 2000).

Kirchoff, Sue, and Hagenbaugh, Barbara, "Savings Enter Negative Territory: First Time Since the Depression." *USA Today Magazine*, January 31, 2006.

Statistics

China Struggles to Publish Accurate Data

Dexter Roberts

- The government moves to shed its reliance on local officials
- "The cadres produce the data, and data produces the cadres"

The figures that go into China's gross domestic product are "man-made" and "for reference only," warned Chinese politician Li Keqiang back in 2007, The comments by the then-regional party head, who is expected to become premier next spring, were revealed in a diplomatic cable published by WikiLeaks in late 2010. Li's remarks are especially relevant now as Chinese officials are expected to announce on July 13 that GDP grew by less than 8 percent in the second quarter, a three-year low.

But how low exactly? Investors, bankers, and economists face a host of difficulties in interpreting the numbers from China's statistics bureau. Combine all officially reported provincial GDP numbers for last year and you come up with a total exceeding national GDP by about 10 percent, Ma Jiantang, head of the National Bureau of Statistics, said in February. Ma said that is due partly to double counting of activities like factory production, and that his bureau was trying to correct the problem.

The fact that China's registered urban unemployment has barely budged, moving between just under 4 and 4.3 percent for the last decade, is harder for officials to explain. Also perplexing: why growth in electricity consumption has slowed much faster than growth in official GDP (dropping to about 4 percent growth in June, according to Chinese media) when usually they move more in tandem. That has some analysts wondering whether GDP figures are being skewed upward in the runup to a leadership transition this fall, "Out of the black box comes a number, and that number doesn't always line up with the other numbers," says Andrew Batson, Beijing-based research director at macroeconomics consulting firm GK Dragonomics. "I wouldn't be surprised if the GDP numbers this year are smoothed."

One legacy of the planned economy is that bureaucrats are given targets by the central government for everything from steel production to harvests and local GDP. These same officials traditionally have been promoted on their success in making their numbers. "We have a saying in China: The cadres produce the data, and data produces the cadres," says Jin Yongjin, a professor of statistics at Renmin University.

There are some pieces of the economy that the government is pretty good at measuring, says Louis Kuijs, an economist at the Fung Global

Institute, a think tank in Hong Kong. Industrial production and profits are considered relatively accurate, he says. Those numbers benefit from a nationwide system of corporate reporting instituted decades ago to help central planners steer the economy. "In the old system it was crucial to have that reporting system in place," says Kuijs. "China's industrial survey is giving us quite good numbers."

The country's statistical system is far less capable of measuring the service economy or getting an accurate reading of consumption by the middle class. "If you look at the number of cars produced in China, you will probably get a more or less accurate number," says Stephen Green, regional head of research for greater China at Standard Chartered. "But the system isn't good at measuring how many karaoke nights people have had or restaurant meals they have had." Measuring retail sales is more oriented to counting purchases by government offices and big state enterprises, says Green. That may explain why retail sales haven't fallen during downturns: State entities are ordered to keep buying even when individual consumption has likely fallen.

Investment banks have searched for the indicator that will predict an economic turning point. Standard Chartered looked at sales of earth-moving equipment before deciding it was a lagging rather than a leading indicator. Bank loans, as well as electricity consumption and rail cargo volume, all cited by Li Keqiang as more reliable than GDP, are still a good proxy for economic activity, says Green. UBS Securities has informally surveyed local developers to get a handle on real estate trends. Perhaps the most ambitious effort is the recently launched *China Beige Book*, a quarterly survey of some 2,000 bankers and company executives, modeled on the U.S. Federal Reserve's Beige Book. It measures growth in eight key industries across China's major regions, says Leland Miller, president of CBB International, which publishes the book.

Chinese policymakers are trying to address the government's statistical shortcomings. More data are now directly reported to Beijing, as opposed to being first filtered through local party offices. The statistics bureau has moved to standardize data collection by China's many ministries and industrial associations. And it has worked with the United Nations, the International Monetary Fund, and the Organization for Economic Cooperation & Development to improve its tracking of the economy.

China still tends to treat its data gathering as a national secret, says Anne Stevenson-Yang, co-founder of Beijing based equities analysis firm J Capital Research. She cites the government's refusal to release the weighting of goods tracked to compile its consumer price inflation index, "Why would you ever lift the hood and show people how you do it? That only reduces your ability to change numbers it' you need to," she says.

The bottom line *China's statistics have numerous discrepancies, but the government is working with the OECD and others to improve data collection.*

Sex, Drugs and a GDP Rethink

Josh Zumbrun

New methods of measuring economies sometimes raise eyebrows. Even more so when they involve prostitutes and mounds of cocaine.

The U.K., Ireland and Italy are among the nations now moving to include Illicit doings when tallying their gross domestic product, the broadest measure of goods and services across an economy.

The U.K. could add as much as $9 billion to the value of its GDP by including prostitution and about $7.4 billion by adding illegal drugs, by one estimate, enough to boost the size of its economy by 0.7%. Not to be outdone, Italy will include smuggling as well as drugs and prostitution. Both changes will begin later this year.

Other nations in Europe are also poised to fall in line with a European Union call to standardize and broaden GDPs. The EU is following a "best practices" directive laid out in 2008 by the United Nations.

Some economists question the merits—and methods—of measuring the shadows. Criminals go to great lengths to hide transactions usually conducted in hard-to-trace cash. Because the activity is beyond the easy reach of tax authorities, it isn't something that can bring in revenue to help a nation pay off its debts. All of which complicates measurement.

Claus Vistesen, chief eurozone economist for Pantheon Macroeconomics, says there is "a trade-off between taking in as much information as you can, and accuracy." Weighing the underground economy, he says, could end up making GDP measures "less accurate."

The argument in favor is simple enough. If drug sales aren't counted in a place where people spend half their income on drugs, one could conclude, wrongly, that the population saved half its money.

The U.N. is blunt in exrolling the need to expand GDP definitions. "Accounts as a whole are liable to be seriously distorted" if governments don't tabulate all transactions, it said as part of its 2008 directive.

The overall changes from adding illicit activity may prove, small, as that is just one component of the statistical revisions sweeping Europe. The U.K., for example, has altered how it will measure nonprofit groups, a shift that will boost its GDP more than the drugs and prostitution, and capital formation and inventories, which will shrink its GDP.

Some European countries have extra incentives to inflate the size of their economies. In addition to bragging rights, a higher GDP helps keep a nation's debt and deficits within the EU's prescribed targets.

If a nation's deficit must remain below 3% of GDP, a profligate government would want the largest possible estimate of GDP. For others, a higher GDP may end up costing governments more. The 28-nation bolc uses measures of GDP to determine how much each country contributes to the EU's collective budget.

Across Europe, Finland and Sweden, hardly nations characterized by vast criminal economies, would see the biggest boosts. The main changes result not from drugs but from technical adjustments such as how to capitalize expenditures on research and development and how to account for pension programs and most types of insurance policies.

Vice Precedent

Estimated impact on gross domestic product from new EU accounting methods, including addition of drugs, prostitution and other activities.

Estimated GDP Increase	
0–1%	Hungary
	Latvia
	Lithuania
	Poland
	Romania
1–2%	Czech Republic
	Estonia
	Ireland
	Italy
	Luxembourg
	Malta
	Portugal
	Slovakia
	Slovenia
	Spain
2–3%	Belgium
	Denmark
	Germany
	France
3–4%	Austria
	Netherlands
	UK.
4–5%	Finland
	Sweden

Source: Eurostat
The Wall Street Journal

The Bureau of Economic Analysis, which calculates U.S. GDP, has "no plans for now to include spending on illicit activities," according to spokes-woman Jeannine Aversa. U.S. GDP would expand by about 3% if all the changes being made in Europe were adopted, according to Eurostat estimates.

The U.K.'s own methodology shows how haphazard it can be to meausre activity far from the reach of cash registers and accountants.

The U.K.'s Office for National Statistics says it will estimate consumption of six drugs: crack cocaine, powder cocaine, herion, cannabis, ecstasy and amphetamines. Officials will first calculate the number of drug users based on crime surveys, and then multiply by an estimate of the average amount of drugs consumed per user.

Then, a series of estimates will hold the accounts in balance. For example, to avoid distorting the statistics on imports, the percentage of cannabis that is homegrown must be estimated. Then, an assumption is made about the volume of seeds and amount of electricity used in production.

For prostitutes, the statisticians will begin with an estimated tally of on-street prostitutes from the London Metropolitan Police and an estimate of off-street prostitutes from a nongovernment group that studies violence against women and girls. The number of prostitutes will be assumed to rise or fall along with the male population. The assumed cost of prostitution services will fluctuate along with the prices of lap dances and escort agencies, "the closest activities we have to prostitution" that are already measured.

Thomas Costerg, an economist for U.K.-based bank Standard Chartered, says governments aren't pushing to expand the definition of GDP "just to fudge the numbers."

But the problem, he says, "is you can get very theoretical and there could be some side effects, including the rising skepticism of statistics in the general population."

Definitions

1. GDP

   Measures the final goods and services produced by an economy within a given period of time.

2. Final goods

   Goods used for final consumption or in the economy.

3. Intermediate goods

   Goods used to produce final goods.

4. Flow variable

   The variable is measured from one point in time to another.

5. Underground economy

   Any kind of economic transaction that results in unreported or undocumented income.

6. Expenditure approach

   Takes into account all variables included in the demand expenditure, such as consumption or investment expenditures.

7. Income approach

   Includes all income received by the economy.

8. Net domestic product

   Output variable because it measures national output minus depreciation.

9. Depreciation

   The wear and tear of capital goods.

10. National income

    Depreciation and indirect business tax.

Multiple Choice

1. The total market value of all final goods and services produced within a given period by factors of production located within a country is
   a. gross national product.
   b. gross domestic product.
   c. net national product.
   d. net national income.

2. Which of the following is an example of a final good or service?
   a. chocolate a bakery purchases to make cakes
   b. coffee beans that are purchased by a restaurant owner from a wholesale food distributor
   c. an economics textbook you purchase with the intent of reselling after your course is over
   d. lumber purchased by a construction company that will be used by the company to build a model house to show to its clients

3. Which of the following is an example of an intermediate good?
   a. the wood you purchase to build yourself bookshelves in your room
   b. the chocolate you buy to make yourself some cookies
   c. the pizza sauce you purchase to make pizzas to sell for a fundraiser for an organization you belong to
   d. all of the above

4. Which of the following is not included in 1977's GDP?
   a. the value of a car produced in the United States and exported to England
   b. the profit earned in 1994 from selling a stock that you purchased in 1990
   c. the value of a computer chip that is used in the production of a personal computer
   d. the commission earned by an employment counselor when she locates a job for a client

5. Gross national product is
   a. the total market value of all final goods and services produced within a given period by factors of production located within a country.
   b. the total market value of all final goods and services produced within a given period by factors of production owned by a country's citizens, regardless of where output is produced.
   c. a nation's total product minus what is required to maintain the value of its capital stock.
   d. the total amount of income received by the factors of production in the economy.

6. Profits earned in the United States by foreign-owned companies are included in
   a. both GDP and GNP.
   b. neither GDP nor GNP.
   c. GNP but not GDP.
   d. GDP but not GNP.

7. In 1994, final sales equal $120 billion and the change in business inventories is –$10 billion. GDP in 1994
   a. is $110 billion.
   b. is $120 billion.
   c. is $ 130 billion.
   d. cannot be determined from this information.

8. In 1994, the change in business inventories is –$20 billion and the GDP is $190 billion. Final sales in 1994
   a. are $170 billion.
   b. are $190 billion.
   c. are $ 210 billion.
   d. cannot be determined from this information.

9. For a year in which there is a negative inventory investment, the final sales
   a. exceed GDP.
   b. are less than GDP.
   c. equal GDP
   d. are zero.

10. The value of net exports is
   a. the ratio of exports to imports.
   b. imports plus exports.
   c. imports minus exports.
   d. exports minus imports.

True/False

Directions: For the following statements, indicate whether the statement is true or false. If the statement is false, make the necessary change(s) in order for it to be a true statement.

1. If a car produced and first sold in 2007 is traded in and resold in 2008, the sale is counted as part of GDP in 2007 and 2008.

2. If McDonald's buys a bun for 10¢ and beef for 30¢, and sells a hamburger for $1, the contribution to GDP is $1.40, as each of these goods are final goods.

3. Firms produce a certain number of goods and services within a period of time, usually per week, month, quarter, or year. This is an example of a flow.

4. Examples of stock variables include the inflation rate and items found on a company's income statement.

5. National income accounting is important because it provides economists with detailed information that can be used to track the health of an economy and to forecast future growth and development.

6. When calculating gross domestic product (GDP), it doesn't matter whether you use the income or expenditure approach because they will always equal each other.

7. The difference between GDP and NDP is indirect business taxes.

8. Two measurement problems with GDP discussed in the chapter include the underground economy and household activities; including both of these would decrease the overall value of GDP.

9. By measuring and adding only the value-added of goods, we can avoid multiple counting and get a better estimate of GDP.

10. The growth rate of an economy is calculated by looking at the ratio of real to nominal GDP.

$$400 + 100 + 120 - 20$$

$$\$ 600$$

Essay Questions

1. Find the GDP if the output of an economy is:
   10,000 computers that cost $2000 each
   200,000 haircuts that cost $15 each
   30,000 bicycles that cost $400 each.

2. You are given the following information for an economy:

	Dollars (in billions)
Consumption	400 C
Net Exports	−20 X−M
Transfer Payments	20
Gross Investment	100 I
Social Security Contributions	10
Government Purchases	120 G
Net Investment	50
Dividends	20
Indirect Business Tax	10
Corporate Income Tax	30
Personal Income Tax	60
Undistributed Corporate Profits	20

Calculate the following:

a. Gross domestic product $GDP = C + I + G + (X-M)$
   $600   400 + 100 + 120 + (-20)$

b. Net domestic product   GDP − CCA
   $550   600 − 50

c. National income   NY = GDP − CCA − IBT
   $540   600 − 50 − 10
             50 = 100 − CCA

3. You are given the following information for an economy:

Year	Real GDP
2005	1,400
2006	1,600
2007	1,100

Calculate the growth rate each year. What is unique about the growth rate trend for each year?

Inflation

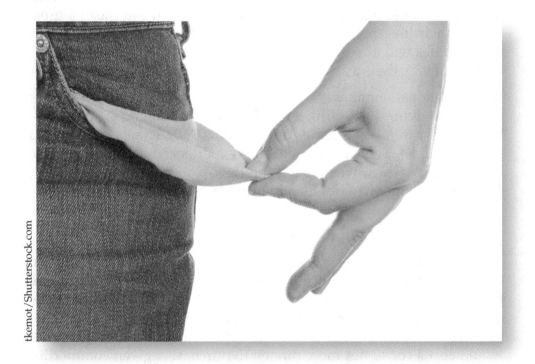

tkemot/Shutterstock.com

OBJECTIVES

1. To define the meaning of inflation.
2. To explain the distinction between the microeconomic and macroeconomic consequences of inflation.
3. To discuss the different types of inflation.
4. To discuss the different measures of inflation.
5. To explain the difference between real versus nominal GDP.

What Is Inflation?

Inflation is a sustained rise in the general level of prices in the economy—called the **price level**. The **inflation rate** is the rate at which the price level increases (conversely, **deflation** is a sustained decline in the price level; it corresponds to a negative inflation rate). Because inflation and deflation are measured in terms of average price levels, it is possible for individual prices to rise or fall continuously without changing the average price level.

The inflation rate is a very important economic indicator because it affects the cost of producing commodities and the cost of living. When the Federal Reserve announces an increase in prices from their statistical surveys, the public listens carefully because it can mean a great deal to their investments. The usual case is that when prices go up, interest rates will also go up to control inflation. The nominal consequence, obviously, is a rise in the interest rate.

By international standards, the U.S. economy has experienced low rates of inflation. From 1980–2010, the U.S. inflation averaged 4.1 percent—far below the inflation rates of Argentina (342.8%), Israel (196.3%), and Mexico (62.2%). The United States has experienced only one extreme inflation rate, which was during the Revolutionary war (1775–1783) when prices more than doubled in a single year.

Microeconomic Consequences of Inflation

The microeconomic effects of inflation are reflected in the distribution of income and wealth and not necessarily in the general decline of economic welfare. The inflation rate is just like a tax, taking income or wealth from some people and giving it to other sectors of the economy. The increase in price reflects the *price effects*. This means that it would cost a consumer more money to purchase a given commodity. Furthermore, an increase in price can also have an income effect. The **income effect** is the reduced consumption of a good whose price has increased that is due to the reduction in a person's buying power, or "real" income; when a person's real income is lower, normally he or she will consume less of all goods, including the higher-priced good. This can result in a decline in purchasing power. On the other hand, an increase in price can also lead to a wealth effect. The **wealth effect** is an increase in spending that accompanies an increase in wealth in absolute terms, or merely a perceived increase in wealth in relative terms. For example, an increase in price can lead to an increase in the value of gold or real assets that a typical consumer is holding. Thus, an increase in price can lead to an increase in the value of wealth.

Macroeconomic Consequences of Inflation

Inflation can alter the rate and mix of output by changing consumption, work, savings, investment, and trade behavior. In the process, our macroeconomic profile takes on a new and possibly unwelcome appearance.

Uncertainty

When prices change, economic decisions become increasingly difficult. The uncertainties created by changing the price level affect production decisions as well. Imagine a firm that is considering building a new factory. If construction costs or price changes rapidly during this period, the firm may find that it is unable to complete the factory or to operate it profitably. Confronted with this added uncertainty, the firm may decide to do without a new plant or at least to postpone its construction until a period of stable price returns.

Speculation

Inflation threatens not only to reduce the level of economic activity but to change its very nature. If you really expect prices to rise, it makes sense for you to buy goods and services or factors of production now for resale later. If prices rise fast enough, you can make a very handsome profit. These are the kinds of thoughts that motivate people to buy houses, precious metals, commodities, and other assets.

Shortened Time Horizon

Even people who don't speculate may find their productive activities disrupted by inflation. If prices are rising exceptionally fast, people must buy basic necessities as quickly as possible, while they can still afford them. For example, during the German Hyperinflation of 1923, prices doubled every week. Confronted with skyrocketing prices, German workers could not afford to wait until the end of the week to do their shopping. Instead, they were paid twice daily and given brief shopping breaks to make their essential purchases.

Tax Effects

Another reason that savings, investments, and work effort decline when prices rise is that taxes go up as well. Federal income tax rates are progressive (that is, tax rates are higher for larger incomes). The intent of these progressive rates is to redistribute income from rich to poor. However, inflation tends to increase everyone's income. In the process, people are pushed into higher tax brackets and thus confront higher tax rates.

Theory to Application
Paying for the American Revolution

Although seigniorage has not been a major source of revenue for the U.S. government in recent history, the situation was very different two centuries ago. Beginning in 1775 the Continental Congress needed to find a way to finance the Revolution, but it had limited ability to raise revenue through taxation. It therefore relied on the printing of fiat money to help pay for the war.

The Continental Congress's reliance on seigniorage increased over time. In 1775 new issues of continental currency were about $6 million. This amount increased to $19 million in 1776, $13 million in 1777, $63 million in 1778, and $125 million in 1779.

Not surprisingly, this rapid growth in the money supply led to massive inflation. At the end of the war, the price of gold measured in continental dollars was more than 100 times what it was only a few years earlier. The large quantity of the continental currency made the continental dollar nearly worthless. This experience also gave birth to a once-popular expression: people used to say something was "not worth a continental," to signify that the item had little real value.

When the new nation won its independence, there was a natural skepticism about fiat money. Upon the recommendation of the first Secretary of the Treasury, Alexander Hamilton, the Congress passed the Mint Act of 1792, which established gold and silver as the basis for a new system of commodity money.

Types of Inflation

There are two major types of inflation: demand-pull inflation, and cost-push inflation.

Demand-Pull Inflation

Inflation in an economy can be the result of an increase in aggregate demand that is unaccompanied by an increase in aggregate supply. This is known as **demand-pull inflation.** A rise in any component of aggregate demand can bring about demand-pull inflation. One reason

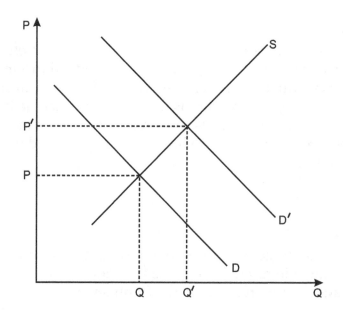

for a sudden, unanticipated rise in aggregate demand can be an unanticipated rise in the supply of money.

A special form of demand-pull inflation is hyperinflation. **Hyperinflation** is inflation that is out of control, a condition in which prices increase rapidly as a currency loses its value. It is a situation when there is a rapid monthly increase in prices, usually 50 percent or more. A good example of hyperinflation would be during the transition period in Russia (1992). The change from a communist to a capitalist economy increased uncertainty among consumers. Russian consumers lost confidence in the ruble (Russian currency); holding or saving rubles caused the depreciation of the currency. People preferred to hold onto some other international currency to exchange goods and services. Another example of hyperinflation is Argentina following the Falklands War in 1982. After they lost the war with the British, the Argentinean government increased money supply more than what the economy needed. The increase in the money supply caused an overvaluation of their currency. It also created a rapid increase in prices as capital moved to other countries.

Theory to Application
Life during the Bolivian Hyperinflation

The following article from the *Wall Street Journal* (1985) shows what life was like during the Bolivian hyperinflation of 1985. What costs of inflation does this article emphasize?

Precarious Peso—Amid Wild Inflation, Bolivians Concentrate on Swapping Currency

LA PAZ, Bolivia—When Edgar Miranda gets his monthly teacher's pay of 25 million pesos, he hasn't a moment to lose. Every hour, pesos drop in value. So, while his wife rushes to market to lay in a month's supply of rice and noodles, he is off with the rest of the pesos to change them into black-market dollars.

Mr. Miranda is practicing the First Rule of Survival amid the most out-of-control inflation in the world today. Bolivia is a case study of how runaway inflation undermines a society. Price increases are so huge that the figures build up almost beyond comprehension. In one six-month period, for example, prices soared at an annual rate of 38,000 percent. By official count, however, last year's inflation reached 2,000 percent and this year's is expected to hit 8,000 percent—though other estimates range many times higher. In any event, Bolivia's rate dwarfs Israel's 370 percent and Argentina's 1,100 percent—two other cases of severe inflation.

It is easier to comprehend what happens to the 38-year-old Mr. Miranda's pay if he doesn't quickly change it into dollars. The day he was paid 25 million pesos, a dollar cost 500,000 pesos. So he received $50. Just days later, with the rate at 900,000 pesos, he would have received $27.

"We think only about today and converting every peso into dollars," says Ronald MacLeans, the manager of a gold-mining firm. "We have become myopic."

And intent on survival. Civil servants won't hand out a form without a bribe. Lawyers, accountants, hairdressers, even prostitutes have almost given up working to become money-changers in the streets. Workers stage repeated strikes and steal from their bosses. The bosses smuggle production abroad, take out phony loans, duck taxes—anything to get dollars for speculation.

The production at the state mines, for example, dropped to 12,000 tons last year from 18,000. The miners pad their wages by smuggling out the richest ore in their lunch pails, and the ore goes by a contraband network into neighboring Peru. Without a major tin mine, Peru now exports some 4,000 metric tons of tin a year.

"We don't produce anything. We are all currency speculators," a heavy-equipment dealer in La Paz says. "People don't know what's good and bad anymore. We have become an amoral society . . ."

It is an open secret that practically all of the black-market dollars come from the illegal cocaine trade with the U.S. Cocaine traffickers earn an estimated $1 billion a year . . .

But meanwhile the country is suffering from inflation largely because the government's revenues cover a mere 15% of its expenditures and its deficit has widened to nearly 25% of the country's total annual output. The revenues are hurt by a lag in tax payments, and taxes aren't being collected largely because of widespread theft and bribery.

Cost-Push Inflation

Inflation can also result from a decrease in aggregate supply that occurs when businesses find that production inputs have risen in price. This

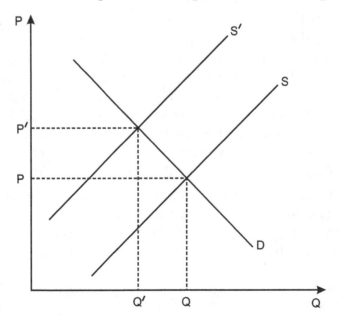

occurs when labor costs and the price of raw materials such as crude oil have risen. Decreases in productivity (the ratio of GDP to inputs) can also have a negative impact on aggregate supply and, therefore, cause a rise in prices. This type of inflation is known as *cost-push inflation*.

A special case of cost-push inflation is stagflation. **Stagflation** refers to stagnant growth and inflation. The usual case is that inflation exists when the economy is expanding. However, there are cases when inflation can occur while the economy is slowing down. This case of stagflation actually happened in the United States in the early 1980s when the second oil crisis occurred.

Measures of Inflation

The practical issue in measuring inflation is how to define the price level. Economists typically look at different measures of the price level or *price indexes*; these indexes include the Consumer Price Index, the Producer Price Index, and the GDP Deflator.

Consumer Price Index

The Consumer Price Index (CPI) measures the prices of a fixed market basket of some 300 consumer goods and services purchased by a typical urban consumer. This is the most important price index and the most commonly used. This type of price index is used widely, especially in the wage bargaining process and in transforming nominal economic variables to real values as in GDP.

As you can see from the table, the CPI gradually increases throughout time. This is primarily explained by the gradual increase in the money supply to meet the market's needs. For example, food and beverages along with energy are necessities, which everyone needs to survive. When the market expands, the demand will increase for these goods, causing prices to rise. It is also important to note that medical care had an inflation rate 3 percent for 2011. One reason that the prices of medical care continue to rise is because the quality continues to improve. Since the CPI does not take this into account, it overstates inflation. Additionally, new medical technology replaces old medical technology, which puts an upward bias into the CPI.

Producer's Price Index

The Producer's Price Index (PPI) is an index that measures inflation in wholesale goods. The Producer Price Index tracks the prices of food, metals, lumber, oil, and gas, as well as many other commodities, but does not measure the price of services. It is reported monthly by the Bureau of Labor Statistics.

GDP Deflator

The GDP deflator is a price index associated with adjusting money or nominal GDP for price changes. GDP deflator is used primarily for

Table 8–1. Consumer Price Indexes for Major Expenditure Classes

Year or month	All items	Food and beverages		Apparel	Housing	Transportation	Medical care	Recreation	Education and communication	Other goods and services	Energy
		Total	Food								
2000	172.2	168.4	167.8	129.6	169.6	153.3	260.8	103.3	102.5	271.1	124.6
2001	177.1	173.6	173.1	127.3	176.4	154.3	272.8	104.9	105.2	282.6	129.3
2002	179.9	176.8	176.2	124.0	180.3	152.9	285.6	106.2	107.9	293.2	121.7
2003	184.0	180.5	180.0	120.9	184.8	157.6	297.1	107.5	109.8	298.7	136.5
2004	188.9	186.6	186.2	120.4	189.5	163.1	310.1	108.6	111.6	304.7	151.4
2005	195.3	191.2	190.7	119.5	195.7	173.9	323.2	109.4	113.7	313.4	177.1
2006	201.6	195.7	195.2	119.5	203.2	180.9	336.2	110.9	116.8	321.7	196.9
2007	207.342	203.300	202.916	118.998	209.586	184.682	351.054	111.443	119.577	333.328	207.723
2008	215.303	214.225	214.106	118.907	216.264	195.549	364.065	113.254	123.631	345.381	236.666
2009	214.537	218.249	217.955	120.078	217.057	179.252	375.613	114.272	127.393	368.586	193.126
2010	218.056	219.984	219.625	119.503	216.256	193.396	388.436	113.313	129.919	381.291	211.449
2011	224.939	227.866	227.842	122.111	219.102	212.366	400.258	113.357	131.466	387.224	243.909

Source: Bureau of Economic Analysis (beau.gov)

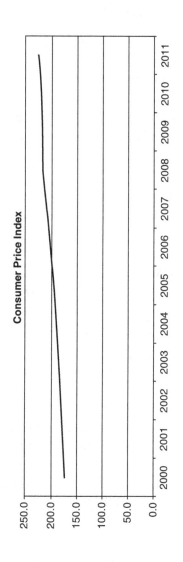

Consumer Price Index

aggregative data (e.g., money supply, industrial production, etc.). The GDP deflator in year t, P_t, is defined as the ratio of nominal GDP to real GDP in year t:

$$P_t = \frac{Nominal\ GDP_t}{RealvGDP_t} \times 100$$

To measure inflation, we use the percentage change formula as follows:

$$\pi = \frac{CPI_t - CPI_{t-1}}{CPI_{t-1}} \times 100$$

Where:

π = **the inflation rate**

t = **the current year or time period**

$t-1$ = **the previous year or time period**

For example: Looking at the historical consumer price index, the annual average CPI for 1998 is 163.0 and for 1997 is 160.5. To solve for the inflation rate, we use the above equation as follows:

$$\pi = \frac{163 - 160.5}{160.5} \times 100 = 1.56 \approx 1.6\%$$

An interpretation of this percentage means that the change in prices from 1997 to 1998 is approximately 1.6 percent.

Real versus Nominal GDP

Real GDP is the GDP that factors in the effects of inflation. The actual or current GDP that is collected from various sectors of the economy is the nominal GDP. If we want to compare different values of GDP over time, the best indicator is the real GDP.

$$Real\ GDP = \frac{Nominal\ GDP}{Price\ Index} \times 100$$

For example, the following table gives us the nominal GDP and Price Index for two different years:

Year	Nominal GDP Price	Index
1998	300	100
1999	350	110

To find the real GDP, we divide nominal GDP by the price index. For 1998, the real GDP is equal to $\frac{300}{100} \times 100 = 300$. For 1999, on the other hand, the real GDP is $\frac{350}{110} \times 100 = 318.18$. If the price index for a given year is equal to 1 or 100, then nominal GDP is the same as the real GDP. This year refers to the *base year*. The base year is the year in which all GDP are actually compared. For 1999, the real GDP of 318.18 means that the value of $350 in 1998 prices is $318.18. It is obviously less than $350 because of the effects of inflation.

This same analysis can be used to explain why salaries in different regions vary. Suppose that your hard work at the job search has paid off—your efforts have rewarded you with two job offers from which to choose. These two positions offer similar responsibilities, titles, and salaries. However, they may not be comparable if one is located in a high-cost city, whereas the other is based in a less-expensive one. If your job search involves different cities, it's helpful to know the cost of living index for those cities. For example, a $25,000 salary will give you more buying power in Omaha than it would in San Diego or Baltimore. But how do you effectively evaluate different offers?

To determine the real value of your salary offers, divide each city's salary by its price index and multiply the result by 100. To the extent the published price indexes reflect your likely living costs, the real salaries will give you a better gauge of a dollar's worth in that city.

$$\frac{Salary_{City\,A}}{Price\;Index_{City\,A}} \times 100 = Real\;Salary$$

For example, a Kansas City firm offers you a position with a salary of $24,000. A Los Angeles firm tops the offer with $30,000. Which position offers the higher real income?

$$Kansas\;City = \frac{\$24,000}{93.1} \times 100 = \$25,779$$

$$Los\;Angeles = \frac{\$30,000}{124.1} \times 100 = \$24,174$$

Based on the data given, the Kansas City job may be a better offer (*The Margin*, 1991).

References

The Margin. (January/February, 1991). 5(3).

The Wall Street Journal, August 13, 1985, p. 1.

Expected Inflation and TIPS

Charles T. Carlstrom and Timothy S. Fuerst

In 1997 the U.S. Treasury introduced a new security. This security, a bond called TIPS, for "Treasury Inflation-Protected Securities," is unique in the sense that its returns are indexed to inflation, thus promising bondholders a sure real return over the life of the bond. Unlike nominal Treasury notes, the real return of a TIPS is fixed at auction time. The face value and the coupon payments are indexed to the inflation rate, so they grow at that rate. Once the security is purchased, increases in inflation do not reduce an investor's real return. This is much different than a nominal Treasury note, where changes in inflation directly influence the realized real return of the bond.

The potential benefit of TIPS, however, goes beyond the inflation protection offered to bondholders. TIPS also promise economists and policymakers a potential way to tease out of the data the market's expectations for the future course of inflation. In principle, subtracting the real yield on TIPS from the nominal yield of Treasury notes of the same maturity should give policymakers and economists a market-based measure of expected inflation.

But thus far the results have been less than encouraging. Ten-year expected inflation rates derived from the TIPS market have run approximately 50 basis points lower than the inflation expectations of professional forecasters (obtained from the Survey of Professional Forecasters), and a full percentage point lower than those of households (as measured by the University of Michigan's Survey of Consumers). Of course, survey measures of expected inflation have a multitude of problems associated with them. However, the available evidence strongly suggests that expected inflation derived from the TIPS market underestimates actual expected inflation.

In this *Economic Commentary* we explore why the TIPS-based measure may have underestimated expected inflation. We show that there are two countervailing factors influencing the measure. First, inflation risk, in and of itself, implies that TIPS-based expected inflation should *overstate* actual expected inflation. Second, and even more important, is the relative illiquidity of the TIPS market, which leads TIPS-based expected inflation to *understate* actual expected inflation.

We demonstrate a method of correcting for the biases caused by the illiquidity of the TIPS market and inflation risk. The method produces a TIPS-based series that can serve as a measure of expected inflation, one that is potentially more accurate than the unadjusted TIPS series.

Using the adjusted series, we examine several interesting time periods. We show instances where the new series uncovers potential movements in expected inflation that the uncorrected TIPS series does not reveal. Similarly, there are periods for which the uncorrected TIPS series incorrectly indicates movements in expected inflation, but for which the adjusted series suggests no change occurred.

Inflation Risk and TIPS-Based Expected Inflation

Remember that, in principle, expected inflation should be accurately measured by subtracting the real yield on TIPS from the nominal yield on Treasury notes of the same maturity. The reason it is supposed to work this way is that the nominal yield on Treasury notes consists of a real return plus compensation for the inflation rate that is expected to occur over the horizon of the security.

But here is the rub: the calculation assumes that the real yields on both securities are equal. Anything that causes these two real returns to differ will cause a bias in a TIPS-based measure of expected inflation.

In 1996, even before the Treasury started issuing inflation-protected securities, two economists, John Campbell and Robert Shiller, suggested that if the Treasury were to introduce such a security, estimating expected inflation from it would probably overstate actual expected inflation by 50 to 100 basis points. They reasoned that in addition to compensation for expected inflation, regular Treasury notes must also pay compensation for *inflation risk,* or the possibility that actual inflation will be higher (or lower) than expected inflation.

To understand their reasoning, consider a 10-year Treasury note with a nominal yield of 6 percent. Say everyone expects inflation to average 2.5 percent over the next 10 years—but this is only what they expect. Actual inflation could turn out to be much lower, say 1.5 percent, or much higher, say 3.5 percent. This implies that the actual real yield from holding the bond may be as low as 2.5 percent or as high as 4.5 percent. On average it may be 3.5 percent, but there is an inflation risk associated with holding this bond that does not exist with an inflation-indexed security such as TIPS. Investors must be compensated for this risk, and the result is that the real yield of a nominal Treasury note tends to exceed the real return of an inflation-indexed security. Expected inflation derived from the inflation-indexed security would thus overstate actual expected inflation.

Campbell and Shiller then produced an estimate of the inflation risk premium. They first estimated historical inflation volatility as a means of quantifying the inflation risk people might be inclined to expect, and then they combined that figure with existing measures of the compensation that households require to accept that sort of risk. The premium they calculated was 50 to 100 basis points, which led them to their prediction that inflation-indexed securities would overstate expected inflation by that much. Given that TIPS appear to understate expected inflation by 50 basis points, we have something of a puzzle.

Liquidity and the TIPS Market

If we combine Campbell and Shiller's estimate of a 100-basis-point *overstatement* of TIPS-based inflation expectations with the 50-basis-point *understatement* that is actually observed, it suggests that the real yield on nominal Treasury notes is 150 basis points lower than the real yield on TIPS. Given that the real yield on nominal Treasury notes is about 2.6 percent, a real TIPS yield of over 4 percent is quite large! We argue that the difference can be explained as compensation for liquidity risk. Although the TIPS market is deepening, it does not approach the depth of nominal Treasury notes, suggesting that the liquidity risk for TIPS might be important. While this liquidity risk also exists for non-inflation-indexed Treasury notes, it does so to a much reduced extent, as markets for the notes are older and more developed than for TIPS.

Nominal Treasury notes are extremely liquid instruments. If one were to buy a 10-year note today and sell it tomorrow, one could do so without a large loss in capital. The reason is that large and active primary and secondary markets exist for these securities. The secondary market is extremely important because most buyers of Treasury notes do not hold the notes to maturity but sell them long before. It is rare for an investor to buy a 10- or 30-year note and still be holding onto it 10 or 30 years later. Circumstances change, and an investor who wants a long-term bond today does not necessarily want that same bond tomorrow.

Imagine the compensation an investor would need if it were impossible to sell a security once it was purchased. Obviously, investors can sell TIPS, but not nearly as easily as regular Treasury notes. This implies that investors in TIPS must be compensated for the relative illiquidity of these securities. The relative illiquidity of TIPS also introduces uncertainty into their pricing, which affects an investor's return when he or she sells the security early.

But can this extra liquidity risk explain the missing 150 basis points? Unfortunately, there are no good measures of TIPS market liquidity. However, there is a measure of the liquidity risk that is associated with nominal Treasury notes. We can safely assume that the liquidity risk for TIPS is correlated with the small liquidity risk that exists for regular nominal Treasury notes. Basically, if there is a small liquidity risk associated with holding nominal Treasury securities, there is an even larger liquidity risk associated with holding TIPS.

One measure of liquidity risk for nominal Treasury notes is the difference between returns for securities of the same maturity in the primary market and the less liquid secondary market. For example, the difference between the return on a 10-year Treasury note purchased in the primary market ("on-the-run") and the return on a 15-year Treasury note with 10 years left purchased in the secondary market ("off-the-run") provides a measure of the liquidity risk associated with that instrument. This liquidity risk does exist and since 1997 has varied from a low of 8 basis points to a high of 37 basis points.

Liquidity Risk and Expected Inflation

We can estimate the compensation needed to insure against the liquidity risk of TIPS by making three reasonable conjectures. First, the liquidity risk for TIPS is larger than the risk of off-the-run nominal Treasury securities because the TIPS market is less developed. Second, the liquidity premium in the TIPS market is correlated with the liquidity premium in the nominal Treasury market. The third conjecture relates the liquidity risk of TIPS to the difference that is observed between two measures of expected inflation—that reported in the Survey of Professional Forecasters and that derived from unadjusted TIPS yields. We assume this difference is largely driven by the liquidity risk.

We use the relationship to correct for the bias in TIPS-derived inflation expectations caused by inflation risk and the illiquidity of the TIPS market. The difference between the corrected series and the uncorrected series is obtained, as you may recall, by subtracting real TIPS yields from nominal Treasury yields. These inflation measures are clearly closely related but some interesting differences do exist.

First, our analysis suggests that inflation over the next 10 years will average around 2.5 percent to 2.6 percent. This is about the same as was expected at the beginning of 2002. Yet the uncorrected series suggests that expected inflation increased by around 85 basis points from 2002 to the present. Without the correction, you might worry that the credibility of the Federal Reserve to keep inflation fairly low and stable was waning, but with the correction, you might conclude the opposite.

A second divergent prediction for the two series occurs in August 1998, after the Asian financial crisis and at the beginning of the Russian default crisis. Looking at the uncorrected series, you might mistakenly conclude that expected inflation dropped precipitously from just over 3 percent in mid-1997 to around 0.8 percent in early 1999. Not surprisingly, however, there were liquidity problems with TIPS around the time and, to a lesser extent, Treasury notes, which affected the liquidity risk of both securities. The corrected series takes this change in risk into account, dropping from just over 3 percent to 1.5 percent.

It is also worth pointing out that our measure suggests that the uncorrected series can also miss changes in expected inflation. Long-term inflation expectations dropped more heading into the 2001 recession than the uncorrected series suggests. Also, from January 2004 to May 2004, our corrected measure of expected inflation increased by nearly

70 basis points, possibly because of inflationary concerns arising from the rapid growth in the U.S. economy at the time. This increase in inflation expectations was reversed only after the initial federal funds rate increase in the summer of 2004. After that, expected inflation once again fell back to its long-term average of around 2.6 percent. The up-tick in inflation expectations before the funds rate hike in June might not have been noticed in the uncorrected series, which increased only half as much over the same time span.

Concluding Thoughts

This *Economic Commentary* has shown a simple way of using TIPS to obtain a reasonable estimate of expected inflation. In particular, this estimate corrects for the inflation risk associated with nominal Treasury notes and the liquidity risk associated with TIPS. Clearly there are other factors that would influence the accuracy of TIPS-based expected inflation measures. The importance of these factors, however, is likely to be very small.

We emphasize that the success of TIPS should not be judged on the basis of how well they can be used to measure expected inflation. Measuring expected inflation is a potential side benefit of these securities; it is not the reason they were introduced. The very fact that their popularity is increasing suggests that they have fulfilled their primary purpose—to provide investors with an inflation hedge.

The Price of Cooking the Books

Buenos Aires

An extraordinarily elaborate deception may come back to haunt the government as the economy deteriorates

History has left Argentines with more than their share of economic trauma. Having twice suffered destructive bouts of hyperinflation in the late 1980s, they are sensitive to rising prices. When they spot inflation their instinct is to dump the peso and buy dollars. But after the economy collapsed in 2001-02, horror at mass unemployment temporarily eclipsed the public's fear of inflation. That has been the successful political calculation of the president, Cristina Fernández, and her late husband and predecessor, Néstor Kirchner. For years they stoked an overheating economy with expansionary policies. Faced with the resulting rise in inflation, their officials resorted to price controls—and to an extraordinarily elaborate deception to conceal the rise.

Since 2007, when Guillermo Moreno, the secretary of Internal trade, was sent into the statistics institute, INDEC, to tell its staff that their figures had better not show inflation shooting up, prices and the official record have parted ways. Private-sector economists and statistical offices of provincial governments show inflation two to three times higher than INEC'S number (which only covers greater Buenos Aires). Unions, including those from the public sector, use these independent estimates when negotiating pay rises. Surveys by Torcuato di Tella University show inflation expectations running at 25–30%.

PriceSlats, a specialist provider of inflation rates which produces figures for 19 countries that are published by State Street, an investment bank, puts the annual rate at 24.4% and cumulative inflation since the beginning of 2007 at 137%, INDEC says that the current rate is only 9.7%, and that prices have gone up a mere 44% over that period (see chart).

INDEC seems to arrive at its figures by a pick-and-mix process of tweaking, sophistry and sheer invention. Graciela Bevacqua, the professional statistician responsible for the consumer-price Index (CPI) until Mr Moreno forced her out, says that he tried to get her to omit decimal points, not round them. That sounds minor—until you calculate that a 1% monthly inflation rate works out at an annual 12.7%, whereas 1.9% monthly compounds to 25.3%.

Threatening letters sent by the government to independent economists also shed light on INDEC'S methods. One was told that since the cost of domestic service was "a wage, not a price", he should not have included it in his CPI calculations. "They have put a lot of effort and lawyers into such arguments," he says.

Ana Maria Edwin, INDEC'S current boss, is unrepentant. In Ms Bevacqua's day, INDEC artificially boosted the inflation rate, perhaps to benefit holders of inflation-linked bonds, she claims. She hints at underhand, possibly criminal, dealings between former INDEC staff, independent Argentine economists and international financiers. The evidence? That agreements between Mr. Moreno and retailers to cap prices of basic products were not reflected in INDEC'S calculations before 2007. That suggests INDEC is now using some government-mandated prices rather than those that consumers actually pay.

When a product's price spikes, INDEC takes it out of the CPI basket. "Poor people don't just keep buying things if their price goes up a lot," Ms Edwin explains. "They think: I will leave those tomatoes for the rich." A proper CPI calculation does indeed involve rules for dealing with changes in buying patterns. But the potential for abuse is clear.

Some Argentine government bodies seem well aware of the true inflation rate. Foreign investors report presentations by the Central Bank mentioning a real (ie, inflation-adjusted) exchange rate that implies annual inflation of around 20%. Economists who have picked through the somewhat suspect figures for economic growth say they can discern a similar rate in the "deflator" used 10 correct some prices. Perhaps most intriguingly, INDEC'S and PriceStats' inflation rates accelerate and decelerate in tandem.

The government has gone to extraordinary lengths involving fines and threats of prosecution, to try to stop independent economists from publishing accurate inflation numbers. The American Statistical Association has protested at the political persecution faced by its Argentine colleagues, and is urging the United Nations to act, on the ground that the harassment is a violation of the right to freedom of expression.

At the government's request, last year the IMF sent experts to help it plan a new national CPI. Ms Edwin says that the new index will not be ready until early 2014.

The longer this deception goes on, the trickier it is for the government to end. Faced with deteriorating fiscal accounts, Ms Fernandez has begun to trim subsidies amounting to 5% of GDP, Their removal will push prices up further–as would a weakening of the peso, So Mr. Moreno's latest wheeze involves responding to a vanishing current-account surplus with strict import controls, which will undermine growth. Argentina has created a statistical labyrinth that might have been dreamed up by Jorge Luis Borges, the country's greatest writer. This story is unlikely to have a happy ending.

WORLD NEWS

Deflation More Than Threat to Some

By Patricia Kowsmann

LISBON—José Teixeira isn't familiar with the word deflation. But he can tell you exactly what Portugal's downward spiral of shrinking paychecks and falling prices has done to Sal-Si-Fré, his modest restaurant.

"My business has been through a lot" in its 20 years, he said. "But this is by far the most difficult crisis."

Since the country's near-bankrupt government started making drastic spending cuts and raising income taxes three years ago, he has lost much of his business. Customers stopped coming in for a €6 ($8) serving of baked cod and started bringing lunch from home.

Desperate to stay afloat, he said he cut prices nearly in half but couldn't lure everyone back.

He figures he is earning 40% less than he did in 2010. That means he is spending less, he says, forcing other businesses to lower prices—and their employees' salaries—to get by.

"No more vacations, or even the occasional pair of jeans or shoes," said the 58-year-old restaurateur, coming up with his own definition of deflation.

"It is very simple," he said. "If we don't sell, we can't buy."

Deflation poses a threat to the fragile recovery across the 18-nation euro zone. But it has already taken hold in Portugal, Greece, Cyprus and Slovakia in recent months.

The European Central Bank's decision Thursday to cut interest rates and stimulate bank lending was aimed at reversing that trend before it becomes more broadly entrenched.

Portugal got in this downward spiral with good intentions. In return for a €78 billion ($106 billion) bailout in 2011, the government promised its lenders—the European Union, the International Monetary Fund and the European Central Bank—to cut spending, raise taxes and bring down its gaping budget deficit.

By cutting labor costs, the thinking went, made-in-Portugal products would become cheaper and thus more competitive abroad, spurring economic growth at home.

Portugal got in its downward spiral with good intentions.

The three-year-bailout program, which ended last month, did help boost exports, and a year ago Portugal emerged from recession.

But the small- and medium-size enterprises that form the backbone of the economy, and aren't so resilient to shocks, have struggled. Many have cut salaries or fired workers, driving overall unemployment above 15%. Gross domestic product slumped in the first quarter of this year, threatening a new recession.

Because people are earning and spending less, households and businesses have a harder time paying off their debts, which total a towering 240% of gross domestic product. Risky loans held by Portuguese banks were above 10% of total credit last year, up from 5% in 2010, according to the Bank of Portugal.

"If you have people who can't consume, are unemployed and have debt, that of course affects banks, which in turn tend to close the tap on giving credit," said Antonio Roldan an analyst at risk consultancy Eurasia Group in London. "As a result, the economy slows down, building a cycle of low growth mixed with deflation."

Mr. Roldan said Thursday's rate cut by the ECB, coupled with an easing up of Portugal's budget-cutting drive, could help reverse the downward spiral and spur growth.

Otherwise, deflation will make it harder for the government to pay off the public debt, which is close to 130% of GDP, and could bring Portugal back to the debt crisis that triggered the bailout.

Not far from Mr. Teixeira's restaurant in central Lisbon, the Iluminadora São Mamede hardware store is offering deep discounts on batteries, light bulbs and other basic products.

Natividade Silva, the 62-year-old owner, said she has cut back on inventory, which in turn has hurt her suppliers.

"Everybody is suffering, from those I buy from, to those I sell to," she said.

"Now you tell me how we are going to get out of this?"

Definitions

1. Inflation

A sustained rise in the general level of prices in the economy.

2. Inflation rate

Affects the cost of producing commodities and the cost of living. Rate at which price level increases.

3. Deflation

Sustained decline in the price level.

4. Income effect

Reduced consumption of a good whose price has increased that is due to the reduction in a person's buying power or real income.

5. Wealth effect

Increase in spending that accompanies an increase in wealth in absolute terms, or merely a perceived increase in wealth in relative terms.

6. Demand-pull inflation

Increase in aggregate demand that is unaccompanied by an increase in aggregate supply.

7. Income approach

Sum of all sources of income from different factors of production.

8. Cost-push inflation

Decreases in productivity have negative impact on aggregate supply, causes increase in prices.

9. Hyperinflation

Inflation that is out of control, a condition in which prices increase rapidly as a currency loses its value.

10. Stagflation

Stagnant growth and inflation.

Multiple Choice

1. Inflation is defined as
   a. any increase in the general price level.
   b. a sustained increase in the weighted average of all prices.
   c. a sustained increase in relative prices.
   d. an increase in the prices of specific products.
   e. a sudden increase in the weighted average of all prices.

2. The purchasing power of money
   a. increases as the level of relative prices decreases.
   b. has been rising in the United States since the 1940s.
   c. is the nominal value of money.
   d. is the nominal value of income.
   e. is the value of goods and services that can be bought with a dollar.

3. During periods of inflation,
   a. everyone's real income falls.
   b. those people benefit who have fixed incomes.
   c. those people benefit whose real income rises faster than the general price level.
   d. those people benefit who enter long-term wage agreements.
   e. those people benefit who hold a lot of cash.

4. If increases in total spending are not offset by increases in the supply of goods and services, the average level of prices will rise. Which of the following is responsible?
   a. cost-push inflation
   b. profit-push inflation
   c. demand-pull inflation
   d. wage-push pressures
   e. unemployment

5. When the economy is operating at full capacity, we might expect.
   a. cost-push inflation.
   b. demand-pull inflation.
   c. profit-push inflation.
   d. wage-push inflation.
   e. no inflation at all.

6. Cost-push inflation is caused by
   a. full employment of resources in the economy.
   b. excessive government spending.
   c. excess raw materials.
   d. the demand side of the market.
   e. the supply side of the market.

7. Annual inflation rates
    a. are about the same across countries.
    b. are higher in developing countries than in industrial countries.
    c. are higher in industrial countries than in developing countries.
    d. are not linked to the monetary policy of a country.
    e. remain relatively stable over time.

8. Hyperinflation
    a. causes the value of a currency to deteriorate so quickly that people become reluctant to hold that currency.
    b. is a situation where people hoard currency.
    c. is a simultaneous increase in the inflation and a decrease in the quality of products.
    d. occurred in the United States in the 1970s.
    e. is a synonym for cost-push inflation.

9. The introduction of a new currency in developing countries is generally a sign of
    a. an economic depression.
    b. a misguided political situation.
    c. social instability.
    d. hyperinflation.
    e. deflation.
10. If a college professor's income has increased by 3 percent at the same time that prices have risen by 5 percent, the professor's real income has
    a. decreased by 2 percent.
    b. increased by 2 percent.
    c. increased by 7 percent.
    d. decreased by 7 percent.
    e. not changed.

RESOURCES

ECONOMICS BOYES/MELVIN

True/False

Directions: For the following statements, indicate whether the statement is true or false. If the statement is false, make the necessary change(s) in order for it to be a true statement.

1. Because inflation and deflation are measured in terms of relative price levels, it is possible for average prices to rise or fall continuously without changing the individual price level.

2. One reason that economists are concerned about the inflation rate is because it affects the cost of living and the cost of inputs.

3. The income and substitution effects are some of the microeconomic effects of inflation mentioned in the chapter.

4. Some of the macroeconomic effects mentioned in the chapter include the wealth effect, uncertainty, price effect, and tax effects.

5. An example of cost-push inflation is when the Federal Reserve decides to increase the money supply in the economy.

6. Cost-push inflation is not as much of a concern to an economy as demand-pull inflation.

7. Stagflation occurs when inflation is increasing and the economy is experiencing negative growth (or recession).

8. Some ways to measure the price level include the Consumer Price Index, the Producer Price Index, and the GDP inflator.

9. The GDP deflator is the most important and most commonly used index when computing the price level.

10. The difference between real and nominal GDP is that nominal GDP factors in the effects of inflation.

11. When calculating the price level, the base year is always defined as the year with the highest price index.

$$\frac{10.30 - 9.70}{9.70} \times 10$$

$$\frac{10.95 - 8.2}{8.2} \times 100$$

$$\frac{9.70 - 4.25}{4.25} \times 100$$

$$\frac{11.77 - 10.95}{10.95} \times 100$$

$$\frac{CY - PY}{4.25 - 2.43} \times 100 = 74.9\%$$

$$2.43 \; PY$$

Essay Questions

The table below shows the actual average nominal income per hour in Country X, and CPI for each year with base period = 1982.

1. Calculate the real income and fill in the cells in the table below.

Year	Nominal Income	CPI	Real Income ($ per hour)
1960	2.43	29.6	8.2
1970	4.25	38.8	10.95
1980	9.70	82.4	11.77
1990	16.30	130.7	12.47

$\dfrac{salary\ city A}{Price\ index\ city A} \times 100$

2. Complete the table below.

Year	Percentage Change in Nominal Income	Percentage Change in Real Income
1960–1970	74.9%	33.5%
1970–1980	128.2%	7.5%
1980–1990	68%	5.9%

3. You worked for Walmart from 1980–1990. From 1980–1989 you earned the same wage of $9.00 an hour. In 1990 you received a 40 percent raise in your hourly wage. Is your real wage in 1990 higher than your real wage in 1980? Show all your work (use CPI information from the table).

$9 \times 1.4 = \$12.4$

$1990 = \$12.4$

$1980 = \$10.9$

$\dfrac{9}{82.4} \times 100 = 10.9$

$.1990 = \$9.64$

$\dfrac{12.4}{130.7} \times 100 = \$9.64$

No, real wage is $10.9 in 1980, and $9.64 in 1990.

Unemployment and the Business Cycle

Just ASC/Shutterstock.com

OBJECTIVES

1. To define the concept of unemployment.
2. To describe the meaning of unemployment rate.
3. To describe the scheme of labor force and explain how unemployment is derived.
4. To explain why the natural rate of unemployment exists.
5. To describe and explain the different types of unemployment.
6. To explain the different problems in measuring unemployment.
7. To discuss the meaning of business cycles.
8. To discuss the different stages of business cycles.
9. To explain the different sources of business cycles.
10. To understand the basic facts about business cycles.

Introduction

In almost any economy at almost any time, many individuals appear to be unemployed. That is, there are many people who are not working but who say they want to work in jobs like those held by individuals similar to them, at the wages those individuals are earning.

The possibility of unemployment is a central subject of macroeconomics. There are two basic issues. The central questions here are whether this unemployment represents a genuine failure of markets to clear, and, if so, what the causes and consequences are. There is a wide range of possible views. At one extreme is the position that unemployment is largely illusory, or the working out of unimportant frictions in the process of matching up workers and jobs. At the other extreme is the view that unemployment largely represents a waste of resources.

Jobs are essential because they provide workers with not only income but also social status and some sense of fulfillment. Employment represents the use of scarce labor resources to produce desired goods and services. Unemployment can be a major problem when the economy slows down. Business cycles, which represent the ups and downs in the economy, can affect the number of available jobs in a given time.

To understand the concept of unemployment, we will start with explaining how the unemployment rate is derived by the government. The unemployment rate is a fraction of the total labor force. We divide the population into two categories: institutionalized versus the civilian noninstitutionalized population (CNIP). The institutionalized segments of the population are those people who are less than 16 years of age, incarcerated, military personnel, or mentally ill. The CNIP includes both people who are employed and people who are unemployed but seeking for a job.

The Bureau of Labor and Statistics takes a survey among 65,000 households and defines the labor force. The total labor force can be defined as all persons over the age of 16 who are either working for pay or actively seeking paid employment. People who are not employed and not actively seeking work are not counted as part of the labor force. Therefore, unemployment rate can be defined as follows:

$$u = \frac{U}{L} \times 100$$

where:

u = **the unemployment rate**

U = **the number of unemployed workers**

L = **the total labor force**

The unemployment rate is the proportion of the labor force that is unemployed. The unemployment rate does not include those people who are out of the labor force. People who voluntarily leave the labor force such as **discouraged workers**—those who would be willing to work but have given up trying to find work—are not factored into the unemployment rate. Therefore, to be considered unemployed, a person must be willing to work *and be actively seeking* employment. Usually, if an individual gives up looking for a job after 3 weeks, he or she is considered to be a discouraged worker.

Other key indicators of the labor market include the **labor force participation rate** and the **employment-to-population ratio**. The labor force participation rate is the ratio of people in the labor force to the working-age population. In the past decade, there was a steady rise in the labor force participation rate, from 62 percent of the labor force in the mid-1970s to 67 percent of the labor force in the mid-1990s. This increase is mainly due to more women entering the labor force, a trend that has been ongoing since the 1950s. In the early 1950s about 30 percent of women were in the labor force; currently that statistic is closer to 60 percent. Possible explanations for this trend include reduced discrimination and the women's movement, which emphasized the attractiveness of paid work outside the home. Another reason is the rise of the dual-income family, which is necessary to maintain a family's expenses. The **employment-to-population ratio**, on the other hand, fluctuates as real GDP fluctuates, but there is an important long-term trend. The employment-to-population ratio has increased from about 57 percent in 1976 to about 63 percent in 1996. The employment-to-population ratio is higher than it has been at any time in U.S. history. In this sense, the U.S. economy is creating more jobs now than at any time in its history (Taylor, 1998).

Scheme of Labor Force

Natural Rate of Unemployment

In the labor market, equilibrium exists when the demand and supply for labor is equal. Theoretically, what this means is that the unemployment rate is equal to zero. However, this is not realistic because there will always be people who are unemployed and looking for work at any given time.

In a normal state of the economy, we refer to the unemployment rate as the **natural rate of unemployment** (denoted u_n). The natural rate of unemployment is the unemployment rate when inflation is stable. In normal times, the average rate of unemployment is somewhere between 4 and 6 percent. The three types of unemployment that can be accounted for in the natural rate of unemployment include frictional, structural, and seasonal unemployment.

Types of Unemployment

Frictional Unemployment

These are brief periods of unemployment experienced by people moving between jobs or into labor market. Of the 4 to 6 percent natural rate of unemployment, 2 to 3 percent is accounted for by frictional unemployment. For example, a student who just recently graduated from college enters the labor market; it is not likely that he or she would have a job immediately upon graduating.

Structural Unemployment

Structural unemployment is caused by a mismatch between skills or location of job seekers and requirements of available jobs. This is a much more serious kind of unemployment because it may take a longer time for a worker to be absorbed into the labor market. Coal miners who lose their jobs when their mines are mechanized, and secretaries who do not know how to use computer programs or processors and need to be retrained are examples of structural unemployment. Between 1 and 2 percent of the natural rate of unemployment is accounted for by structural unemployment.

Seasonal Unemployment

Seasonal unemployment results from seasonality in demand or supply of any particular goods or services. Summer resort workers, lifeguards, Santa Clauses, Easter bunnies, construction workers, and landscapers all represent seasonal workers. About 0.5 percent of the natural rate of unemployment is accounted for by seasonal unemployment.

Cyclical Unemployment

Cyclical unemployment is unemployment caused by a low level of aggregate demand associated with recession in the business cycle. It is a temporary downturn in the job market. Cyclical unemployment, when workers are temporarily laid off, is the most common form of unemployment. Cyclical unemployment is not included as part of the natural rate of unemployment.

The definition of unemployment is not without ambiguity. Remember that persons are counted as unemployed *only* if they are available for and actively seeking work or are awaiting recall from a layoff. These criteria can lead to some paradoxical outcomes. For example, a person who quits looking for work because his or her job-seeking efforts have been discouraging is not counted as unemployed. On the other hand, a well-paid northern construction worker drawing unemployment compensation while vacationing in Florida during an annual winter-weather layoff is numbered among the unemployed.

One can argue that the statistical definition of unemployment results both in people being excluded even though they would prefer to be working (or working more) and people being included who are not seriously seeking employment. Discouraged workers are those whose employment prospects are so bleak that they no longer consider it worthwhile to search for employment. Though not counted as unemployed, many of them would be willing to accept employment if it was available. When the economy turns down, the number of workers in the discouraged category rises substantially. For example, during the 1991 recession the Department of Labor estimated there were 1 million discouraged workers (approximately 0.8 percent of the labor force) in the United States—up from 715,000 prior to the recession.

The method of classifying part-time workers may also result in an understatement of the number of unemployed workers. Part-time workers who desire full-time employment are classified as employed rather than unemployed if they work as much as a single hour per week. Yet these people are certainly underemployed, if not unemployed.

On the other hand, some people who claim to be searching for work and are thus classified as unemployed are not seriously seeking employment. For example, an individual who rejects available employment because it is less attractive than the current combination of household work, continued job search, unemployment benefits, food stamps, and other government welfare programs is numbered among the unemployed. Since recipients of several government income-assistance programs, including food stamps and Aid to Families with Dependent Children (AFDC), are required to register for employment, many of them are classified as unemployed even though they have no plans to search for and accept employment. According to a study by Lawrence Summers and Kim Clark of Harvard University, these work-registration requirements push the official unemployment rate up by approximately 0.5 to 0.8 percent (600,000 to 1 million potential employees) (Gwartney & Stroup, 1997).

The measurement of unemployment is also complicated by other factors. Unemployment insurance benefits tend to increase the measured unemployment rate by reducing the incentive of recipients to accept available jobs as long as they qualify for the benefits. If they are not otherwise gainfully employed, people engaged in criminal activities (e.g., drug pushers, gamblers, and prostitutes) or working "off the book" in the underground economy may also be classified as unemployed. Although estimates are difficult to project, some researchers believe that as many as 1 million people fall into this category.

The financial crises of 2008 led to a significant increase in unemployment rate to 10.2 percent as of October 2009. This marks the first time in 26 years that it has been above 10 percent. According to the data released by the Economic Policy Institute, the underemployment rate is about 17.5 percent, which includes people who have been unable to find full-time work and working either part time or not at all. The number of consecutive months of job loss during this recession is 22 months. The last time the United States saw a double-digit unemployment rate was in 1983.

This is the only recession since the Great Depression to have wiped out all of the job growth from the previous business cycle. In the article by the Upjohn Institute, various ideas were innovative local solutions through community collaboration was the best way to overcome the drastic consequences of the Great Depression—widespread unemployment and poverty. There were some suggestions coming from various countries, particularly European countries that can serve as a safety net to alleviate the effects of the recession.

The first policy suggestion is the automatic stabilizers such as unemployment compensation, which is popular especially in Germany and France. An important part of the social safety net in Germany, France, and a number of European countries is short-time compensation, which provides pro-rated unemployment benefits to workers whose hours have been reduced and thereby helps companies avoid layoffs. Short-time compensation—also known as work-sharing benefits—is available in only 17 U.S. states and is little used in the majority of states with such programs. The absence of the STC (short-time compensation) benefits is a significant gap in U.S. social insurance policy that should be plugged. By fostering work-sharing in lieu of layoffs, STC benefits can help firms make needed workforce adjustments in a more efficient and equitable way. Companies that implement work-sharing arrangements can avoid the loss of valued employees during a temporary downturn. Work-sharing is more equitable because the burden of a recession is spread across workers rather than being concentrated among a few (Abraham and Houseman, 2009).

Another policy to fight high national or regional unemployment is a new job tax credit (NJTC). This tax credit was provided to businesses for additions to their overall employment in 1977–78. The program at its peak provided such subsidies to 1.1 million businesses for adding more than 2.1 million workers, at an annual cost of a little less than $4 billion, which in today's dollars is around $13 billion (Bartik, 2009). These credits would be made refundable in order to make it more relevant to businesses that are less profitable. It should also apply to any employer that pays Social Security taxes which includes many small and medium-sized businesses and nonprofit organization that do not file corporate income taxes. Studies suggest that wage subsidies are more effective for smaller employers, who face greater financing constraints (Bartik, 2009).

The third policy to reduce unemployment is through a workforce development system. To help people find jobs, the American Recovery and Reinvestment Act of 2009 has more than doubled the appropriations for programs to assist dislocated workers, disadvantaged adults, and youth from the amount appropriated in the 2009 budget. These services are critical to the economy's recovery; they help workers get back to work by assisting them in the job-search process and in retooling their skills. For the recovery effort to work, all entities that have a responsibility for these programs—federal, state and local—must implement them quickly and effectively. Yet, it is not enough simply to spend money and enroll participants. Rather, the services need to be effective at getting people into decent-paying jobs (Ebberts, 2009).

Theory to Application

Henry Ford's $5 Workday

In 1914, the Ford Motor Company started paying its workers $5 per day. The prevailing wage at the time was between $2 and $3 per day, so Ford's wage was well above the equilibrium level. Not surprisingly, long lines of job seekers waited outside the Ford plant gates hoping for a chance to earn this high wage.

What was Ford's motive? Henry Ford later wrote, "We wanted to pay these wages so that the business would be on a lasting foundation. We were building for the future. A low wage business is always insecure. . . The payment of five dollars a day for an eight hour day was one of the finest cost cutting moves we ever made."

From the standpoint of traditional economic theory, Ford's explanation seems peculiar. He was suggesting that *high* wages imply *low* costs. But perhaps Ford had discovered efficiency-wage theory. Perhaps he was using the high wage to increase worker productivity.

Evidence suggests that paying such a high wage did benefit the company. According to an engineering report written at the time, "The Ford high wage does away with all the inertia and living force resistance. . . The workingmen are absolutely docile, and it is safe to say that since the last day of 1913, every single day has seen major reductions in Ford shops' labor costs." Absenteeism fell by 75 percent, suggesting a large increase in worker effort. Alan Nevins, a historian who studied the early Ford Motor Company, wrote, "Ford and his associates freely declared on many occasions that the high wage policy had turned out to be good business. By this they meant that it had improved the discipline of the workers, given them a more loyal interest in the institution, and raised their personal efficiency" (Bulow & Summers, 1986).

Business Cycles

Business cycles are defined as the alternating periods of economic growth and contraction.

Graphical Representation of a Business Cycle

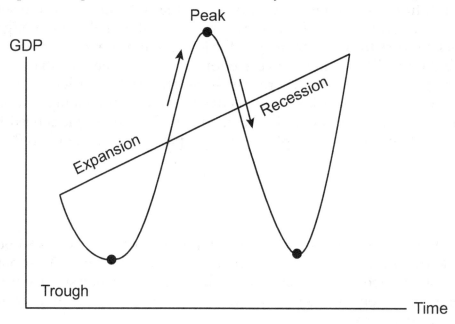

Between 1921 and 1927 the stock market's value more than doubled, adding billions of dollars to the wealth of American households. The roaring stock market made it look easy to get rich in America. The party ended abruptly on October 24, 1929. On what came to be known as Black Thursday, the stock market crashed. In a few short hours, the market value of U.S. corporations fell abruptly. The effect of this crash was that by 1933, 25 percent of the labor force was unable to find work. In 1938, 20 percent of the workforce was still unemployed. The Great Depression shook not only the foundations of the world economy but also the assured self-confidence of the economics profession because nobody had predicted the Depression and few could explain it.

Stages of Business Cycles

1. **Trough:** The bottom of the economy. A trough is usually characterized by high unemployment and low levels of consumer demand (in relation to the capacity of industry to produce goods for consumption). A good example of a trough is the Great Depression.

2. **Expansion or Recovery:** When something sets off a recovery, the lower turning point of the cycle has been reached. Worn-out machinery will be replaced; employment and income begin to rise.

3. **Peak or Boom Stage:** At this stage, a high degree of utilization of existing capacity exists. Labor shortages may be severe, and shortages of raw materials may develop.

4. **Turning Points or Recession:** When GDP falls for two successive quarters, we face a recession. It is usually characterized

by a falling demand and unemployment. While recessions are usually looked at negatively, they do help the economy substantially. Recessions eliminate inefficiencies in the economy. An example of this is to look at the housing and credit markets during 2007 and 2008. As the subprime mortgage market began to deteriorate, the market started clearing out the inefficiencies in the form of housing foreclosures, and businesses such as the investment bank Bear Stearns being bailed out by the government (*Wall Street Journal*, March 18, 2008) (and then being acquired by J. P. Morgan) (*Wall Street Journal*, March 17, 2008). Once these inefficiencies are cleared, the business cycle starts again, leading to an expansion in the economy.

Sources of Business Cycles

The behavior of buyers and sellers may be responsible for our erratic economic performance. The following are the different sources of business fluctuations:

1. **Aggregate Demand Shocks:** For example, a change in consumption, a change in government expenditures, and changes in investment can contribute to the fluctuations of the economy.

2. **Aggregate Supply Shocks:** If we want to predict actual sales, we also need to know something about potential sellers. How much output will businesses be willing and able to produce at various prices? Aggregate supply reflects the various quantities of real output that firms are willing and able to produce at alternative price levels in a given time period.

Our failure to achieve full employment may result from the unwillingness of producers to provide more goods at existing prices. That unwillingness may originate in simple greed, in rising costs, in revenue shortages, or in government taxes and spending.

3. **Eclectic Explanations:** The word *eclectic* means "various ideas." This theory supports the premise that business cycles draw from both sides of the market. It can be a price-level change, as in the case of price-ceiling or price floor.

Basic Facts about Business Cycles

While economists have collected and poured over an inordinate number of pieces of information related to recessions and expansions over the years, six basic facts are crucial to understanding the fundamental properties of business cycles (Knoop, 2004):

Business cycles are not cyclical. The term *business cycle* is really a misnomer, because it implies that recessions and expansions follow a regular, predictable pattern. They do not. In fact, business cycles vary considerably in size and duration. The shortest recession in U.S.

history was in 1980–1981 (though it was a very sharp recession), lasting only 6 months. It was followed by the shortest expansion, which lasted only 12 months. The longest modern recession lasted 43 months, between 1933 and 1937, while the longest expansion ended in 2001 and lasted 121 months—more than 10 years. Between the shortest and longest recessions and expansions other cycles have exhibited a wide variety of spacing and length. The length of one business cycle is not a reliable indicator of the length of the next business cycle.

Business cycles are not symmetrical. In the United States, expansions average 43 months, while recessions average only 14 months. Thus, expansions are about three times longer than recessions on average. However, output changes tend to be much larger during recessions than they are during expansions. These asymmetries between recessions and expansions hold internationally as well. There is a great deal of similarity across countries in the length of recessions. Excluding Spain and Germany, expansions also tend to last roughly the same amount of time across countries.

Business cycles have not changed dramatically over time. Ten years ago, economists generally believed that business cycles had changed dramatically and were much shorter and less severe during the postwar period than in the prewar period. However, newer and better historical data has given economists a clearer picture of historical business cycles in the United States. Based on historical data, recessions are somewhat shorter but expansions are significantly longer in the postwar period.

The Great Depression and the World War II expansion dominate all other recessions and expansions. GDP fell by 50 percent between 1929 and 1932, while unemployment rose to a peak of 25 percent in 1933. The Great Depression dwarfs the next largest recession, which took place during 1973–1975, in which GDP declined by 4.2 percent and unemployment rose to 9 percent. Likewise, the expansion that began in 1938 and continued throughout World War II was unparalleled, with GDP rising by 64 percent between 1941 and 1944.

Business cycles are associated with big changes in the labor market. Unemployment is strongly countercyclical, and changes in employment are much larger during recessions than the changes in other inputs into production. Over the long run, increases in the capital stock account for roughly one-third of trend per capita GDP growth, while increases in productivity account for the other two-thirds. Changes in employment account for essentially none of the increases in trend per capita GDP. (This makes sense if employment and the population grow at roughly the same rate, which they do.) However, during business cycles (times when output is growing at a rate different from trend), the story is exactly the opposite. In other words, during recessions and expansions, changes in employment appear to be driving a large portion of the changes in output. This seems to suggest that any plausible theory of business cycles has to give a prominent role to the cyclical behavior of the labor market.

Bubbles

With the recent economic crisis in the United States, business cycles have been somewhat link to the concept of "bubbles." In the past, bubbles in the economy existed due to inflationary expectation or simply overvalued assets. In the seventeenth century, there was tulipmania, in which the Dutch people became obsessed with holding onto the rare tulips, which could command a very high market price. Other kinds of historic bubbles included the South Seas bubble when stock prices for the South Seas company that held a monopoly for South American goods were overpriced. In today's market, the housing market is an example of a bubble. In recent years, housing prices have gone up 40 percent or more in various regions of the United States. The U.S. housing market created a bubble as prices doubled or even quadrupled in the last couple of years. The recent financial crisis can be attributed to the housing bubble as it cannot sustain the rate at which the value of the housing market increases.

References

Abraham, G. & Houseman. (2009, July). Easing labor market troubles in the short run and developing a skilled workforce in the long run: Some ideas. Upjohn Institute of Employment Research.

Bartik, T. J. (2009, July). The new jobs tax credit: A tested way to fight high unemployment. Upjohn Institute of Employment Research.

Bulow, J. I. & Summers, L. H. (1986, July). A theory of dual labor markets with application to industrial policy, discrimination, and Keynesian unemployment. *Journal of Labor Economics, 4*, 376–414.

Ebberts, R. W. (2009, July). Improving performance measures for the nation's workforce development system. Upjohn Institute of Employment Research.

Gwartney, J. & Stroup, R. (1997). *Economics: Private and public choice* (8th ed.). Orlando, FL: Dryden Press.

Knoop, T. (2004). *Recessions and depressions: Understanding business cycles*. Westport, CT: Praeger Publishers.

Raff, D. M. G., & Summers, L. H. (1987, October). Did Henry Ford pay efficiency wages? *Journal of Labor Economics, 5*, Part 2, S57–S86.

Taylor, J. (1998). *Inflation, unemployment, and monetary policy*. Boston: MIT Press, 173–174.

The Wall Street Journal. (2008, March 17). J. P. Morgan rescues Bear Stearns.

The Wall Street Journal. (2008, March 18). U.S. mulls next steps in crisis.

Phillips Curve and the Role of Expectations

Phillips Curve

In 1958, A.W. Phillips of the London School of Economics published a paper, "The Relation between Unemployment and the Rate of Change of Money Wages in the United Kingdom, 1861–1957," in the economics journal Economica. He plotted the inflation rate against the unemployment rate for each year. What he found is a curve that looks similar to the graph below:

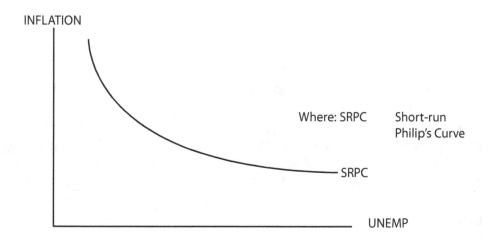

This curve later became known as the Phillips Curve. He found that inflation and unemployment are inversely related. This inverse relationship between inflation and unemployment suggests that there is a tradeoff between prices and unemployment. The higher the unemployment rate is, the lower the inflation rate is, or, conversely, the higher the inflation rate, the lower the unemployment rate.

The implication of this relationship led policymakers to conclude that it was impossible to both lower inflation and unemployment. That policymakers could only do one or the other suggested a tradeoff between inflation and unemployment.

A theoretical reasoning behind the Phillips Curve can be explained using our aggregate demand concept. When aggregate demand is increasing, business production increases and more workers are hired. As the unemployment rate decreases, employers find it harder to hire workers at the old wages. Businesses will soon offer a higher wage for workers, thus increasing prices and causing overall inflation. This reasoning can be shown using the model below:

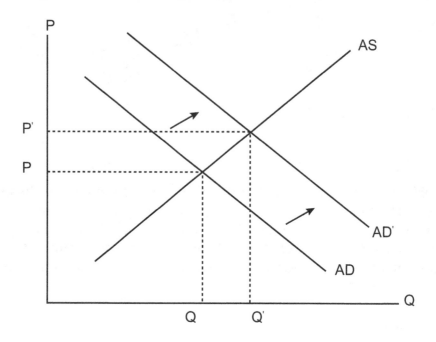

Long-Run Phillips Curve

In the 1970s and 1980s, economists began to question the conclusions of the Phillips Curve. There were periods, especially from 1970–1994, when events did not really suggest a tradeoff between inflation and unemployment. In 1981 and 1982, there were periods suggesting stagflation—high unemployment and high inflation. Furthermore, cycles of unemployment and inflation rates appear to move around a 6 percent unemployment rate, identified by a vertical line as shown below:

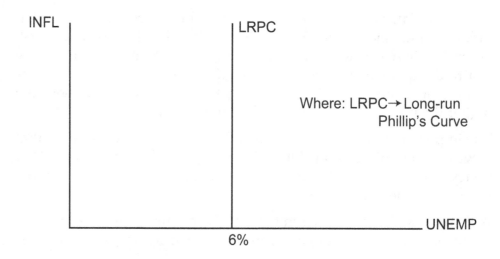

This model suggests that the unemployment rate tends to move toward some natural level in the long run. Thus, the Phillips Curves were divided into two categories: (a) short-run Phillips Curve (SRPC); and (b) long-run Phillips Curve (LRPC). One explanation for the LRPC is Friedman's natural rate theory. This idea suggests that in the long run the natural rate of unemployment prevails. Within the Phillips Curve model, the natural rate theory specifies that there is an LRPC, which suggests that the curve is vertical at the natural rate of unemployment. This natural rate of unemployment is around 4 to 6 percent.

The Role of Expectations in the Long-Run Phillips Curve

In the early 1970s, Robert Lucas of the University of Chicago challenged the concept of short-run tradeoff between inflation and unemployment. Essentially, what Lucas did was combine the natural rate theory with rational expectations.

Expectation viewpoints can be divided into two categories: (a) adaptive expectations, and (b) rational expectations.

In the case of adaptive expectations, people form their expectations about what will happen in the future based on what has happened in the past. If inflation has been higher than expected in the past, then people would revise expectations for the future. Another example is in the case of non-unionized workers; the only time people would ask for a pay raise was when inflation affected the workers. In short, there was a time lag between changes in prices and change in wages. People responded to what happened in the past to form their decisions. Using our Phillips Curve model, adaptive expectation can be shown as a movement from A to B to C. In short, there is an error-learning process in the decision-making process of individuals.

Rational expectations, on the other hand, contend that businesses, consumers, and workers generally understand how the economy functions and effectively use available information to protect or further their own self-interest. In particular, people understand how government policies will affect the economy and anticipate these impacts in their own decision making. For example, when government implements an expansionary policy, workers anticipate inflation and a subsequent decline in real wages. Therefore, workers incorporate this expected inflation into their nominal wage demands. A good example for this model is the case of unionized workers. Workers can anticipate inflation in the future and can incorporate the anticipated inflation into their nominal wage in the collective bargaining agreement. This model is shown as follows:

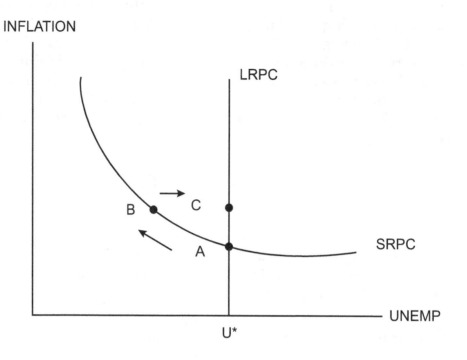

The Natural Rate of Interest

Natural rate theorists view attempts to achieve lower interest rates that are consistent with individual decisions as self-defense. By definition, an interest rate is the annual monetary premium paid for the use of money. Interest rates vary almost as much as wage rates or other prices. The different interest rates paid by borrowers to lenders reflect, among other considerations, risk, length of time to maturity, availability of credit, and legal constraints. When all of these factors are included, we refer to these interest rates as *nominal interest rates*.

In this section, we will make a distinction between *real interest rates* and nominal interest rates. Real interest rates are the annual percentage of purchasing power paid by a borrower to a lender for the use of money. The formula for the real interest rate is as follows:

Real Interest Rate = Nominal Interest Rate − Expected Inflation
$$(r) \quad = \quad (n) \quad - \quad E(P)$$

The formula indicates that the real interest rate is the difference between the nominal interest rate and expected inflation. If inflation is expected, lenders try to charge higher interest to ensure that they will not lose purchasing power. For example, during the late 1970s housing prices increased by 10 percent. Mortgage rates for housing were around 7 percent. Looking at the formula, the real interest rate for mortgages was about 3 percent. Thus, it was better to borrow money to purchase a house during this time than to do nothing. It also tells us that banks were subsidizing mortgages in this period.

Definitions

1. Unemployment rate

2. Business cycles

3. CNIP

4. Labor force

5. Natural rate of unemployment

6. Frictional unemployment

7. Structural unemployment

8. Seasonal unemployment

9. Recession

10. Bubbles

Multiple Choice

1. Business cycles are
   a. variations in the economy that are all equal in intensity.
   b. seasonal variations in the economy that occur every year.
   c. fluctuations in economic output that show a declining growth pattern over time.
   d. periodic but irregular variations in economic activity.
   e. exactly alike in the amount of time that passes from peak to peak.

2. In the business cycle, a trough marks the end of a(n) _____ and the beginning of a new _____.
   a. contraction; expansion
   b. peak; expansion
   c. expansion; contraction
   d. peak; contraction
   e. expansion; peak

3. The period between a peak and a trough is known as
   a. boom.
   b. recovery.
   c. expansion.
   d. business cycle.
   e. contraction.

4. The Bureau of Labor Statistics defines a person as unemployed if he or she
   a. does not work full time.
   b. does not have a job but is actively seeking one.
   c. does not earn a wage above the minimum wage rate.
   d. does not earn enough income to be above the poverty level.
   e. does not work as much as he or she desires.

5. Including the discouraged workers in the labor market statistics would
   a. reduce the labor force and increase the unemployment rate.
   b. increase the labor force and increase the unemployment rate.
   c. increase the labor force and reduce the unemployment rate.
   d. reduce the labor force and decrease the unemployment rate.
   e. affect neither the size of the labor force nor unemployment rate.

6. Which of the following is true in respect to seasonal unemployment?
   a. It results from downturns in economic activity.
   b. It is likely to be associated with jobs that are affected by changes in the weather.
   c. It is the type of unemployment associated with discouraged workers.
   d. It is likely to be affected by changes in consumer preferences.
   e. It is difficult to predict since it involves all kinds of workers.

7. Very short-term unemployment is most likely to be
   a. full employment.
   b. involuntary unemployment.
   c. frictional unemployment.
   d. structural unemployment.
   e. cyclical unemployment.

8. Which of the following is the product of technological change and other changes in the structure of the economy?
   a. seasonal unemployment
   b. underemployment
   c. structural unemployment
   d. frictional unemployment
   e. cyclical unemployment

9. The number of people classified as employed is 550,000 and the number of people classified as unemployed is 150,000. The size of the labor force
   a. equals 700,000.
   b. equals 550,000.
   c. equals 400,000.
   d. cannot be determined from this information.

10. If the number of people classified as unemployed is 20,000 and the number of people classified as employed is 230,000, what is the unemployment rate?
    a. 8 percent
    b. 8.7 percent
    c. 9.2 percent
    d. 11.5 percent

References

Principles of Macroeconomics Case & Fair

Economics Boyles/Melvin

True/False

Directions: For the following statements, indicate whether the statement is true or false. If the statement is false, make the necessary change(s) in order for it to be a true statement.

1. Changes in the price of oil are likely to cause a change in the natural rate of unemployment.

2. Those who serve in the U.S. military are counted as part of the labor force.

3. People who are not part of the CNIP are factored into the labor force and unemployment rate.

4. The Bureau of Economic Analysis is the government agency responsible for surveying households and defining the labor force.

5. The unemployment rate does not factor in people who voluntarily leave the labor force such as homemakers and discouraged workers.

6. A discouraged worker is a person who has stopped actively seeking employment after 3 weeks of job searching.

7. Under normal circumstances, the natural rate of unemployment is between 0 and 3 percent.

8. The three types of unemployment that make up the natural rate of unemployment are frictional, cyclical, and structural unemployment.

9. Frictional unemployment accounts for the majority of the natural rate of unemployment.

10. When analyzing business cycles, the trough is the recovery phase.

11. A recession helps the economy by eliminating inefficiencies in the economy.

12. The Great Depression and the technology boom of the 1990s dominate all historic recessions and expansions.

Essay/Short Answer Questions

1. Complete the table below.

	Counted as Unemployment		If yes, which type of unemployment
Rosalind, who is 14, has been actively looking for a job	Yes	No	
Mr. Tomacruz, a prison inmate, has not landed a job in the 4 years he has been in prison	Yes	No	
Jenny lost her job as a TV commercial writer when the economy moved into a recession	Yes	No	
Ms. Smith's skills as an expert handmade quilt maker were no longer enough to get her a good job	Yes	No	
Joe quit his job as a medical sales person and looked for a job that better suited his training as a physician	Yes	No	
Donna Starkman was given a 20 hours a week, part-time job in place of a full-time job she had	Yes	No	
John Goodman decided to stay home, take care of his son, cook meals, and not look for work	Yes	No	
Anthony Givens looked for a job for years and finally gave up looking	Yes	No	

2. Given the following information, calculate the following:
    a. Number of unemployed   7000   The labor force is_____
    b. Number of employed   120,000   The unemployment rate is_____

Chapter 10

Aggregate Demand and Aggregate Supply

Olga Langerova/Shutterstock.com

OBJECTIVES

1. To explain the meanings of aggregate demand and aggregate supply.
2. To describe the circular flow of economic activity
3. To discuss the reasons there is an inverse relationship between aggregate demand and prices.
4. To describe the three regions of aggregate supply.
5. To explain the different components of aggregate demand.
6. To explain the importance of consumption and investment to aggregate demand.
7. To analyze the meaning of equilibrium income.
8. To solve the equilibrium income using models.
9. To explain the concepts of inflationary and recessionary gaps.
10. To apply the concept of investment multiplier.
11. To explain the link between equilibrium income and investment multiplier.

National output can be derived based on the different component of the market. Previously, we have discussed that GDP is more accurate using expenditure approach. By expenditures, we are summing all the elements of **aggregate demand.** Aggregate demand includes all the expenditures incurred in the different sectors of the economy.

$$AD = GDP = Y = C + I + G + (X - M)$$

Aggregate demand includes all the expenditures incurred in the household sector (consumption), business sector (investment), government sector (government expenditures), and foreign sector (net exports). Aggregate demand can be analyzed by a simplified circular flow of economic activity. What this means is that goods and services move from one sector to another, and the flow of funds contributes to the growth of the economy.

Circular Flow of Economic Activity

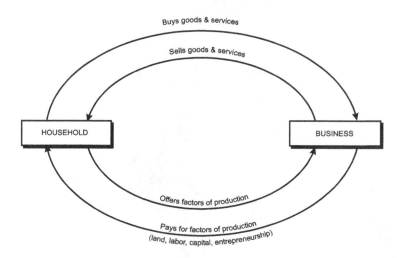

From the factor market, households offer factors of production (land, labor, capital, and entrepreneurship) to the business sector. The business (or private) sector pays wages and salaries (compensation) for rendering services or factors of production. In the product market, the business sector sells final goods and services to households while the household sector buys final goods and services from the business sector.

If we include the government (or public) sector in this circular flow, then we will introduce the concept of withdrawals and injections. By withdrawals, we mean that there are leakages into the economy. Taxes are a form of withdrawal, or leakage, because they have a negative effect on the economy. However, taxes are transformed into government expenditures, which can be an injection of funds to the economy. If we introduce the foreign sector to the model, exports are an injection (since money is coming into the country) and imports represent a withdrawal (since money is going out of the country).

Aggregate Demand and Prices

From a microeconomic standpoint, we know that there is a negative or inverse relationship between quantity demanded and prices. We have also studied the reasons why the inverse relationship exists. We have identified price effectsand **income effect** as the main reasons for the inverse relationship. From a macroeconomic perspective, there is also a negative relationship between aggregate demand and prices. The only difference is that we will not use a ceteris paribus assumption. We will simply discuss the relationship between aggregate demand and prices.

From a macroeconomic viewpoint, the income effect is still relevant because when price increases, the value of our money income tends to decrease. Another term for income effect on a macro level is **purchasing-power effect.**

When prices increase, the pool of money supply circulating in the public will decrease, causing an increase in money demand. If there is not enough money available for credit, businesses will resort to other methods in order to pay for their current expenditures. One way of generating capital funds, aside from borrowing, is to issue bonds. When people start selling their bonds, the price for bonds decreases (because there are too many bonds circulating in the public). A decrease in the price for bonds leads to an increase in interest rates. An increase in interest rates reduces investments, causing GDP to decrease. We refer to this as the **interest rate effect.**

The third reason is the **international trade effect.** When domestic prices increase, the value of the dollar relative to other currency tends to appreciate. As the dollar becomes stronger, it becomes more expensive for foreigners to buy U.S. goods and cheaper for U.S. consumers to buy imported goods. Thus, the volume of our exports declines and the volume of imports increases. This leads to a decline in net exports and eventually to a decline in GDP.

Aggregate Supply

Aggregate supply refers to the relationship between prices and quantity supplied from a macroeconomic viewpoint. We view production from an aggregate level and link it to prices. In the previous chapter, we discussed the elements and composition of aggregate supply.

In this section we will analyze aggregate supply from three different approaches: Keynesian, classical, and intermediate range. The commonly viewed supply curve (the upward-sloping aggregate supply curve) is what is called intermediate range. What is more interesting in this discussion is the difference between the Keynesian and classical approach.

Regions of Aggregate Supply

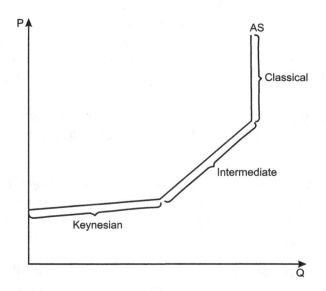

The aggregate supply curve from the Keynesian perspective is flat or horizontal. It means that the prices are too low and that the economy is stagnant and has no growth incentive. Another term for this is called **liquidity trap.** In a recession, or slow times, people would rather horde their money than invest it in stocks and bonds because there is no incentive for a positive or greater return. According to prominent British economist John Maynard Keynes, the only way to stimulate the economy is through government intervention (fiscal policy).

Classical aggregate supply, on the other hand, is vertical. It means that no matter what the price is, the economy will always stay at the same output level (the natural rate of output). This idea of a vertical aggregate supply curve is consistent with the natural market correction theory in which government intervention is irrelevant or ineffective.

Shifts in Aggregate Demand and Supply

The aggregate demand curve can shift by any of the following changes:

- Changes in consumption expenditures.
- Changes in investments.
- Changes in government expenditure.
- Changes in the foreign sector.

Changes in Consumption Expenditure

Personal consumption is the most important component of GDP. As of 2006, personal consumption made up 70 percent of the total GDP for the United States. Personal consumption is the expenditure incurred by consumers from the household sector.

The most important economic variable that can affect consumption is income. There is a positive relationship between consumption and income. When income increases, personal consumption tends to go up. There are various ways of interpreting the link between consumption and income. One of the more common ways of linking the two is through the **marginal propensity to consume (MPC).** Marginal propensity to consume is the change in consumption caused by a change in income. This is one of the most powerful ways of explaining an incremental value of a given variable. Most economists would explain things in a marginal concept because it is relevant from a strategic perspective. A marginal propensity to consume of 10 percent means that for every dollar increase in income, 10 percent goes to additional consumption.

Savings, on the other hand, is the fraction of our income that is not spent. Marginal propensity to save (MPS) is the change in savings caused by a change in income. In theory, if the marginal propensity to consume is 10 percent, the marginal propensity to save is 90 percent. This is on the assumption that income can either be consumed or saved. Therefore, the sum of the marginal propensity to consume and the marginal propensity to save is equal to 1.

We can analyze personal consumption and its effects by looking at the consumption function:

$$C = Ca + bY$$

Where

Ca = **autonomous consumption**

b = **marginal propensity to consume**

Y = **personal disposable income**

Autonomous consumption is independent of income, meaning that there are other factors that can affect consumption, which we will discuss in the next section.

Another way of analyzing consumption and income relationship is through the concept called **average propensity to consume (APC).** The average propensity to consume can be defined as the ratio of consumption relative to income:

$$APC = \frac{Consumption}{Income}$$

APC is an important concept especially when we link it to savings. Savings rate or **average propensity to save (APS)** is the ratio of savings relative to income:

$$APS = \frac{Savings}{Income}$$

Currently, this news about savings rate has been a big issue especially in the U.S. economy. In recent years, our savings rate has been declining for many reasons. Aside from the fact that a fraction of our income goes more toward consumption, it is also important to relate it to how people save. Some people save through their 401Ks or their individual retirement accounts (IRAs). These are investments that are not necessarily traditional savings mechanisms.

External Factors Affecting Consumption

Wealth

Wealth can exert a significant influence on consumer spending. Quantitatively, however, wealth effects tend to be far overshadowed by income changes. Nevertheless, the rise of stock prices in 1997 alone lifted the wealth of Americans by $2 trillion. That is more than 50 percent greater than the total stock of consumer installment credit.

Consumer Confidence

Given low unemployment and inflation plus strong equity prices, it is not too surprising that consumer confidence is high. Consumer confidence is based on the general expectation of the public about the economy. The recession of 1991–1992 can be attributed to the low expectation given by consumers. However, in 1998, consumer sentiment was high in absolute terms. Stock market volatility, job layoffs, and political developments may all combine to lower confidence.

During the recent financial crisis, consumer sentiment has been a major indicator for the downturn. The University of Michigan formulated an index to represent consumer confidence. It serves as a weathervane for assessing whether the economy is in a downturn or recovery. If individuals expect lower future income, then it can also lead to lower consumption. This can lead to a decrease in aggregate demand.

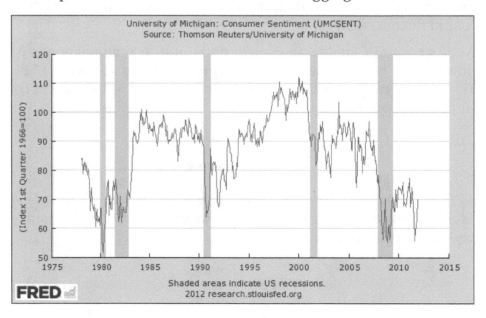

Interest Rates

The interest rate is the cost of borrowing money. For consumers who buy goods and services through credit, an increase in the interest rate means lower consumption. In 2008, the interest rate was at its lowest level in years. A low interest rate environment, however, is not sufficient to guarantee a buoyant economy. Interest rates fall in recession, too, but do you see strong auto sales and capital spending at those times? No. The economy needs favorable expectations in addition to lower interest rates for people to part with their resources.

Taxes

Changes in taxes can also affect consumption. Taxes are a cost on the part of consumers. For example, an increase in sales tax can reduce the sales of consumer goods. Taxes are a leakage, and therefore the effect on disposable income is negative.

We can also consider the effects of personal income taxes. A tax that people pay on their income can also affect their consumption habits. As income taxes increase, personal disposable income decreases. When people have less take-home pay, people tend to spend less. Eventually this can also lead to a decrease in aggregate demand. In the past, government policy tended to favor a reduction in taxes especially during a recession. The assumption is that if taxes were cut, this could lead to an increase in disposable income for consumers, thus increasing consumer spending.

Changes in Investment

Investment is the expenditures incurred by the business sector. In national income accounting, investment can also refer to the gross private domestic investment. There are three elements of investments:

1. Changes in inventory.

2. Durable capital equipment.

3. Residential construction expenditures.

Of all the different expenditure variables in national income accounts, investment is the most volatile (meaning it varies a lot). There are many reasons for this volatility, but the most important is volatility of interest rates. The most influential variable affecting investment is interest rates. The interest rate is the cost of borrowing money. Most investors would borrow money to purchase their inventories, capital equipment, and start their construction projects. If the interest rate increases, then it costs more for investors to pursue their projects. Some investors have less incentive to invest as the interest rate increases. This is because it becomes more lucrative to keep money in savings with a high interest rate. Decisions on investments depend on how sensitive investments are to fluctuations in interest rates.

Other factors affecting investments are similar to factors that affect consumption. Factors such as disposable income, taxes, expectations, and cost of capital can all affect investments. Disposable income has a positive effect on investment. Taxes and other costs of capital have negative effects. The effects of expectations depend entirely on how investors perceive the health of the economy. Businesses invest because of future profits. If the business sector perceived a future greater return on a given investment, then it is more likely that investment spending will grow. If, however, business investors become pessimistic about the economy, then investment spending will contract. Eventually this can also affect aggregate demand.

Business taxes are another major factor affecting overall investments. Businesses naturally consider after-tax profits when making investment decisions. An increase in business taxes decreases after-tax profitability. Thus, this can lead investors to invest less. This leads us to a well-known supply-side economic theory called Reaganomics. The premise behind this theory is the effect of a capital-gains tax cut. By cutting capital gains taxes, the public can boost savings and investment. Eventually this can also lead to a boost in aggregate demand and GDP.

Paradox of Thrift

In the previous sections, we discussed savings as the difference between income and consumption. Savings is an important factor in the economy as it can be transformed into investments that can eventually lead to growth and productivity. In the recent events, "savings" or "thrifts" have been widely reported as the economy shrinks and we have experienced the so-called Great Recession of 2008. Prior to the recession, reports about the U.S. savings rate were negative, which basically tells us that people in general are not saving. The driving force in the U.S. economy was consumption. In fact, 70 percent of our GDP accounts for personal consumption. In a recession, as much as we want to see a countercyclical phenomena, our savings rate in fact increases. People save more when the economy is contracting. But what is the effect of such case? If savings increases, it means that consumption is decreasing. Since consumption is a component of GDP, it eventually exacerbates the slowdown in the economy. Savings from an individual basis is a virtue. However, from a macro perspective, savings has a negative effect when the economy is contracting. This phenomena is called a "paradox of thrift or savings."

In an article in *The Economist* (September 18, 2010), another example of a paradox of thrift was explained from the perspective of interest rates. With the credit crunch of 2007–2008, interest rates were at their lowest at about 1 percent or below in most rich countries. Investors seem to have two reactions to the prospect of a prolonged period of low rates. For the bulls, it is a sign that investors will eventually decide to reject the safety of cash in return for the higher returns available from riskier assets. For the bears, low rates are a sign of the desperation of central bankers, and an indication that economic growth will be subdued for some time to come.

A long period of low rates has found consequences for savers. For example, whether pension schemes are funded by the public or private sector, or are structured as defined benefits (final salary) or defined contribution plans, the fundamental principle is the same. Schemes try to build up a capital pot, which is used to buy an income in retirement, for example, in the form of an annuity. Low rates increase the liabilities of pension schemes. In addition, deflation is a hidden risk for pension schemes. If it occurs, it will cut the nominal incomes of those who have to fund future pensions, creating another potential gap between assets and liabilities.

The effects of low interest rates do not stop there. Rates are low in real as well as in nominal terms, which makes it harder to accumulate as given capital sum. Since less of the work is performed by investment returns, more of the work has to be done by the saver. Interest rate cuts hurt savers' incomes even as they make borrowers better off. If this income effect were to become powerful enough, it would be a nice irony. Low interest rates, which have the main aim of encouraging spending, could have the perverse effect of encouraging savings (*Economist*, 2010).

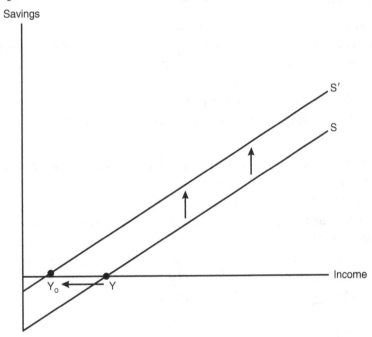

Just like we did with consumption, we can analyze the effect of investment on the economy. At the moment, we will assume that investment is autonomous. In this case, our investment function is represented by:

$$I = Ia$$

Although we can say that there are other factors affecting investment, for simplicity purposes, we safely assume that investment expenditure is an exogenous shock to the system.

Foreign Exchange and the Liquidity Trap

Owen F. Humpage and William R. Melick

The federal funds rate—the interest rate that the Federal Reserve uses to guide monetary policy—currently stands at 1 percent, its lowest level since the recession of 1958. Overnight reserve market interest rates are similarly low in the euro area and are essentially at zero in Japan. Rates this low raise concerns among economists and policymakers about the ability of central banks to conduct monetary policy. The problem is that when prices are falling and short-term interest rates approach zero, banks may become indifferent between lending and holding money in their portfolios. If banks have no incentive to lend, the standard method for conducting monetary policy—cutting short-term interest rates by purchasing government securities to add reserves to commercial bank portfolios—becomes ineffective because reserves stay in banks and are not lent out to trickle through the economy. With this mechanism closed, central banks may find offsetting any downward momentum in prices and economic activity inordinately difficult.

Economists often refer to this situation as a liquidity trap, and they have proposed a wide variety of ways to make an escape. Some economists, notably Ben McCallum of Carnegie Mellon University and Lars Svensson of Princeton University, suggest that central banks buy foreign exchange instead of domestic government securities and use an exchange rate target to help guide monetary policy out of a liquidity trap.

While not everyone agrees that liquidity traps are a serious possibility, in this *Economic Commentary,* we assume they are and discuss the merits and the drawbacks of these exchange-rate-based escapes. We show that while these foreign-exchange-based recommendations are theoretically feasible, they rely on rather esoteric and largely untried transmission mechanisms. Moreover, they raise potential beggar-thy-neighbor issues that would likely require the domestic monetary authorities to coordinate with foreign monetary authorities.

The Japanese Experience

Japan's economic experience over the past 12 years, and the fear that similar problems could develop in the United States or in Europe, have motivated much of the current discussion about liquidity traps.

While the issue of whether Japan is truly stuck in a liquidity trap or is instead the victim of persistent structural banking problems remains contentious, the country exhibits most of the hallmarks that economists associate with a liquidity trap. Real growth in Japan began to stagnate in 1990, by 1995, prices started to fall, and short-term interest rates reached their zero limit. Frustrated by the inability of standard monetary procedures to combat these symptoms, the Bank of Japan switched its operating procedure in March 2001 from targeting a nominal overnight interest rate to targeting reserves held by Japanese banks. The Bank has since increased its reserve target roughly four-fold and tripled the amount of long-term Japanese government bonds that it purchases each month. These policy changes resulted in a rapid increase in the monetary base, but the broader money stock has not grown apace. Commercial banks in Japan apparently are still holding the additional reserves instead of using them to support more lending.

From the perspective of the banks, holding reserves makes economic sense. With nominal short-term interest rates stuck at zero, reserves and short-term interest-bearing assets become close substitutes in Japanese banks' portfolios—especially portfolios weakened by questionable loans. The situation becomes even more intractable if, as is the case in Japan, prices are falling and the balance sheets of many potential borrowers are in poor condition. With falling prices, cash in a bank's vault will increase in value and offer a return that may be greater than a loan to a struggling business. In this type of environment, how might a central bank operate?

Inflation, Credibility, and the Expectations Channel

When Princeton University economist Paul Krugman first suggested that Japan was caught in a liquidity trap, he emphasized the importance of policy credibility to making an escape. A central bank caught in a liquidity trap faces the daunting task of convincing the public that it is committed to raising the rate of inflation substantially. The expectation that prices will soon rise should have two effects on economic activity. First, a public that expects prices to be higher in the future will spend today on both consumption and investment in order to beat the coming price increases. Second, as prices rise and inflation expectations firm, loan demand will strengthen, and interest rates will also begin to rise. Banks will no longer be content to hold excess reserves, since idle cash in vaults will lose value as prices rise. Lenders will look to satisfy a rising loan demand and earn a positive rate of return. Economic activity will expand.

Krugman advocated that the Bank of Japan simply announce an inflation target and expand its open market operations accordingly. But a simple announcement may not be sufficiently convincing for central banks like the Bank of Japan or the Federal Reserve System, which have consistently demonstrated an aversion to inflation. If people doubt the central bank's resolve to generate inflation, economic activity will continue to stagnate.

Lars Svensson's plan for escaping a liquidity trap primarily offers a mechanism for enhancing credibility. Not all economists agree in their interpretation of the nuts and bolts of Svensson's proposal, but in the main, he seems to exploit a mechanism known as the expectations channel.

Svensson suggests that the Bank of Japan—and, by extension, any central bank caught in a liquidity trap—announce a long-term target path for the price level (necessarily embodying a significant inflation rate) and a long-term target path for the exchange rate (necessarily embodying a significant depreciation) that is consistent with the target path for the price level. Svensson argues that this twin announcement will be more credible, since the Bank of Japan can guarantee the exchange rate depreciation by flooding the world with yen by purchasing essentially unlimited amounts of foreign exchange, such as dollars or euros. Except for the instruments involved—foreign currencies instead of domestic securities—such an operation is equivalent to a standard central bank open market operation. How then does this mechanism enhance credibility? What encourages Japanese banks to lend out these yen reserves instead of holding on to them?

The essential element in Svensson's proposal is that the Bank of Japan must persuade the public that the yen will remain at the depreciated rate until the price target is achieved and convincingly maintained. Since exchange rates are quoted minute by minute—unlike price indexes, which appear at a monthly frequency and only after a significant lag—the Bank of Japan's efforts to depreciate the yen are immediately and always visible. Market participants can continuously monitor the central bank's commitment to depreciate the currency. The transparency of this mechanism enhances the central bank's credibility more than standard open market operations aimed solely at an inflation rate. The hope is that once the central bank announces the twin target paths and depreciates the yen, people will anticipate the inflation rate embodied in the price-level target and will immediately alter their behavior.

While Svensson's plan has the benefit of being more transparent with respect to the inflation objective than a typical open market operation, it is far from foolproof. Ultimately, it relies on the public seeing the immediate depreciation of the yen and therefore completely believing the central bank's commitment to the price-level target and higher inflation. However, the plan could go awry if the public instead believes that the immediate depreciation of the yen is only temporary and perhaps likely to be reversed. Given that the yen has basically appreciated against the dollar over the past 30 years, this possibility cannot be ignored, as emphasized by Stanford economist Ronald McKinnon.

Portfolio-Balance Channel

Ben McCallum's proposal for a foreign-exchange-based escape from a liquidity trap introduces a channel of influence—the portfolio-balance mechanism—that does not depend on affecting expectations. In a liquidity trap, the purchase of foreign exchange can produce a depreciation—even if expectations about a future depreciation and inflation do not change—by altering the currency composition of assets in investors' portfolios. If, for example, the Bank of Japan acquires dollars (or other foreign currencies), private investors across the globe necessarily end up holding more yen-denominated base money and securities in their portfolios relative to dollar-denominated assets. Although short-term Japanese securities and currency may be perfect substitutes in a liquidity trap, yen- and dollar-denominated assets probably will not be perfect substitutes. Consequently, international investors may only acquire additional yen assets if compensated for the risk of loading their portfolios with them. Their initial aversion to additional yen assets induces a spot depreciation. With the expected future exchange rate unchanged, the initial depreciation implies that the yen will appreciate in the future and will provide holders of the yen assets with a valuation gain. This implied valuation gain compensates investors for their added risk.

This portfolio-balance effect offers a mechanism through which the spot exchange rate will immediately depreciate even if domestic short-term interest rates are stuck at zero. As we discuss in the next section, the yen depreciation will lower the foreign currency prices of Japanese goods and raise the yen price of foreign goods. This change in relative prices shifts worldwide demand—at least temporarily—toward Japanese goods and services. If the depreciation is large enough, it could provide a sufficient boost to lift economic activity out of the liquidity trap.

Although theoretically sound, the portfolio-balance mechanism lacks convincing empirical support. At best, empirical studies suggest that to exploit the portfolio-balance channel, a central bank would have to undertake an extremely large amount of foreign exchange purchases—an amount well beyond the typical central bank foreign exchange intervention. However, for a central bank caught in a liquidity trap, these large purchases may indeed be technically feasible. A central bank can essentially print an unlimited amount of its own currency, and the pool of foreign currencies available for purchase is vast.

Beggar-Thy-Neighbor

Along with questions about their feasibility, proposals to escape a liquidity trap through planned currency depreciation have raised concerns about their potential consequences for other countries. The depreciating country would gain competitiveness—at least initially—at the expense of its trading partners. Economist Michael Mussa, for example, contends that such proposals, if narrowly construed, might violate the prohibition in the International Monetary Fund's Articles of Agreement against "manipulating exchange rates... to gain an unfair competitive advantage over other members." Even though the ultimate objective is to generate inflation, and even though any competitive gain would dissipate as prices rose, the technical legality of these proposals might be problematic.

Clearly the fault lies solely in the explicit yen depreciation, since any monetary expansion that successfully freed Japan from its liquidity trap—no matter how it was induced—would depreciate the yen. Because exchange rates tend to respond to monetary policy changes faster than goods prices, a yen depreciation would initially improve Japan's price competitiveness, thereby boosting its exports and reducing its imports. An accelerating inflation rate, however, would eventually erode the competitive gains from the depreciation, and import demand would rise with the revival of GDP growth.

Empirical studies are unclear about how these offsetting influences play out over time. Many suggest that a monetary expansion could eventually worsen Japan's trade balance because renewed growth would increase that country's imports more than enough to offset the temporary gain in price competitiveness resulting from the yen depreciation. Claims that exchange-rate-based proposals violate international law may be technically correct, but largely overblown. The proposals are not likely to do much damage to other countries.

Some commentators have been especially concerned that a depreciation of the yen will have dramatic effects in East Asia. These commentators fear that floating East Asian currencies, especially the Singapore dollar, South Korean won, and Taiwan dollar, will depreciate in sympathy with the yen and put excessive pressure on those currencies maintaining a fixed parity with the dollar, particularly China's.

These concerns also seem exaggerated. Detailed trade data reveal that Chinese exports compete most closely with exports from Indonesia, Thailand, Taiwan, and Malaysia—countries whose exchange rates do not move all that closely with the yen. This finding suggests that the competitive effects of yen depreciation on China are likely to be modest. Moreover, the share of China's exports destined for Japan has increased rapidly, from 13.9 percent in 1995 to 20.8 percent in 2000. China stands to gain enormously from a Japanese economic revival, even one entailing a weaker yen.

Global Liquidity Trap?

What works well for one can fail miserably for many. Although the exchange-rate-based proposals for escaping a liquidity trap rely on rather uncertain transmission mechanisms, they are theoretically feasible. If it were willing to commit the resources, Japan probably could escape a liquidity trap by following the exchange-rate-based approaches. But if the United States and the euro area face liquidity traps and adopt similar strategies, this route will be unavailable. All three currencies cannot simultaneously depreciate against each other.

AHEAD OF THE TAPE

Output Gap Helps Deflate Inflation Talk

Mark Gongloff

A weak economy is keeping inflation from catching fire, but a recovery won't necessarily spark it, either.

The Bureau of Labor Statistics releases the March consumer-price index on Wednesday. Economists think CPI fell 0.1% and that "core" CPI, which excludes food and energy prices, rose 0.1%.

Such mild results belie the conflicting tectonic forces at work on prices. On the one band are aggressive government spending and a busy Federal Reserve printing press. Both are designed to fight the recession, and both are raising inflation anxiety.

But the more powerful force is a deflationary one: the wide and growing gap between the economy's output and its potential, or what it would produce if it were making full use of its work force and production capacity. The excess supply of idle workers and drill presses means there is no kindling for an inflationary bonfire.

A clear example could come Thursday, when the Fed releases March industrial production data. Economists expect the report to show the nation's factories, mines and utilities running at less than 70% of capacity, a record low. More important unemployment is at 8.5% and expected to rise to more than 9% by next year.

With so much slack, U.S. GDP growth could be 7% below potential for the next two years, the Congressional Budget Office estimates, the deepest underperformance since the 1981-82 recession. Goldman Sachs economists suggest the gap could yawn to 10% next year, the widest since the Great Depression.

Getting GDP back to trend will require unusually fast catch-up growth—4.75% per year in order to close the output gap by 2015, or 3.75% per year to close it in a decade, Goldman estimates.

Such speedy growth closed the wide output gap of the early 1980s, Goldman notes, and it didn't create inflation.

Appendix 10

Equilibrium Income Analysis

With the consumption function and investment function, we are now able to analyze two sectors of the economy: the household sector (consumption) and the business sector (investment). In a macroeconomic perspective, it is important to look at the overall market stability. When aggregate demand is equal to aggregate supply, then we consider the system as in equilibrium. The income or national output that corresponds to this point is called "equilibrium income." In order to find the equilibrium income (Y_e) for the economy, we must solve the following system of equations simultaneously[1]:

Given:

$$Y = C + I$$
$$C = Ca + bY$$
$$I = Ia$$

To solve for Ye,

$$Y = C + I = (Ca + bY) + Ia$$
$$Y - bY = Ca + Ia$$
$$Y(1-b) = Ca + Ia$$

Therefore,t

$$Y_e = \frac{Ca + Ia}{1 - b}$$

Given the numbers for income, consumption, savings and investments:

Income (Y)	Consumption (C)	Savings (S)	Investment (I)	AD ($C+I$)
0	30	−30	50	80
50	60	−10	50	110
100	90	10	50	140
150	120	30	50	170
200	150	50	50	200
250	180	70	50	230
300	210	90	50	260
350	240	110	50	290
400	270	130	50	320
450	300	150	50	350

Using the table above, the consumption equation is:

$$C = 30 + .6Y$$

The savings equation is:

$$S = -30 + .4Y$$

The investment equation is:

$$I = 50$$

Applying the formula for the equilibrium income (Y_e):

$$Y_e = (30 + 50)/(1 - .6)$$

$$= 200$$

By plotting Y versus $C + I$, equilibrium income can be shown by the point of intersection between Y and $C + I$:

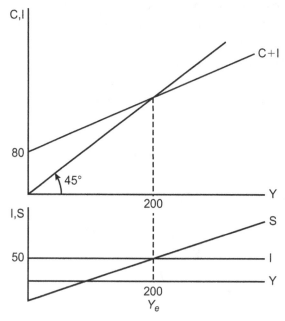

At equilibrium, the economy is assumed to be stable. Both aggregate demand and supply are equal at this point. However, in the real world, the economy is not always stable. There will always be a point in which aggregate demand is not equal to aggregate supply. Equilibrium income analysis exists only in the product market. If we introduce the factor markets (markets for factors of production and labor), a full-employment income, Y_f, is assumed. It is not always assumed that when the product market is stable, the factor market is stable as well. In a situation when $Y_f > Y_e$, aggregate demand is less than aggregate supply (see the table above). Looking at the graph, the vertical distance between Y_f and the aggregate demand corresponding to the full employment level is the **recessionary gap**.

However, if $Y_f{}^1 < Y_e$, then aggregate demand is greater than aggregate supply. The vertical distance between Y_f and the aggregate demand corresponding to the full employment level is called an **inflationary gap**.

Table A:

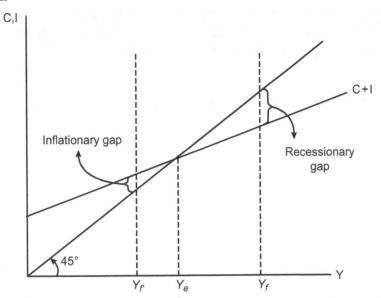

To solve for the gap, we take the difference between the full-employment income (Y_f) and the aggregate demand at full employment (AD at Y_f). Aggregate demand at full-employment can be computed as:

$$(AD \mid Y_f) = Ca + bY_f + Ia$$

Multiplier Effect

In our model, we assume that investment is an autonomous variable. By autonomous we mean that it is independent of any other variables. For example, a Chinese investor tries to expand his business in the United States by building a steel factory in northeast Ohio. The money that he would invest in the United States represents a shock to the economy. It will be used to hire workers, buy construction materials, and hire consultants, among other things. On a macro level, there would be a multiplier effect as a result. This is called the **investment multiplier**.

The investment multiplier is the average number of times by which the equilibrium income changes owing to a one-dollar change in investment. The investment multiplier is a function of the marginal propensity to consume (MPC). In general terms, the formula for the investment multiplier is as follows:

$$\frac{\Delta Y}{\Delta I} = \frac{1}{1 - MPC} = \frac{1}{MPS}$$

In our example, our MPC = .6, therefore the multiplier effect is $\frac{1}{1-0.6}$ = 2.5 That is, for every one dollar that is invested in the economy, the economy will grow 2.5 times.

Notice that the formula for investment multiplier depends on the marginal propensity to consume (MPC). One way of interpreting this in terms of the economy is that the economy will grow depending on the willingness of people to consume other goods.

Endnotes

[1]Further information on how to solve these systems of equations can be found in the math review appendix at the end of this book.

Definitions

1. Aggregate demand
   includes all expenditures incurred in the different sectors of the economy.

2. Price effects
   one of the main reasons for inverse relationship.

3. Income effects
   Part of the change in quantity demanded caused by a change in real income.

4. Purchasing-power effect

5. Interest rate effect
   An increase in interest rates reduces investments, causing GDP to increase.

6. International trade effect
   When domestic prices increase, the value of the dollar relative to other currency tends to appreciate.

7. Aggregate supply
   Refers to the relationship between prices and quantity supplied from a macroeconomic standpoint.

8. Keynesian approach – Aggregate supply curve is flat or horizontal. Prices are too low, economy is stagnant and has no growth incentive.

9. Liquidity trap

10. Classical aggregate supply
    Vertical - no matter what the price is, the economy will always stay at same output level.

11. Personal consumption
    most important component of GDP.

12. Marginal propensity to consume

The change in consumption caused by a change in income.

13. Consumption function

a relationship showing the determinants of C consumption

14. Autonomous consumption

Independent of income

15. Induced consumption

Portion of consumption that changes with income.

16. Investment

Goods produced by individuals and firms to add to their stock of capital.

17. Equilibrium income

State of balance between opposing forces

18. Recessionary gap

The amount by which equilibrium income/output falls short of full employment income/output.

19. Inflationary gap

The amount by which equilibrium income/output exceeds full employment income/output.

20. Aggregate demand at full employment

21. Full employment income

22. Autonomous investment

The Portion of investment that is unaffected by changes with income

23. Investment multiplier

one divided by marginal propensity to save.

234

Multiple Choice

1. Given the consumption function $C = Ca + bY_D$, the variable b can be described as
   a. marginal propensity to consume
   b. autonomous consumption
   c. marginal propensity to save
   d. marginal income
   e. none of the above

2. The most important factor affecting consumption is
   a. investment
   b. savings
   c. marginal propensity to consume
   d. income
   e. none of the above

3. The marginal propensity to consume (MPC) is best defined as
   a. the percentage of new or added income that is consumed
   b. an increase in personal consumption
   c. an increase in personal disposable income
   d. the change in personal disposable income from consumption
   e. none of the above

4. The equilibrium income model is best explained by

   a. $P = \dfrac{Ca + 1a}{Y}$

   b. $Y_e = Ca + bY$

   c. $Y_e = \dfrac{(Ca + 1a)}{1 - b}$

   d. $Y_e = \dfrac{Ca}{1a}$

   e. none of the above

5. In equilibrium income analysis, the economy is considered stable when _____ and _____ are equal.
   a. factor market; product market
   b. consumption; investment
   c. aggregate demand; aggregate supply
   d. aggregate spending; savings
   e. none of the above

6. When full employment income is less than equilibrium income ($Y_f < Y_e$), we know that _____ exceeds _____.
    a. aggregate demand; aggregate supply
    b. aggregate supply; aggregate demand
    c. income; investment
    d. income; consumption
    e. none of the above

Use the following graph to answer questions 7 and 8.

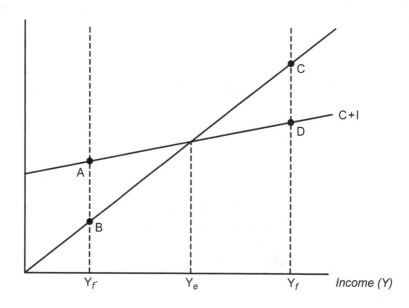

7. The distance between points A and B can be described as a(n)
    a. inflationary gap
    b. recessionary gap
    c. income gap
    d. investment gap
    e. none of the above

8. The distance between points C and D can be described as a(n)
    e. inflationary gap
    f. recessionary gap
    g. income gap
    h. investment gap
    i. none of the above

9. The model $\dfrac{\Delta Y}{\Delta I}$ is known as the
    a. marginal propensity to consume (MPC)
    b. marginal propensity to save (MPS)
    c. marginal propensity to invest (MPI)
    d. marginal income
    e. none of the above

10. Investment is assumed to be an autonomous variable. This means that
    a. investment is a function of income
    b. investment is a dependent variable
    c. investment would represent a shock in the economy
    d. investment would not have an effect on the economy
    e. none of the above

11. The wealth effect refers to the theory that
    a. a rise in the price level causes an increase in purchasing power and aggregate expenditures.
    b. a rise in real wealth causes an increase in the price level.
    c. a rise in the price level causes a decrease in real wealth and aggregate expenditures.
    d. a lower price level brings about a lower real GNP rate.
    e. real wealth is not affected by price level changes.

12. The interest rate effect suggests that an increase in the price level will cause
    a. a decline in the interest rate.
    b. a decrease in planned investment.
    c. an increase in the equilibrium level of income.
    d. a decrease in the supply of financial assets.
    e. an increase in real wealth.

13. Higher investment spending is the result of
    a. a decline in purchasing power.
    b. a higher demand for money.
    c. an increase in the price level.
    d. higher government investment.
    e. lower interest rates.

14. When domestic prices fall relative to foreign prices
    a. domestic exports will rise.
    b. international tariffs will increase.
    c. domestic exports will fall.
    d. domestic imports will rise.
    e. domestic net exports will remain unchanged.

15. A decrease in the aggregate quantity demanded means that
    a. the equilibrium level of income has risen.
    b. the equilibrium level of income has fallen.
    c. the average price level has fallen.
    d. aggregate production has risen.
    e. aggregate expenditures have risen

16. If people expect the economy to do well in the future, we should see
    a. a decrease in consumption.
    b. a rise in aggregate demand.
    c. a decrease in aggregate expenditures.
    d. a decrease in aggregate demand.
    e. no change in either aggregate expenditures or aggregate demand.

17. Economists consider households to be suppliers in which of the following markets?
    a. Product and labor markets.
    b. Labor and capital markets.
    c. Product and capital markets.
    d. product market only.

18. According to classical economists, aggregate supply is
    a. horizontal.
    b. vertical.
    c. upward sloping.
    d. backward bending.
    e. vertical in the short run but upward sloping in the long run.

19. In the classical model, a decline in output
    a. is temporary and will be quickly corrected.
    b. is usually the result of shifts in aggregate supply.
    c. is permanent and calls for active correction by government.
    d. is the result of the instability of investment.
    e. both b and c are correct.

20. According to Keynesian economists, when real output is very low, the aggregate supply curve is
    a. vertical.
    b. horizontal.
    c. upward sloping.
    d. backward bending.
    e. likely to shift to the right.

Resources

Principles of Macroeconomics Case & Fair

Economics Boyes/Melvin

Economics Malbry/Ulbrich

Essay/Short Answer Questions

Use the information below to answer questions 1 and 2.

$C = 1000 + .75\,Y$

$I = 850$

1. Calculate the equilibrium level of GDP.

2. What is the multiplier (MPC)?

3. Using the investment multiplier formula ($\dfrac{1}{1 - MPC}$), explain briefly and algebraically what the effect is when MPC = 0.6.

4. Using the consumption function presented in this chapter, provide some examples that would cause a shift of the consumption function.

5. Complete the following table:

Disposable Income (in $)	Consumption (in $)	$\frac{C}{DI}$ APC	APS	Savings
500	510	1.02	−0.02	−10
600	600	1	0	0
700	690	.99	0.01	10
800	780	.98	0.025	20
900	870	.97	0.033	30
1,000	960	.9u	0.04	40

$S = (Di - C)$

$APS = \dfrac{S}{Di} = \dfrac{(Di - C)}{Di}$

a. Plot the consumption and savings schedules on the graph above.

b. Determine the marginal propensity to consume and the marginal propensity to save.

$$mPS = .1 \qquad mPC = .9$$

c. Determine the average propensity to consume and the average propensity to save for each level of income. $see \ chart$

6. Consider the following table, then answer the questions below it:

Annual Consumption (in $)	Annual Income (in $)	APC
$ 5 ⟩ 75	$ 0 ⟩₁₀₀	
80	100	
155	200	

$$c = 5 + .75Y$$

a. What is the APC at annual income level $100? At $200?

$$At \ \$100, \ APC = .85$$
$$At \ \$200, \ APC = .775$$

b. What happens to the APC as annual income rises?

$$It \ lowers$$

c. What is the MPC as annual income goes from $0 to $100? From $100 to $200?

$$From \ \$0 \ to \ \$100, \ mPC = .75$$
$$From \ \$100 \ to \ \$200, \ mPC = .75$$

d. What happens to the MPC as income rises?

$$It \ stays \ the \ same.$$

e. What number is the APC approaching?

$$O$$

f. What is the equation for the consumption function in this table?

$$C = 5 + .75Y$$

g. Of what significance is a positive y-intercept in this equation?
The y intercept tells us our initial consumption is greater than initial income.

7. Assume that the consumption function is $C = \$150 + .8Y$, that desired investment is $500, and no other forms of expenditure exists.
   a. Complete the following table (all numbers in billions of dollars per year).

Income	C	I	C + I
$500	550	500	1050
700	710	700	1410
1000	950	1000	1950
1200	1110	1200	2310
1500	1350	1500	2850
2000	1750	2000	3750

   b. If full employment is $2,000, how large is the recessionary or inflationary gap?

   c. Illustrate the gap on the graph.

8. Calculate the multiplier for the following cases.
   a. MPC = .8

   b. MPS = .2

   c. MPS = .10

   d. $C = 80 + .7Y$

   e. $S = -60 + .3Y$

9. Given a two-sector economy with all expenditures summarized in the following equations:

C = $200 billion per year + .8Y
I = $300 billion

   a. Solve for the equilibrium income.

   b. Compute for the size of the recessionary gap when full employment income equals $2,800 billion.

   c. What is the value of the multiplier?

   d. What would happen to equilibrium income if the investment increased to $350 billion per year?

   e. Illustrate your answers on a graph.

Chapter 11

Government Expenditures and Fiscal Policy

S. Borisov/Shutterstock.com

OBJECTIVES

1. To explain the meaning of fiscal policy.
2. To describe the three kinds of fiscal policy.
3. To discuss the concept of the crowding out effect.
4. To discuss the different ways of supporting a budget deficit.
5. To discuss the economic implication of issuing bonds to support a deficit.

Of all the sectors in the economy, government policy is one of the most influential/significant factors affecting the economy. You might want to ask the following: How well are the roads maintained where you live? Is the government doing a good job in maintaining city streets, state and interstate highways? Why do we need government policy? We have government because without government we cannot cooperate efficiently. In other words, if law and order are absent, we cannot make good choices because rational self-interest is defeated by market failures (Millman, 1990). Think about it this way: as a college student or recent graduate, if you had the choice, how much of your income would you give to national defense? How about social programs such as Medicare, Medicaid, and/or Social Security? How much of your income would you be willing to give up to ensure the streets in your city or state are properly maintained? Would you give up a lot of your income or would you say, "Well, I'll leave it to someone else who can afford it?" Or maybe what you would consider to be a significant charitable donation would be pennies from another person's perspective. With government regulation (taxes, in this example), we are able to have a central authority make these kinds of determinations.

What Is Fiscal Policy?

Fiscal policy is federal spending and taxation policies designed to affect the business cycle and attain price stability, sustained economic growth, and full employment.

There are three types of fiscal policy. The first kind is **discretionary fiscal policy** (or *spending*). Discretionary fiscal policy is a category of federal spending subject to the annual appropriations process. It includes such things as funding for transportation, environmental programs, job training, and education programs. It refers to the fact that fiscal expenditure is solely determined by Congress, and that Congress has the discretion to change the amount of fiscal expenditure through budget approval. The second type is called **mandatory fiscal policy**. Mandatory fiscal spending accounts for more than half of all government spending; this kind of spending is authorized by permanent laws. It includes social programs and entitlements such as Social Security, Medicare, and Food Stamps—programs through which individuals receive benefits based on their age, income, or other criteria. Figure 11.1 compares the levels of mandatory versus discretionary spending in 1962 and 2007. The third type of policy, **automatic stabilizers**, is designed to reduce the lags associated with fiscal policy. Automatic stabilizers are policies that stimulate or depress the economy when necessary without any deliberate policy change. For example, the system of income taxes automatically reduces taxes when the economy goes into a recession, without any change in the tax laws, because individuals and corporations pay less tax when their incomes fall. Similarly, the unemployment insurance and welfare systems automatically raise transfer payments when the economy moves into a recession because more people apply for benefits. Automatic stabilizers act countercyclically to the fluctuations in the economy.

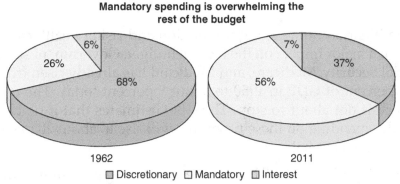

Mandatory spending is overwhelming the rest of the budget

6%
26%
68%
1962

7%
37%
56%
2011

☐ Discretionary ☐ Mandatory ☐ Interest

Figure 11.1

Theory to Application

The Troubling Outlook for Fiscal Policy

What does the future hold for fiscal policymakers? Economic forecasting is far from precise, and it is easy to be cynical about economic predictions. But good policy cannot be made if policymakers only look backward. As a result, economists in the Congressional Budget Office (CBO) and other government agencies are always trying to look ahead to see what problems and opportunities are likely to develop. When these economists conduct long-term projections of U.S. fiscal policy, they paint a troubling picture.

One reason is demographic. Advances in medical technology have been increasing life expectancy, while improvements in birth-control techniques and changing social norms have reduced the number of children people have. Because of these developments, the elderly are becoming a larger share of the population. In 1950, the elderly population (aged 65 and older) was about 14 percent of the working-age population (aged 20 to 64). Now the elderly are about 21 percent of the working-age population, and that figure will rise to about 40 percent over the next 50 years. About one-third of the budget of the U.S. federal government is devoted to providing the elderly with pensions (mainly through the Social Security program) and health care. As more people become eligible for these "entitlements," as they are sometimes called, government spending will automatically rise.

A second, related reason for the troubling fiscal picture is the rising cost of health care. The government provides health care to the elderly through the Medicare system and to the poor through Medicaid. As the cost of health care increases, government spending on these programs increases as well. Policymakers have proposed various ways to stem the rise in health care costs, such as reducing the burden of lawsuits, encouraging more competition among health care providers, and promoting greater use of information technology, but most health economists believe such measures will have only limited impact. The main reason for rising health care costs is medical advances that provide new, better, and often expensive ways to extend and improve our lives.

The combination of the aging population and rising health care costs will have a major impact on the federal budget. Government spending on Social Security, Medicare, and Medicaid has already risen from less than 1 percent of GDP in 1950 to about 8 percent today. The upward trajectory is not about to stop. The CBO estimates that if no changes are made, spending on these programs will rise to about 20 percent of GDP over the next half century.

How the United States will handle these spending pressures is an open question. Simply increasing the budget deficit is not feasible. A budget deficit just pushes the cost of government spending onto a future generation of taxpayers. In the long run, the government needs to raise tax revenue to pay for the benefits it provides.

The big question is how the required fiscal adjustment will be split between tax increases and spending reductions. Some economists believe that to pay for these commitments we will need to raise taxes substantially as a percentage of GDP. Given the projected increases in spending on Social Security, Medicare, and Medicaid, paying for these benefits would require increasing all taxes by approximately one-third. Other economists believe that such high tax rates would impose too great a cost on younger workers. They believe that policymakers should reduce the promises now being made to the elderly of the future and that, at the same time, people should be encouraged to take a greater role in caring for themselves as they age. This might entail increasing the normal retirement age, while giving people more incentive to save during their working years to prepare for their own retirement and health costs. Resolving this debate will likely be one of the great policy challenges in the decades ahead.

A recent policy change for 2010 is the health care reform plan. Some elements of this health care reform plan includes health care insurance for 95 percent of the population. The policy also includes mandatory insurance for all citizens, and insurance for people with preexisting conditions. It makes insurance more **affordable** by providing the largest middle-class tax cut for health care in history, reducing premium costs for tens of millions of families and small business owners who are priced out of coverage today. This helps 32 million Americans afford health care who do not get it today—and makes coverage more affordable for many more. It sets up a **new competitive health insurance market** giving millions of Americans the same choices of insurance that members of Congress will have. It brings **greater accountability** to health care by laying out commonsense rules of the road to keep premiums down and prevent insurance industry abuses and denial of care. It will **end discrimination** against Americans with preexisting conditions. In the reform plan, it will put our **budget and economy on a more stable path** by reducing the deficit by more than $100 billion over the next 10 years—and more than $1 trillion over the second decade—by cutting government overspending and reining in waste, fraud, and abuse.

Health care reform is needed because rising health care cost will outstrip Medicare and Medicaid payment and devastate our federal budget in our lifetime. The U.S. health care contributes $2.5 trillion dollars and accounts for 18 percent of our GDP. Proponents for health care reform indicates that 25 percent of all American have little or no health care insurance. Half of all bankruptcies result from medical costs despite the fact that some of them are insured. Furthermore, health care reform can also curb the economic cost of fraud. Two major critics of this reform is the question of deficit neutral. The fact that this is an "entitlement," it questions the issue of controlling cost relative to the tax revenues that can support this program. Furthermore, it also questions whether employers would rather pay the penalty instead of insuring their employees. This would lead to a more government-subsidized care purchase on a new insurance exchange.

Taxes and Government Finance

Table 11.1 shows the federal government's receipts, outlays, and debts. The largest component of government spending in the recent years was income transfer programs such as Social Security, Medicare, and public assistance to the poor (which make up more than 50 percent of government spending). According to the Congressional Budget Office (CBO), from 1995 to 2005 mandatory spending increased at an average annual rate of 6 percent (CBO, 2007). Increases in the Earned Income Tax Credit (EITC) and the child tax credit, rising spending in health care programs, a drop in deposit insurance collections, increases in the subsidy costs of student loans, higher spending for farm programs, and a shift in the timing of payments that raised outlays in 2005 all contributed to strong growth over that period. Buoyed by robust growth in Medicare spending, mandatory outlays increased by 6.9 percent in 2006. Over the next 10 years, the CBO estimates, mandatory outlays are expected to climb at a faster rate than the economy—5.9 percent per year, on average—thereby increasing as a share of GDP from 10.8 percent in 2006 to 12.1 percent by 2017. The next largest expenditure is national defense, which has been around 20–22 percent of government spending on average for the past several years. Many people might argue that defense spending is too high, but if we compare the level of spending on national defense today with that of the 1950s and 1960s, we can see that the percentage is much lower now. During the 1950s and 1960s, defense spending constituted the bulk of federal spending.

Table 11.1

[Billions of dollars]

Fiscal year or period	Total			On-budget			Off-budget			Federal debt (end of period)	
	Receipts	Outlays	Surplus or deficit (−)	Receipts	Outlays	Surplus or Deficit (−)	Receipts	Outlays	Surplus or deficit (−)	Gross Federal Debt	Held by the Public
1992	1,091.2	1,381.5	−290.3	788.8	1,129.2	−340.4	302.4	252.3	50.1	4,001.8	2,999.7
1993	1,154.3	1,409.4	−255.1	842.4	1,142.8	−300.4	311.9	266.6	45.3	4,351.0	3,248.4
1994	1,258.6	1,461.8	−203.2	923.5	1,182.4	−258.6	335.0	279.4	55.7	4,643.3	3,433.1
1995	1,351.8	1,515.7	−164.0	1,000.7	1,227.1	−226.4	351.1	288.7	62.4	4,920.6	3,604.4
1996	1,453.1	1,560.5	−107.4	1,085.6	1,259.6	−174.0	367.5	300.9	66.6	5,181.5	3,734.1
1997	1,579.2	1,601.1	−21.9	1,187.2	1,290.5	−103.2	392.0	310.6	81.4	5,369.2	3,772.3
1998	1,721.7	1,652.5	69.3	1,305.9	1,335.9	−29.9	415.8	316.6	99.2	5,476.2	3,721.1
1999	1,827.5	1,701.8	125.6	1,383.0	1,381.1	1.9	444.5	320.8	123.7	5,605.5	3,632.4
2000	2,025.2	1,789.0	236.2	1,544.6	1,458.2	86.4	480.6	330.8	149.8	5,628.7	3,409.8
2001	1,991.1	1,862.8	128.2	1,483.6	1,516.0	−32.4	507.5	346.8	160.7	5,769.9	3,319.6
2002	1,853.1	2,010.9	−157.8	1,337.8	1,655.2	−317.4	515.3	355.7	159.7	6,198.4	3,540.4
2003	1,782.3	2,159.9	−377.6	1,258.5	1,796.9	−538.4	523.8	363.0	160.8	6,760.0	3,913.4
2004	1,880.1	2,292.8	−412.7	1,345.4	1,913.3	−568.0	534.7	379.5	155.2	7,354.7	4,295.5

2005	2,153.6	2,472.0	−318.3	1,576.1	2,069.7	−493.6	577.5	402.2	175.3	7,905.3	4,592.2
2006	2,406.9	2,655.1	−248.2	1,798.5	2,233.0	−434.5	608.4	422.1	186.3	8,451.4	4,829.0
2007	2,568.0	2,728.7	−160.7	1,932.9	2,275.0	−342.2	635.1	453.6	181.5	8,950.7	5,035.1
2008	2,524.0	2,982.5	−458.6	1,865.9	2,507.8	−641.6	658.0	474.8	183.3	9,986.1	5.803.1
2009	2,105.0	3,517.7	−1,412.7	1,451.0	3,000.7	−1,549.7	654.0	517.0	137.0	11,875.9	7,544.7
2010	2,162.7	3,456.2	−1,293.5	1,531.0	2,901.5	−1,370.5	631.7	554.7	77.0	13,528.8	9,018.9
2011	2,303.5	3,603.1	−1,299.6	1,737.7	3,104.5	−1,366.8	565.8	498.6	67.2	14,764.2	10,128.2
2012 estimate	2,468.6	3,795.5	−1,326.9	1,896.5	3,290.4	−1,393.9	572.1	505.2	67.0	16,350.9	11,578.1
2013 estimate	2,902.0	3,803.4	−901.4	2,224.5	3,169.3	−944.7	677.4	634.1	43.3	17,547.9	12,636.7
Cumlative total first 3 months;[1]											
Fiscal Year 2010	488	876	−389	345	740	−395	143	137	6	404	9,278
Fiscal Year 2011	532	903	−371	396	788	−392	136	115	21	464	10,592

[1]Data from current issue *Monthly Treasury Statement*.

NOTE.- Data (except as noted are from *Budget of the United States Government, Fiscal Year 2013*, issued February 13, 2012. SOURCES: Department of the Treasury and Office of Management and Budget.

[Billions of dollars]

Fiscal year or period	Total			On-budget			Off-budget			Federal debt (end of period)	
	Receipts	Outlays	Surplus or deficit (−)	Receipts	Outlays	Surplus or Deficit (−)	Receipts	Outlays	Surplus or deficit (−)	Gross Federal Debt	Held by the Public
1992	1,091.208	1,381.529	−290.321	788.783	1,129.191	−340.408	302.426	252.339	50.087	4,001.787	2,999.737
1993	1,154.335	1,409.386	−255.051	842.401	1,142.799	−300.398	311.934	266.587	45.347	4,351.044	3,248.396
1994	1,258.566	1,461.753	−203.186	923.541	1,182.380	−258.840	335.026	279.372	55.654	4,643.307	3,433.065
1995	1,351.790	1,515.742	−163.952	1,000.711	1,227.078	−226.367	351.079	288.664	62.415	4,920.586	3,604.378
1996	1,453.053	1,560.484	−107.431	1,085.561	1,259.580	−174.019	367.492	300.904	66.588	5,181.465	3,734.073
1997	1,579.232	1,601.116	−21.884	1,187.242	1,290.490	−103.248	391.990	310.626	81.364	5,369.206	3,772.344
1998	1,721.728	1,652.458	69.270	1,305.929	1,335.854	−29.925	415.799	316.604	99.195	5,478.189	3,721.099
1999	1,827.452	1,701.842	125.610	1,382.984	1,381.064	1.920	444.468	320.776	123.690	5,605.523	3,632.363
2000	2,025.191	1,788.950	236.241	1,544.607	1,458.185	86.422	480.584	330.765	149.819	5,628.700	3,409.804
2001	1,991.082	1,862.846	128.236	1,483.563	1,516.008	−32.445	507.519	346.838	160.681	5,769.881	3,319.615
2002	1,853.136	2,010.894	−157.758	1,337.815	1,655.232	−317.417	515.321	355.662	159.659	6,198.401	3,540.427
2003	1,782.314	2,159.899	−377.585	1,258.472	1,796.890	−538.418	523.842	363.009	160.833	6,760.014	3,913.443
2004	1,880.114	2,292.841	−412.727	1,345.369	1,913.330	−567.961	534.745	379.511	155.234	7,354.657	4,295.544
2005	2,153.611	2,471.957	−318.346	1,576.135	2,069.746	−493.611	577.476	402.211	175.265	7,905.300	4,592.212

Year										
2006	2,406.869	2,655.050	−248.181	1,798.487	2,233.961	−434.494	608.382	422.069	186.313	8,451.350	4,828.972
2007	2,567.985	2,728.686	−160.701	1,932.896	2,275.049	−342.153	635.089	453.637	181.452	8,950.744	5,035.129
2008	2,523.991	2,982.544	−458.553	1,865.945	2,507.793	−641.848	658.046	474.751	183.295	9,986.082	5,803.050
2009	2,104.989	3,517.677	−1,412.688	1,450.980	3,000.661	−1,549.681	654.009	517.016	136.993	11,875.851	7,544.707
2010	2,162.724	3,456.213	−1,293.489	1,531.037	2,901.531	−1,370.494	631.687	554.682	77.005	13,528.807	9,018.882
2011	2,303.466	3,603.061	−1,299.595	1,737.678	3,104.455	−1,366.777	565.788	498.606	67.182	14,764.222	10,128.206
2012 estimate	2,468.599	3,795.547	−1,326.948	1,896.459	3,290.381	−1,393.922	572.140	505.166	66.974	16,350.885	11,578.083
2013 estimate	2,901.956	3,803.364	−901.408	2,224.545	3,169.287	−944.742	677.411	634.077	43.334	17,547.936	12,636.689

Cumlative total first 3 months;[1]

Fiscal Year 2010	487.776	876.284	−388.507	345.036	739.744	−394.708	142.740	136.539	6.201	404.040	9,278.029
Fiscal Year 2011	531.797	902.619	−371.822	396.022	787.962	−391.940	135.755	114.657	21.118	464.254	10,592.460

[1]Data from current issue *Monthly Treasury Statement*

NOTE.- Data (except as noted are from *Budget of the United States Government, Fiscal Year 2013, issued February 13, 2012. SOURCES: Department of the Treasury and Office of Management and Budget.*

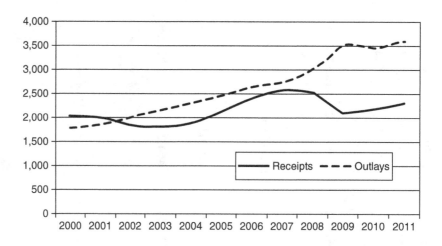

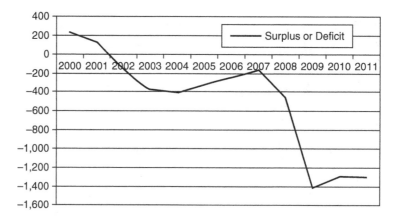

Another category that is significant from an expenditures perspective is the interest on public debt. As we incurred a budget deficit, the government issued Treasury bonds and securities. When these securities mature, investors are paid the face value plus interest earned.

The source of federal revenues is basically personal income tax, which is paid by the household sector and individual businesses and partnerships. There are also corporate profit taxes and other miscellaneous taxes such as estate taxes, tariffs, licenses, and value-added taxes. The average tax rate for the United State is about 30 percent of domestic income. Other nations, like Canada, Sweden, and Germany have an average tax rate of over 50 percent. A fair tax system is usually regarded as being based on people's ability to pay taxes, although some have contended that taxes should also be based on the benefits received from public expenditures. According to the benefits-received principle of taxation, taxes should be paid in proportion to the benefits that taxpayers derive from public expenditures. The ability-to-pay principle, on the other hand, is based on the idea that people with greater income should pay a higher tax rate.

There are three types of taxation systems: proportional, progressive, and regressive. Proportional taxes are taxes take a constant fraction of income as income rises. Progressive taxes take a larger fraction of income as income rises. Regressive taxes take a smaller fraction of income as incomes rises.

Budget Deficits and Surplus

One of the major problems in analyzing fiscal policy is the way we balance the difference between government expenditures and taxes. When government expenditures exceed income through taxes, we have a budget deficit. On the other hand, when government expenditures are less than taxes, we have a budget surplus. In recent years, most of the problems faced by the government have dealt with the budget deficit.

There are three ways of supporting a budget deficit. The first way is by lowering government expenditures. If the government was to cut expenditures, however, the economy could slow down, as contractions occur when government programs are cut. The second way is by increasing taxes. This can be very unpopular, as people naturally desire to keep more of their income rather than have the government take it away from them. People can also be shortsighted in that they only remember the bad things that a certain administration implements, such as an increase in the tax level. Thus, it is very unlikely that an incumbent administration would increase taxes during an election period.

Another way of supporting a deficit is by issuing Treasury bonds to cover the difference. When shortfalls persist year after year, the outstanding debt of the federal government rises. With an 11-year string of triple digit deficits, the ratio of U.S. publicly held debt rose from 26.5 percent of gross domestic product (GDP) in 1981 to 51.1 percent of GDP in 1992. According to the conventional view, deficits can be both a blessing and a curse. When the economy is in a recession or otherwise operating below its full potential, an increase in government spending or a decrease in taxes can provide stimulus, particularly if the government borrows to finance this fiscal program. As the effects of the initial tax cut or federal spending program ripple throughout the economy, aggregate demand expands by a substantial multiple of the fiscal initiative, and employment increases. The deficit may put some upward pressure on interest rates, but because the private sector is operating below its full capacity, conventional-view proponents consider this effect rather mild compared to the more direct, favorable effects of the fiscal stimulus on aggregate spending.

Theory to Application

Deficits, Consumption, and Investment in the United States during World War II

In 1939, the share of U.S. government spending on goods and services in GDP was 15 percent. By 1944, it had increased to 45 percent (Blanchard, 2006). The increase was owing to increased spending on national defense, which went from 1 percent of GDP in 1939 to 36 percent in 1944.

Faced with such a massive increase in spending, the U.S. government reacted with large tax increases. For the first time in U.S. history, the individual income tax became a major source of revenues; individual income tax revenues, which were 1 percent of GDP in 1939, increased to 8.5 percent in 1944. But the tax increases were still far less than the increase in expenditures. The increase in federal revenues, from 7.2 percent of GDP in 1939 to 22.7 percent in 1944, was only a little more than half the increase in expenditures.

The result was a sequence of large budget deficits. By 1944, the federal deficit reached 22 percent of GDP. The ratio of debt to GDP, already high at 53 percent in 1939 because of the deficits the government had run during the Great Depression, was 110 percent.

Was the increase in government spending achieved at the expense of consumption or private investment? (It could, in principle, have come from higher imports and a current account deficit. But the United States had nobody to borrow from during the war. In fact, it was lending to some of its allies. Transfers from the U.S. government to foreign countries were 6 percent of U.S. GDP in 1944.)

The 30 percent increase in the share of GDP going to government purchases was met, in large part, by a decrease in consumption. The share of consumption in GDP decreased by 23 percentage points, from 74 percent to 51 percent. Part of the decrease in consumption may have been due to anticipations of higher taxes after the war; part was also the result of the unavailability of many consumer durables; patriotism probably also played a role in leading people to save more and buy the war bonds issued by the government to finance the war. But the increase in government purchases was also met by a 6 percent decrease in the share of (private) investment in GDP—from 10 percent to 4 percent. Part of the burden of the war was, therefore, passed on in the form of lower capital accumulation to those living after the war.

Graphical Model of "Crowding-out" Effect

In a similar way, government can rely on fiscal policy—this time tax hikes, expenditure cuts, and budget surpluses—to rein in economic activity when the economy returns to its full potential. The government budget then becomes an instrument with which to finance real economic activity around its optimal growth path. Consider first the effects of an increase in government purchases by an amount ΔG.[1] The immediate impact is to increase the demand for goods and services by ΔG. But since total output is fixed by the factors of production, the increase in government purchases must be met by a decrease in some other category of demand. Because disposable income remains

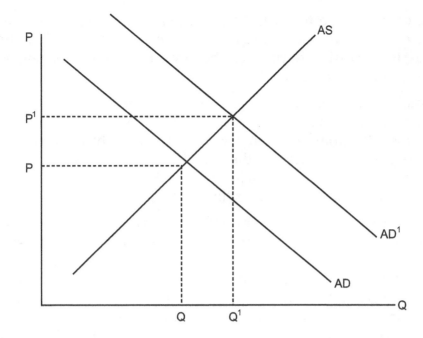

unchanged, consumption is unchanged. The increase in government purchases must be met by an equal decrease in investment.

To induce investment to fall, the interest rate must rise. Therefore, the increase in government purchases causes the interest rate to increase and investment to decrease. Government purchases, therefore, **crowd out** investment.

According to common view, when output is below par a fiscally induced expansion of current income does not come at the expense of future economic growth. Problems can arise, however, if the government continues to borrow after the economy reaches full employment. To sustain long-term growth, the nation must save and invest in productive capacity.

The deficit places private and public borrowers in competition for the available supply of national savings. Interest rates will rise to encourage private investment. Government borrowing, however, is insensitive to higher interest rates. With some luck, the most immediate effect of this crowding out of private investment may only be a change in the composition of national output: an increase in the relative size of the government sector. However, conventional beliefs hold that a persistent deficit will lower the economy's long-term potential growth path, implying an inevitable reduction in the nation's standard of living.

The Link between Budget Deficit and Trade Deficit

The exact nature of this crowding-out effect depends on the extent to which capital is internationally mobile. If persistent government borrowing increases domestic interest rates relative to foreign interest rates, offshore investors will begin acquiring interest-earning assets in the country with the higher rates. This capital inflow will mitigate the rise in domestic interest rates, thereby limiting the crowding out of private domestic investment.

To purchase assets in the domestic economy, however, foreigners must first acquire the domestic currency in the foreign exchange market. This causes the domestic currency to appreciate, which then increases the foreign-currency price of the deficit country's exports and lowers the domestic-currency price of its imports. All else equal, the trade balance will then deteriorate, according to the conventional view.

As the discussion reveals, the inflow of foreign capital does not eliminate crowding out. It merely shifts this effect from interest-rate-sensitive to exchange-rate-sensitive sectors of the economy. When financed internally, persistent deficits lower private investment, leaving future generations with a smaller stock of capital to sustain real economic growth at potential. When financed externally, persistent deficits do not lower future stock of capital, but the deficit country must now devote a greater portion of its future output to servicing its foreign debts. The domestic standard of living (what is remaining per capita for domestic consumption) may then be lower. Proponents of the conventional view often point to events of the past decade—the rapid appreciation of the dollar early on, the subsequent record deterioration of the U.S. trade balance, and the eventual shift in our international investment position to debtor status—as a classic example of this type of crowding out.

Why Deficits Don't Matter

An alternative view claims that under certain assumptions deficits and taxes are equivalent. Although the types of levels of government spending might affect economic activity, the method of financing those activities is irrelevant. Deficits do not matter. This approach rests on two plausible presumptions. First, governments must ultimately pay for their debts, so the present value of their expenditures must equal the present value of their expected receipts. Second, taxpayers realize that deficits imply a future tax liability for themselves or their heirs and therefore increase their current saving by an amount equal to the present discounted value of this future tax bill. In this case, taxes and government debt become equivalent means of financing government spending. Because an offsetting increase in private saving matches any rise in the deficit, public borrowing has no effect on real interest rates or real exchange rates. This is known as the **Ricardian equivalence theorem**, which is named after nineteenth-century economist David Ricardo.

Although many find its assumptions rather stringent, the equivalence theorem nevertheless presents an internally consistent model, which empirical tests have not clearly refuted. One can therefore consider how changes in its underlying premise might invalidate the theorem and create the conventional linkage between budget deficits, interest rates, and exchange rates. An important assumption concerns the nature of taxes.

The equivalence theorem presupposes that taxes are lump sum—that is, they are straightforward dollar assessments as opposed to being a proportion of income, wages, or expenditures. Lump-sum taxes do not affect individuals, savings, and working decisions. Assume, for example, that the equivalence theorem holds and that the government offers a deficit-producing tax cut. The inclination of taxpayers is to offset their implied future tax liabilities, and they will do this exactly if the tax reduction is lump-sum. The effects of the deficit and tax cut on national savings will net out with no impact on interest rates.

Technical Model for a Three-Sector Economy

In Chapter 10, we discussed the implications of a two-sector model in the equilibrium income analysis. In this section, we will discuss the effects of including the third sector, government expenditure. Our model will be given as follows:

1. $Y = C + I + G$
2. $C = Ca + bY_D$
3. $I = Ia$
4. $G = Ga$
5. $Y_D = Y - T$
6. $T = Ta$

To solve for the equilibrium income in this model, we will substitute equation 2, 3, 4, 5 and 6 into equation 1. The result of the model is as follows:

$$Y = C + I + G$$
$$Y = Ca + bY_D + Ia + Ga$$
$$Y = Ca + b(Y - Ta) + Ia + Ga$$
$$Y = Ca + bY - bTa) + Ia + Ga$$
$$Y = Ca + b(Y - Ta) + Ia + Ga$$
$$Y(1 - b) = Ca - bTa + Ia + Ga$$

The equilibrium income can solved as:

$$Y_e = \frac{Ca - bTa + Ia + Ga}{(1 - b)}$$

The equilibrium income can be graphed as follows:

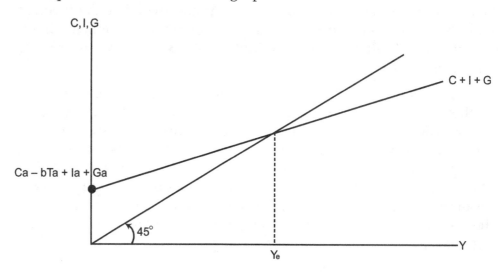

From this equilibrium income formula we can derive the different multiplier effects as shocks in the market are imposed. For example, if there is a change in government spending (Ga), then its multiplier effect can be given as follows:

$$\frac{\Delta Y}{\Delta G} = \frac{1}{1-b}$$

The government spending multiplier can be defined as the average number of times by which equilibrium income changes due to a dollar change in government spending. For example, if the marginal propensity to consume is 0.6, then the government spending multiplier effect is 2.5. This multiplier effect tells us that for every $1.00 change in government spending, equilibrium income will increase by 2.5.

Furthermore, we can also derive the effects of a change in tax. The formula for the tax multiplier is as follows:

$$\frac{\Delta Y}{\Delta T} = \frac{-b}{1-b}$$

The tax multiplier is the average number of times by which equilibrium income changes due to a $1.00 change in taxes. In our previous model, if the MPC or the marginal propensity to consume is 0.6, then the tax multiplier effect is –1.5. The tax multiplier effect tells us that for every $1.00 change in tax, equilibrium income will decrease by 1.5. Since there is an inverse relationship between taxes and income, we would expect a negative value for the tax multiplier.

Notice the difference in the value of the government multiplier and tax multiplier given the marginal propensity to consume. In theory, we can say that government spending has more impact than taxes. In our model, the impact of government spending is 2.5 times whereas the tax effect is only 1.5 times. This has a significant implication, especially when governments debate the implication of a tax cut versus government spending. In both scenarios we are looking at an expansionary effect in the economy. However, a tax cut may not necessarily have the same impact as government spending.

Current and past studies showed various calculation of the tax versus government multipliers. In the article by Romer and Bernstein (2009), they indicated that the effects of tax cuts, especially temporary ones, and fiscal relief to the states are likely to create a smaller impact than direct increases in government purchases. However, because there is a limit on how much government investment can be carried out efficiently in a short time frame, and because tax cuts and state relief can be implemented quickly, they are crucial elements of any package aimed at easing economic distress quickly. However, Ramey (2011) indicated that government spending multipliers range from 0.6 to 1.2. The Ramey-Shapiro suggests that that key differences in approaches is the timing.

Endnotes

[1] ΔG is simply a constant representing a change (increase or decrease) in the level of government expenditure.

Learning From Greece

Paul Krugman

The debt crisis in Greece is approaching the point of no return. As prospects for a rescue plan seem to be fading, largely thanks to German obduracy, nervous investors have driven interest rates on Greek government bonds sky-high, sharply raising the country's borrowing costs. This will push Greece even deeper into debt, further undermining confidence. At this point it's hard to see how the nation can escape from this death spiral into default.

It's a terrible story, and clearly an object lesson for the rest of us. But an object lesson in what, exactly?

Yes, Greece is paying the price for past fiscal irresponsibility. Yet that's by no means the whole story. The Greek tragedy also illustrates the extreme danger posed by a deflationary monetary policy. And that's a lesson one hopes American policy makers will take to heart.

The key thing to understand about Greece's predicament is that it's not just a matter of excessive debt. Greece's public debt, at 113 percent of G.D.P., is indeed high, but other countries have dealt with similar levels of debt without crisis. For example, in 1946, the United States, having just emerged from World War II, had federal debt equal to 122 percent of G.D.P. Yet investors were relaxed, and rightly so: Over the next decade the ratio of U.S. debt to G.D.P. was cut nearly in half, easing any concerns people might have had about our ability to pay what we owed. And debt as a percentage of G.D.P. continued to fall in the decades that followed, hitting a low of 33 percent in 1981.

So how did the U.S. government manage to pay off its wartime debt? Actually, it didn't. At the end of 1946, the federal government owed $271 billion; by the end of 1956 that figure had risen slightly, to $274 billion. The ratio of debt to G.D.P. fell not because debt went down, but because G.D.P. went up, roughly doubling in dollar terms over the course of a decade. The rise in G.D.P. in dollar terms was almost equally the result of economic growth and inflation, with both real G.D.P. and the overall level of prices rising about 40 percent from 1946 to 1956.

Unfortunately, Greece can't expect a similar performance. Why? Because of the euro.

Until recently, being a member of the euro zone seemed like a good thing for Greece, bringing with it cheap loans and large inflows of capital. But those capital inflows also led to inflation — and when the music stopped, Greece found itself with costs and prices way out of line with Europe's big economies. Over time, Greek prices will have to come back down. And that means that unlike postwar America, which inflated away part of its debt, Greece will see its debt burden worsened by deflation.

That's not all. Deflation is a painful process, which invariably takes a toll on growth and employment. So Greece won't grow its way out of debt. On the contrary, it will have to deal with its debt in the face of an economy that's stagnant at best.

So the only way Greece could tame its debt problem would be with savage spending cuts and tax increases, measures that would themselves worsen the unemployment rate. No wonder, then, that bond markets are losing confidence, and pushing the situation to the brink.

What can be done? The hope was that other European countries would strike a deal, guaranteeing Greek debt in return for a commitment to harsh fiscal austerity. That might have worked. But without German support, such a deal won't happen.

Greece could alleviate some of its problems by leaving the euro, and devaluing. But it's hard to see how Greece could do that without triggering a catastrophic run on its banking system. Indeed, worried depositors have already begun pulling cash out of Greek banks. There are no good answers here — actually, no nonterrible answers.

But what are the lessons for America? Of course, we should be fiscally responsible. What that means, however, is taking on the big long-term issues, above all health costs — not grandstanding and penny-pinching over short-term spending to help a distressed economy.

Equally important, however, we need to steer clear of deflation, or even excessively low inflation. Unlike Greece, we're not stuck with someone else's currency. But as Japan has demonstrated, even countries with their own currencies can get stuck in a deflationary trap.

What worries me most about the U.S. situation right now is the rising clamor from inflation hawks, who want the Fed to raise rates (and the federal government to pull back from stimulus) even though employment has barely started to recover. If they get their way, they'll perpetuate mass unemployment. But that's not all. America's public debt will be manageable if we eventually return to vigorous growth and moderate inflation. But if the tight-money people prevail, that won't happen — and all bets will be off.

A version of this op-ed appears in print on April 9, 2010, on page A27 of the New York edition with the headline: Learning From Greece.

ECONOMIC VIEW

The Rock And the Hard Place On the Deficit

Christina D. Romer

Dealing with our nation's gaping budget deficit is going to hurt. So here is a question for policy makers: What would hurt more, raising taxes or reducing spending?

The Republicans who walked out of budget negotiations the other week think they know the answer. They insist that higher taxes would threaten our fragile economic recovery and do serious long-term damage. Better to cut federal spending, they say.

President Obama pressured Republicans last week to accept higher taxes, in addition to reduced spending, as part of a plan to pare the deficit.

The economic evidence doesn't support the anti-tax view. Both tax increases and spending cuts will tend to slow the recovery in the near term, but spending cuts will likely slow it more. Over the longer term, sensible tax increases will probably do less damage to economic growth and productivity than cuts in government investment.

Why tax increases should be part of any comprehensive budget plan

Tax increases and spending cuts hurt the economy in the short run by reducing demand. Increase taxes, and Americans would have less money to spend. Reduce spending, and less government money would be pumped into the economy.

Professional forecasters estimate that a tax increase equivalent to 1 percent of the nation's economic output usually reduces gross domestic product by about 1 percent after 18 months. A spending cut of that size, by contrast, reduces G.D.P. by about 1.5 percent—substantially more.

Some in Washington and in the news media have seized on a study 1 conducted with David Romer, my husband and colleague, that they say shows tax increases having a bigger short-term effect on the economy than spending cuts.

They are mistaken.

Our study, which examined only federal tax policy, found that conventional analysis underestimates the effect of tax changes on the economy substantially. The key problem we address is that changes in taxes are often linked to what is happening in the economy.

A tax surcharge in 1968, for instance, raised taxes because output was rising rapidly and was expected to keep surging. That the economy's growth rate was about average even after that step might be interpreted as evidence that the surcharge did little. But considering the motive for it, and the fact that the economy had been predicted to continue growing quickly when it was introduced, this tax increase appears to have had a substantial chilling effect on the economy.

If there were a similar study on government spending, it would likely show that spending cuts also have larger effects than conventionally believed. Like tax actions, spending changes are often correlated with other factors affecting economic activity. For example, large cuts in military spending, like those after World War II and the Korean War, were typically accompanied by the end of wartime taxes and production controls. Those probably lessened the economic impact of the spending cuts, leading many researchers to underestimate the reductions' effects.

There is a basic reason why government spending changes probably have a larger short-term impact than tax changes. When a household's tax bill rises by, say, $100, that household typically pays for part of that increase by reducing its savings. Its spending tends to fall by less than $100. But when the government cuts spending by $100, overall demand goes down by that full amount.

Wealthier households typically pay for more of a tax increase out of savings, and so they reduce their spending less than ordinary households. This implies that tax increases on wealthy households probably have less effect on the economy than those on the poor or the middle class.

All of this argues against any form of fiscal austerity just now. Even some deficit hawks warn that immediate tax increases or spending cuts could push the economy back into recession. Far better to pass a plan that phases in spending cuts or tax increases over time.

But if federal policy makers do decide to reduce the deficit immediately, reducing spending alone would probably be the most damaging to the recovery. Raising taxes for the wealthy would be least likely to reduce overall demand and raise unemployment.

What about the long-term health of the economy? Here, too, the relative costs of tax increases and spending cuts are often misstated.

Higher tax rates reduce the rewards of work and investing. This can have supply-side effects that lower economic growth over decades.

But a large number of academic studies has found that these effects are relatively small. An excellent survey due to be published in the Journal of Economic Literature found that raising current tax rates by 10 percent would reduce reported income—the end result of work and entrepreneurial effort—by less than 2 percent. That is far less than what was hypothesized by prominent Reagan-era supply-siders like Arthur B. Laffer. He and others postulated that raising taxes 10 percent would ultimately reduce income by more than 10 percent, leading to a decline in tax revenue.

Certain spending cuts may also have small effects on long-run growth. Entitlement spending on Social Security and Medicare could probably be slowed without reducing the nation's productive ability. But as the bipartisan National Commission on Fiscal Responsibility and Reform emphasized in a report in December, such changes can and should be made in a way that protects the most vulnerable Americans.

Government spending on things like basic scientific research, education and infrastructure, on the other hand, helps increase future productivity. This type of spending often produces high social returns, but the private sector is unlikely to step up if the government pulls back. Case studies described in a recent survey found that less than half of the returns from research-and-development spending were captured by the private investor, so corporations shy away from such endeavors. Cutting federal funds for R.&D., would leave a void and could have significant long-run effects on growth.

These long-term considerations, like the short-run concerns, point to a plan for reducing the deficit that combines spending cuts and tax increases. The cuts should spare valuable investment spending. On the tax side, nearly every economist. I know agrees that the best way to raise revenue would be limit tax breaks for households and corporations.

The fiscal commission proposed a concrete plan that would trim a wide range of credits and exemptions, including the preferential treatment of employer-provided health insurance. It would use part of the revenue to reduce tax rates and the rest to cut the deficit. This would help deal with the deficit while actually improving incentives.

The bottom line is that tax increases should be part of any comprehensive budget plan. Opinion polls suggest that many Americans understand this. It is time for policy makers to accept this economic reality.

'Fiscal Cliff' Has Many Perils

CBO Warns of Recession, or More Big Deficits, Depending on Congressional Action

Damian Paletta and Sara Murray

WASHINGTON—The U.S. economy likely would slide into a "significant recession" next year if Congress doesn't avert tax increases and spending cuts set to begin in January, the Congressional Budget Office said Wednesday.

But if they are postponed for at least a year, the federal government faces the prospect of a fifth straight year with a budget deficit greater than $1 trillion, the CBO said.

These dueling pressures came into sharp focus as the nonpartisan agency released its final budget and economic forecast ahead of the November elections.

The fight over how to address tax and spending policies has frozen Washington into political paralysis. And Democrats and Republicans aren't expected to begin negotiating a way to avoid tax increases and spending cuts until after the elections.

The report was immediately seized on by the White House and presumptive Republican presidential nominee Mitt Romney, as the economy remains a top issue on the campaign trail.

"We can see what's happening over in Europe . . . people have spent more than they have taken in year after year after year, borrowed, more and more money, made promises they couldn't fulfill and finally something which had to end did end," Mr. Romney said in Bettendorf, Iowa.

White House press secretary Jay Carney pointed the blame at House Republicans, saying they "have chosen to double down on the same failed policies that led to the economic crisis in the first place. They're willing to hold the middle class hostage unless we also give massive new tax cuts to millionaires and billionaires—tax cuts we can't afford that would do nothing to strengthen the economy."

The CBO painted two starkly different scenarios for next year, depending on which path lawmakers take.

Under current law, the Bushera tax cuts are scheduled to expire at year-end, raising tax rates on more than 100 million Americans. These tax increases, combined with roughly $100 billion in required spending cuts on military and other government programs, would shrink projected deficits from $1.13 trillion in the fiscal year ending Sept, 30 to $641 billion for the year that ends Sept, 30, 2013.

That would reduce the deficit from roughly 7.3% of the nation's gross domestic product to roughly 4% of GDP, the CBO said, the largest one-year reduction since 1969.

But as a consequence, the economy would contract at a projected annualized rate of 2.9% in the first half of 2013, and by 0.5% over the entire year. The unemployment rate would rise to 9.1% at the end of the year from just above 8% now, the CBO estimated.

If Congress were to postpone the tax increases and spending cuts, the deficit would shrink just slightly in the next fiscal year, to $1.037 trillion, or 6.5% of GDP. The unemployment rate at the end of 2013 would be 8%, a difference of roughly two million jobs from the other scenario, CBO said. The economy would grow by 1.7% over the year.

Democrats have advocated using a combination of tax increases on upper-income Americans and spending cats in a number of programs to reduce the deficit over time. The White House has called for extending all of the Bush-era tax cuts except on the portion of income that tops $250,000 for families. The CBO estimated this change would boost tax collections $42 billion in 2013 and $824 billion, over the next 10 years.

Many Republicans have called for extending all of the Bush-era tax cuts for at least another year and cutting spending on many programs. Mr. Romney has called for a one-year extension of all the tax cuts and has called for postponing spending cuts into next year, giving him time to develop his own deficit-reduction plan if he is elected.

A number of members from both parties have said Democrats and Republicans will have to compromise to reach a deal after the election, but so far party leaders have shown no willingness to do so.

References

Blanchard, O. (2006). *Macroeconomics* (4th ed.). Upper Saddle River, NJ: Prentice Hall, p. 566.

Congressional Budget Office. (2007, January). *The budget and economic outlook: Fiscal years 2008 to 2017.*

Millman (1990)

Ramey (2011)

Romer and Bernstein (2009)

CHAPTER 11

Definitions

1. Fiscal policy

Federal spending and taxation policies designed to affect the business cycle and attain price stability, sustained economic growth and full employment.

2. Mandatory fiscal policy

Spending authorized by permanent law rather than annual appropriations.

3. Discretionary fiscal policy

Those elements of the federal budget not determined by past legislative or executive commitments.

4. Automatic stabilizer

The property of taxes and certain government spending that they help stimulate aggregate demand when the economy is declining and hold down aggregate demand as the economy is expanding.

5. Budget deficit

A shortfall of receipts from government expenditure.

6. Budget surplus

An excess of receipts over expenditure.

7. Lump-Sum Taxes

Taxes that do not change when income changes.

8. Crowding Out Effect

Reduction in investment that results when expansionary fiscal policy raises the interest rate.

9. Government multiplier

10. Tax multiplier

Multiple Choice

1. Fiscal policy refers to
   a. the use of fines to penalize unfair business practices.
   b. the purchase and sale of U.S. government securities to regulate the money supply.
   c. the adjustment of the GNP for inflation.
   d. a policy action by congress to overrule unpopular budget cuts by the President.
   (e.) the use of government spending and taxation to influence the level of economic growth and inflation.

2. Fiscal policy affects which two aggregate expenditures either directly or indirectly.
   (a.) government spending and consumption
   b. net exports and savings.
   c. investment and net exports
   d. consumption and investment
   e. taxes and consumption

3. Treasury bonds are:
   (a.) short term government securities
   b. long term government securities
   c. taxes paid by consumers
   d. stocks issued by corporation
   e. none of the above

4. Which of the following statements about taxation is true.
   a. a tax cut would affect aggregate expenditures directly.
   (b.) a tax cut would raise income and expenditures.
   c. cutting taxes by $20 is the same as increasing government expenditure by $20.
   d. a change in taxes would not affect consumption.
   e. the spending multiplier is the same as the tax multiplier

5. Taxes affect aggregate expenditures
   (a.) indirectly by changing autonomous consumption.
   b. indirectly by changing autonomous investment spending.
   c. indirectly by changing autonomus net exports.
   d. directly by changing the 45 degree line.
   e. directly through government spending.

6. When aggregate expenditures are less than the potential level of national income, there exists
   a. high inflation
   (b.) a recessionary gap
   c. a budget gap
   d. full employment
   e. a balanced budget

7. Crowding out private borrowing as a result of increased federal government borrowing occurs because:
   a. the government borrows to take advantage of investment opportunities that otherwise would have attracted private borrowers.
   b. Interest rates on investment opportunities fall as government takes over more high yielding projects.
   c. The government is interest-rate sensitive in its borrowing decisions, whereas households and businesses are not.
   d. Increased government borrowing drives up the interest rates on borrowed funds.

8. Pete's total income is $ 10,000 and his net taxes are $ 2000. Pete's disposable income is
   a. $ 8,000
   b. $ 10,000
   c. $ 12,000
   d. $ 2,000

9. The size of the national debt increases when the federal government runs a:
   a. deficit budget
   b. balanced budget
   c. surplus budget
   d. contractionary budget

10. A budget deficit is when
   a. government expenditure exceeds taxes
   b. taxes exceeds government expenditure
   c. exports exceeds imports
   d. imports exceeds exports
   e. none of the above

Resources

Priciples of Macroeconomics Case & Fair

Economics Boyes/Melvin

270

True/False

Directions: For the following statements, indicate whether the statement is true or false. If the statement is false, make the necessary change(s) in order for it to be a true statement.

1. Both discretionary fiscal policy and mandatory fiscal policy are subject to the annual appropriations process.

2. Mandatory fiscal policy includes social welfare programs such as Medicare, Medicaid, and Social Security.

3. The federal minimum wage is an example of an automatic stabilizer discussed in this chapter.

4. Compared to the mid-20th century, discretionary spending has consumed most of the federal budget.

5. The average tax rate for the United States is about 30 percent higher than other countries such as Canada, Germany, and Sweden.

6. A budget deficit occurs when taxes exceed government expenditure.

7. The concept of crowding out is when businesses work together to increase barriers to entry to new businesses, leading to a decrease in investment.

8. The government spending and tax multipliers both measure the change in equilibrium income with a $1 change in government spending or taxes.

9. The tax multiplier shows that there is a greater impact on the economy with a change in taxes as opposed to a change in government spending.

Short Answer/Essay Questions

1. Consider the following model:

$$C = 30 + 0.75Y_D$$
$$I = 25$$
$$Y_e = 220$$

   a. If government expenditures of $5 were added to $C + I$, what would be the new equilibrium level of national income?

   b. What is the government spending multiplier?

2. Consider the following model:

$$Y = C + I + G$$
$$C = 125 + 0.75Y_D$$
$$T = 100$$
$$I = 100$$
$$G = 110$$

   a. Solve for equilibrium income.

   b. Assume that government spending decreases by $10, what is the new equilibrium income level?

   c. What is the government spending multiplier?

   d. Assume a corresponding decrease in tax by $10; what is the new equilibrium?

3. Suppose the economy's full employment equilibrium (Y_f) is $2 trillion per year and that the spending desires of market participants are as follows:

$$C = \$400 \text{ billion} + 0.5Y_D$$
$$I = \$300 \text{ billion}$$
$$G = \$400 \text{ billion}$$

a. Given Y_f and after solving for Y_e, what problem is this economy confronted with?

b. How could the government eliminate the problem with:
   (1) a change in tax?
   (2) a change in government spending?

4. Given an MPC of 0.9, answer the following questions:
   a. If government expenditures fall by $500, how much will the aggregate expenditure curve shift? How much would equilibrium change?

   b. If taxes fell by $500, by how much will the aggregate expenditure curve shift up? $(500) = 250 by how much will equilibrium income change?

Money and Banking

Tischenko Irina/Shutterstock.com

OBJECTIVES

1. To define the concept of money.
2. To explain the economic meaning of money markets.
3. To describe the different types of money demand.
4. To describe the different types of money supply.
5. To describe and explain the process of money creation.

Introduction

When we say that a person has a lot of money, we usually mean that he or she is wealthy. By contrast, economists use the term money in a more specialized way. To an economist, money does not refer to all the wealth but only to one type of it: **money** is the stock of assets that can be readily used to make transactions. Roughly speaking, the dollars in the hands of the public make up the nation's stock of money.

Money plays an important role in the economy. Money is used by people to facilitate trade and commerce. Money plays an important role in making markets efficient so that people can specialize in producing some goods or service, thus making the standard of living higher.

The Functions of Money

Money has three purposes. It can serve as a medium of exchange, it serves a store of value, and it can be use as a unit of account.

Money can serve as a **medium of exchange** because we use money in our daily lives. We use money to buy goods and services. "This note is legal tender for all debts, public and private" is printed on the U.S. dollar. When we walk into stores, we are confident that the shopkeepers will accept our money in exchange for the items that they are selling. The ease with which money is converted into other things—that is, goods and services—is known as **liquidity**.

Money is a standard of value; that is, money can be used as a **unit of account**. As a unit of account, money provides the terms in which prices are quoted and debts are recorded. Microeconomics teaches us that resources are allocated according to relative prices—prices of goods relative to other goods—yet stores post their prices in dollars and cents. A car dealer tells you that a car costs $20,000, not 400 shirts. Similarly, most debts require the debtor to deliver a specified number of dollars in the future, not a specified amount of some commodity. Money is the yardstick with which we measure economic transactions.

As a **store of value**, money is a way to transfer purchasing power from the present to the future. You store value in it, just like pioneers stored value in the grain they held until the next harvest. If I work today and earn $100, I can hold the money and spend it tomorrow, next week, or next month. Of course, money is an imperfect store of value: if prices are rising, the amount you can buy with any given quantity of money is falling. Even so, people hold money because they can trade the money for goods and services at some time in the future.

Without money, we would have to rely on bartering. Bartering is a system in which one person provides a good, service, or resource to another in exchange for some other good, service, or resource. Such trade requires that there be a **double coincidence of wants**, which means each person has what the other person wants and wants what the other person has. That would be a rare occurrence. For example, if you tried to trade some surplus pencils for a bike, it could take years to make a trade. Economists call the time plus other things of value that are given up when making exchanges **transaction costs**. People who hate to spend time shopping and to endure crowds know about such costs. When people do comparison-shopping to find the best deal, they deliberately increase their transaction costs.

Money makes more indirect transactions possible. For example, a college professor uses his or her salary to purchase books; the book publisher uses its revenue from the sale of books to buy paper; the paper company uses its revenue from the sale of paper to pay the lumberjack; the lumberjack uses his income to send his child to college; and the college uses its tuition receipts to pay the salary of the professor.

The three functions of money are not independent of each other. For example, if prices rise extremely rapidly, money will be useless as a store of value. People would resort to barter for many exchanges, and money would cease to be used as a medium of exchange.

Money takes many forms. In the U.S. economy we make transactions with an item whose sole function is to act as money: dollar bills. These pieces of green paper with small portraits of famous Americans would have little value if they were not widely accepted as money. Money that has no intrinsic value is called **fiat money** because it is established as money by government decree, or fiat. While most economies today operate with fiat money, many societies in the past used a commodity with some intrinsic value as money (such as gold standard, which was the standard in the United States). This type of money is called **commodity money**.

The Money Market

The quantity of money available in an economy is called the **money supply**. In modern economies, the government controls the supply of money: legal restrictions give the government a monopoly on the printing of money. The control over the money supply is called **monetary policy**.

In the United States, monetary policy is delegated to the **Federal Reserve**, more commonly called the Fed. If you look at a U.S. dollar bill, you will notice that it is called a *Federal Reserve Note*. The primary way in which the Fed controls the supply of money is through **open-market operations**—the purchase and sale of government bonds. When the Fed wants to increase the money supply, it uses some of the dollars it has to buy government bonds from the public. Because these dollars have left the Fed and enter into the hands of the public, the purchase increases the quantity of money in circulation. Conversely, when the Fed wants to decrease the money supply, it sells some government bonds from its own portfolio. This open-market sale of bonds takes some dollars out of the hands of the public and, thus, decreases the quantity of money in circulation.

In Chapter 13 we discuss in more detail how the Fed controls the supply of money. For our current discussion, it is sufficient to assume that the Fed directly controls the supply of money.

The money market in economics deals with the equality between the demand and supply for money. From a laymen's perspective, the money market may be interpreted as money that is actually invested in a bank. From an economist's point of view, the money market refers to the different composition of money demand and money supply.

Types of Money Demand

There are three types of money demand: transaction demand for money; speculative demand for money; and precautionary demand for money.

Transaction demand for money is the money we use for daily business transactions. We use money to purchase goods and services. Transaction demand for money is a function of disposable income. There is a positive relationship between disposable income and transaction demand for money. As disposable income increases, the transaction demand for money also increases.

Speculative demand for money is the money we use to buy stocks and bonds. We use this type of money to speculate, hoping that it will bring us more money in the future. Speculative demand for money is sensitive to interest rates. There is an inverse relationship between interest rates and speculative demand for money.

The third kind of demand for money is **precautionary demand**. This is not a function of any variable. It is a discretionary demand we use for hoarding purposes.

Money Supply

Money supply is determined by the Federal Reserve. The classification of money supply depends on how one can turn the type of money supply into cash or goods and services. It depends on liquidity.

Because money is the stock of assets used for transactions, the quantity of money is the quantity of those assets. In simple economies, this quantity is easy to measure; but how can we measure the quantity of money in more complex economies? The answer is not obvious, because no single asset is used for all transactions. People can use various assets, such as cash in their wallets or deposits in their checking accounts, to make transactions, although some assets are more convenient than others.

The most obvious asset to include in the quantity of money is **currency**, the sum of outstanding paper money and coins. Most day-to-day transactions use currency as the medium of exchange.

A second type of asset used for transactions is **demand deposits,** the funds people hold in their checking accounts. If most sellers accept personal checks, assets in a checking account are almost as convenient as currency. In both cases, the assets are in a form ready to facilitate a transaction. Demand deposits are therefore added to currency when measuring the quantity of money.

Once we admit the logic of including demand deposits in the measured money stock, many other assets become candidates for inclusion. Funds in savings accounts, for example, can be easily transferred into checking accounts; these assets are almost as convenient for transactions. Money market mutual funds allow investors to write checks against their accounts, although restrictions sometimes apply with regard to the size of the check or number of checks written. Because these assets can be easily used for transactions, they should arguably be included in the quantity of money.

Because it is hard to judge which assets should be included in the money stock, various measures are available. Below are the four measures of the money stock that the Federal Reserve calculates for the U.S. economy, together with a list of which assets are included in each measure. From the smallest to the largest, they are designated C, M_1, M_2, and M_3. The most common measures for studying the effects of money on the economy are M_1 and M_2. There is no consensus, however, about which measure of the money stock is best. Disagreements about monetary policy sometimes arise because different measures of money are moving in different directions.

The different types of money supply are the following:

1. C = Currency

2. M_1 = M_1 consists of (a) currency outside the U.S. Treasury, Federal Reserve Banks, and the vaults of depository institutions; (b) travelers' checks of nonbank issuers; (c) demand deposits at commercial banks (excluding those amounts held by depository institutions, the U.S. government, and foreign banks and official institutions) less cash items in the process of collection and Federal Reserve float; and (d) other checkable deposits (OCDs), consisting of negotiable order of withdrawal (NOW) and automatic transfer service (ATS) accounts at depository institutions, credit union share draft accounts, and demand deposits at thrift institutions (Federal Reserve Bank, 2008).

3. M_2 = M_1 plus (a) savings deposits (including money market deposit accounts); (b) small-denomination time deposits (time deposits in amounts of less than $100,000), less individual retirement account (IRA) and Keogh balances at depository institutions; and (c) balances in retail money market mutual funds, less IRA and Keogh balances at money market mutual funds (Federal Reserve Bank, 2008).

4. $M_3 = M_2$ plus large time deposits, repurchase agreements, eurodollars, and institution-only money-market mutual-fund balances.

Theory to Application

How Do Credit and Debit Cards Fit into the Monetary System?

Many people use credit or debit cards to make purchases. Because money is the medium of exchange, one might naturally wonder how these cards fit into the measurement and analysis of money.

Let's start with credit cards. Although one might guess that credit cards are part of the economy's stock of money, measures of the quantity of money do not take credit cards into account. Credit cards are not really a method of payment, but a method of *deferring* payment. When you buy an item with a credit card, the bank that issued that card pays the store the amount that is due. Later, you will have to repay the bank. When the time comes to pay your credit card bill you will likely do so by writing a check against your checking account. The balance in this checking account is part of the economy's stock of money.

The story is different with debit cards, which automatically withdraw funds from a bank account to pay for items bought. Rather than allowing people to postpone payment for their purchases, a debit card allows users immediate access to deposits in their bank accounts. Using a debit card is similar to writing a check. The account balances that lie behind debit cards are included in measures of the quantity of money.

Even though credit cards are not a form of money, they are still important for analyzing the monetary system. Because people with credit cards can pay many of their bills all at once at the end of the month, rather than sporadically as they make purchases, they may hold less money on average than people without credit cards. Thus, the increased popularity of credit cards may reduce the amount of money that people choose to hold. In other words, credit cards are not part of the money supply, but they may affect the demand for money.

Creation of Money

Once we've decided what money is, we still have to explain where it comes from. Part of the explanation is simple. Currency must be printed. Some nations use private printers for this purpose, but all U.S. currency is printed by the Bureau of Engraving and Printing in Washington, D.C. Coins come from the U.S. mints located in Philadelphia and Denver. As we've noted in the previous section, however, currency is a small fraction of our total money supply. So we need to look elsewhere for the origins of most money. Specifically, where do all the transactions accounts come from? How do people acquire transactions deposits? How does the total amount of such deposits—and therefore the money supply of the economy—change?

Most people assume that all transactions account balances come from cash deposits. But this isn't the case. Direct deposits of paychecks, for example, are carried out by computer, not by the movement of cash. Moreover, the employer who issues the paycheck probably didn't make any cash deposits. It's more likely that she covered those paychecks with customer's checks that she deposited or with loans granted by the bank itself.

The ability of banks to lend money opens up a whole new set of possibilities for creating money. *When a bank lends someone money, it simply credits that individual's bank account.* The money appears in an account just as it would with a cash deposit. And the owner of the account is free to spend that money as with any positive balance. Hence, *in making a loan, a bank effectively creates money because transactions account balances are counted as part of the money supply.*

To understand the origins of our money supply then, we must recognize two basic principles:

1. Transactions account balances are a large portion of the money supply.

2. Banks can create transactions account balances by making loans.

The following two sections examine this process of **deposit creation** more closely. We determine how banks actually create deposits and what forces might limit the process of deposit creation.

Bank Regulation

Banks' deposit creation activities are regulated by the government. The most important agency in this regard is the Federal Reserve System. "The Fed" puts limits on the amount of bank lending, thereby controlling the basic money supply. We'll discuss the structure and functions of the Fed in the next chapter; here we focus on the process of deposit creation itself.

There are thousands of banks, of various sorts, in the United States. To understand how banks create money, however, we'll simplify reality greatly. We'll assume for the moment that there's only one bank around, National Bank. Imagine also that you've been saving some of your income by putting loose change into a piggy bank. Now, after months of saving, you break the bank and discover that your thrift has yielded $100. You immediately deposit this money in a new checking account at National Bank. How will this deposit affect the money supply?

Your initial deposit will have no immediate effect on the money supply. The coins in your piggy bank were already counted as part of the money supply (M1 and M2) because they represented cash held by the public. *When you deposit cash or coins in a bank, you're simply changing the composition of the money supply.* The public (you) now holds $100 less of coins but $100 more of transactions deposits. Accordingly, no money is created by the demise of your piggy bank (the initial deposit). This accounting income is reflected in the following "T account" of National Bank and the composition of the money supply.

National Bank		Money Supply	
Assets	Liabilities	Cash held by the public	−$100
+$100	+$100	Transactions deposits at bank	+$100
in coins	in deposits	Change in M	0

The T account shows that your coins are now held by National Bank. In exchange, the bank has credited your checking account $100. This balance is a liability for the bank since it must allow you to withdraw the deposit on demand.

The total money supply is unaffected by your cash deposit because two components of the money supply change in opposite directions (i.e., less cash, more bank deposits). This initial deposit is just the beginning of the money creation process, however. Banks aren't in business for your convenience; they're in business to earn a profit. To earn a profit on your deposit, National Bank will have to put your money to work. This means using your deposit as the basis for making a loan to someone who's willing to pay the bank interest for use of money. If the function of banks was merely to store money, they wouldn't pay interest on their accounts or offer free checking services. Instead, you'd have to pay them for these services. Banks pay you interest and offer free (or inexpensive) checking because they can use your money to make loans that earn interest.

The Initial Loan

Typically, a bank doesn't have much difficulty finding someone who wants to borrow money. Someone is always eager to borrow money. The question is: How much money can a bank lend? Can it lend your entire deposit? Or must National Bank keep some of your coins in reserve, in case you want to withdraw them?

To answer this question, suppose the National Bank decided to lend the entire $100 to Auto USA. Auto USA wants to buy new parts but doesn't have any money in its own checking account. To acquire the antenna, Auto USA must take out a loan.

When National Bank agrees to lend Auto USA $100, it does so by crediting the account of Auto USA. Instead of giving Auto USA $100 cash, National Bank simply adds $100 to Auto's checking account balance. That is, the loan is made with a simple bookkeeping entry as follows:

National Bank		Money Supply	
Assets	Liabilities	Cash held by the public	no change
$100 in coins	$100 in your account balance	Transactions deposits at bank	+$100
$100 in loans	$100 Auto USA account	Change in M	+$100

This simple bookkeeping procedure is the key to creating money. When National Bank lends $100 to the Auto USA account, it "creates" money. Keep in mind that transactions deposits are counted as part of the money supply. Once the $100 loan is credited to it account, Auto USA can use this new money to purchase its desired auto parts, without worrying that its check will bounce.

Or can it? Once National Bank grants a loan to Auto USA, both you and Auto USA have $100 in your checking accounts to spend. But the bank is holding only $100 of **reserves** (your coins). In other words, the increased account balance obtained by Auto USA doesn't limit your ability to write checks. There's been a net *increase* in the value of transactions deposits but no increase in the bank reserves.

Secondary Deposits

What happens if Auto USA actually spends the $100 on new car parts? Won't this "use up all" the reserves held by the bank, endangering your check-writing privileges? The answer is no.

Consider what happens when Atlas Auto Parts receives the check from Auto USA. What will Atlas do with the check? Atlas could go to National Bank and exchange the check for $100 of cash (your coins). But Atlas may prefer to deposit the check in its own checking account at National Bank (still the only bank in town). This way, Atlas not only avoids the necessity of going to the bank (it can deposit the check by mail) but also keeps its money in a safe place. Should Atlas later want to spend the money, it can simply write a check. In the meantime, the bank continues to hold its entire reserves (your coins), and both you and Atlas have $100 to spend.

Fractional Reserves

Notice what's happened here. The money supply has increased by $100 as a result of deposit creation (the loan to Auto USA). Moreover, the bank has been able to support $200 of transaction deposits (your account and either the Auto or Atlas account) with only $100 of reserves (your coins). In other words, *bank reserves are only a fraction of total deposits*. In this case, National Bank's reserves (your $100 in coins) are only 50 percent of total deposits. Thus the bank's reserve ratiois 50 percent—that is,

Reserve ratio = bank reserves/total reserves

The ability of National Bank to hold reserves that are only a fraction of total deposits results from two facts: (a) people use checks for most transactions, and (b) there's no other bank. Accordingly, reserves are rarely withdrawn from this monopoly bank. In fact, if people *never* withdrew their deposits and *all* transactions accounts were held at National Bank, National Bank wouldn't need *any* reserves. In this most unusual case, National Bank could make as many loans as it wanted. Every loan it made would increase the supply of money.

In reality, many banks are available, and people both withdraw cash from their accounts and write checks to people who have accounts in other banks, In addition, bank lending practices are regulated by the Federal Reserve System. *The Federal Reserve System requires banks to maintain some minimum reserve ratio.* This reserve requirement can be readily seen. Suppose that the Federal Reserve imposed a minimum reserve requirement of 75 percent on National Bank. Such a requirement would prohibit National Bank from lending $100 to Auto USA. That loan would result in $200 of deposits, supported by only $100 of reserves. The actual ratio of reserves to deposits would be 50 deposit ($100 of reserves ÷ $200 of deposits), which would violate the Fed's assumed 75 percent reserve requirement. A 75 percent reserve requirement means that national Bank must hold *required reserves* equal to 75 percent of *total* deposits, including those created through loans.

The bank's dilemma is evident in the following equation:

Required reserves = required reserve ratio × total deposits

To support $200 of total deposits, National Bank would need to satisfy this equation:

Required reserves = 0.75 × $200 = $150

But the bank has only $100 of reserves (your coins) and so would violate the reserve requirement if it increased total deposits to $200 by lending $100 to Auto USA.

National Bank can still issue a loan to Auto USA. But the loan must be less than $100 in order to keep the bank within the limits of the required reserve formula. Thus, *a minimum reserve requirement directly limits deposit-creation possibilities.* It's still true, however, as we'll now illustrate, that the banking system taken as a whole, can create multiple loans (money) from a single deposit. Because we don't live with a monopoly bank we'll assume that legally required reserves must equal at least 20 percent of transaction deposits. Now when you deposit $100 in your checking account, National Bank must hold at least $20 as required reserves.[1]

The remaining $80 the bank obtains from your deposit is regarded as *excess reserves*. These reserves are "excess" in that your bank is *required* to hold in reserves only $20 (equal to 20 percent of your $100 deposit):

Excess reserves = total reserves–required reserves

The $80 excess reserves aren't required and may be used to support additional loans. Hence, the bank can now lend $80. In view of the fact that banks earn profits (interest) by making loans, we assume that National Bank will try to use these excess reserves as soon as possible.

A Multibank World

To keep track of the changes in reserves, deposit balances, and loans that occur in a multibank world we'll have to do some bookkeeping. For this purpose we'll again use the same balance sheet, or T account, that banks themselves use. On the left side of the balance sheet, a bank lists all its assets. *Assets* are things the bank owns or is owed by others, including cash held in a bank's vaults, IOUs (loan obligations) from bank customers, reserve credits at the Federal Reserve (essentially the bank's own deposits at the central bank), and securities (bonds) the bank has purchased.

On the right side of the balance sheet a bank lists all its liabilities. *Liabilities* are what the bank owes to others. The largest liability is represented by the deposits of bank customers. The bank owes these deposits to its customers and must return them "on demand."

Notice how the balance of National Bank now looks immediately after it receives your initial deposit. Your deposit of coins is entered on both sides of National's balance sheet. On the left side, your deposit is regarded as an asset, because your piggy bank's coins have an immediate market value and can be used to pay off the bank's liabilities. The coins now appear as *reserves*. The reserves these coins represent are further divided into required reserves ($20, or 20 percent of your deposit) and excess reserves ($80).

On the right side of the balance sheet, the bank reminds itself that it has an obligation (liability) to return your deposit when you so demand. Thus, the bank's accounts balance, with assets and liabilities being equal. In fact, *a bank's books must always balance because all the bank's assets must belong to someone (its depositors or its owners).*

National Bank wants to do more than balance its books, however; it wants to earn profits. To do so, it will have to make loans—that is, put it excess reserves to work. Suppose that it lends $80 to Auto USA.[2] This loan alters both sides of National Bank's balance sheet. On the right-hand side, the bank creates a new transactions deposit for (credits the account of) Auto USA; this item represents an additional liability (promise to pay). On the left-hand side of the balance sheet, two things happen. First, the bank notes that Auto USA owes it $80 ("loans"). Second, the bank recognizes that it's now required to hold $36 in *required* reserves, in accordance with its higher level of transactions deposits ($180). (Recall we're assuming that required reserves are 20 percent of total transactions deposits.) Since its total reserves are still $100, $64 is left as *excess* reserves. Note again that *excess reserves are reserves a bank isn't required to hold*.

Changes in the Money Supply

Before examining further changes in the balance sheet of National Bank, consider again what's happened to the economy's money supply during these first two steps. In the first step, you deposited $100 of cash in your checking account. This initial transaction didn't change the value of the money supply. Only the composition of the money supply (M1 or M2) was affected ($100 less cash held by the public, $100 more in transactions accounts).

Not until step 2—when the bank makes a loan—does all the excitement begin. In making a loan, the bank automatically increases the total money supply by $80. Why? Because someone (Auto USA) now has more money (a transactions deposit) than it did before, *and no one else has any less*. And Auto can use its money to buy goods and services, just like anybody else.

This second step is the heart of money creation. Money effectively appears out of thin air when a bank makes a loan. To understand how this works, you have to keep reminding yourself that money is more than the coins and currency we carry around. Transactions deposits are money too. Hence, *the creation of transactions deposits via new loans is the same thing as creating money*.

More Deposit Creation

Suppose again that Auto USA actually uses its $80 loan to buy car parts. In step 3, Auto USA buys the $80 parts, the balance in its checking account at National Bank drops to zero because it has spent all its money. As National Bank's liabilities fall (from $180 to $100), so does the level of its required reserves (from $36 to $20). (Note that required reserves are still 20 percent of its remaining transactions deposits.) But National Bank's excess reserves have disappeared completely! This disappearance reflects the fact that Atlas Auto Parts keeps *its* transactions account at another bank (Eternal Savings). When Atlas deposits the check it received from Auto USA, Eternal Savings does two things: First it credits Atlas's account by $80. Second, it goes to National Bank to get the reserves that support the deposit.[3] The reserves later appear on the balance sheet of Eternal Savings as both required ($16) and excess ($64) reserves.

Observe that the money supply hasn't changed during step 3. The increase in the value of Atlas Auto Parts' transactions account balance exactly offsets the drop in the value of Auto USA's transactions account. Ownership of the money supply is the only thing that has changed.

In step 4, Eternal Savings takes advantage of its newly acquired excess reserves by making a loan to Hammon's Hardware. As before, the loan itself has two primary effects. First, it creates a transactions deposit of $64 for Hammon's Hardware and thereby increases the money supply by the same amount. Second, it increases the required level of reserves at Eternal Savings.

The Money Multiplier

By now it's perhaps obvious that the process of deposit creation won't come to an end quickly. On the contrary, it can continue indefinitely, just like the income multiplier process. Indeed, people often refer to deposit creation as the money multiplier process, with the **money multiplier** expressed as the reciprocal of the required reserve ratio.[4] That is,

Money multiplier = 1 / required reserve ratio

The figure below illustrates the money multiplier process. When a new deposit enters the banking system, it creates both excess and required reserves. The required reserves represent leakage from the flow of money since they can't be used to create new loans. Excess reserves, on the other hand, can be used for new loans. once those loans are made, they typically become transactions deposits elsewhere in the banking system. Then some additional leakage into required reserves occurs, and further loans are made. The process continues until all excess reserves have leaked into required reserves. Once excess reserves have completely disappeared, the total vale of new loans will equal initial excess reserves multiplied by the money multiplier.

The potential of the money multiplier to create loans is summarized by the equation

Excess reserves of banking system × money multiplier = potential deposit creation

Notice how the money multiplier worked in or previous example. The value of the money multiplier was equal to 5, since we assumed that the required reserve ration was 0.20. Moreover, the initial level of excess reserves was $80, as a consequence of your original deposit (step 1). According to the money multiplier, then, the deposit-creation potential of the banking system was

Excess reserves ($80) × money multiplier (5) = potential deposit creation ($400)

When all the banks fully utilized their excess reserves at each step of the money multipliers process, the ultimate increase in the money supply was in fact $400). While you're struggling through the table, note the

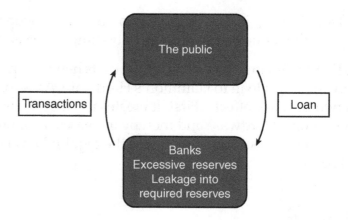

critical role that excess reserves lay in the process of deposit creation. A bank can make additional loans only if it has excess reserves. Without excess reserves, all of a bank's reserves are required, and no further liabilities (transactions deposits) can be created with new loans. On the other hand, a bank with excess reserves can make additional loans. In fact,

- *Each bank may lend an amount equal to its excess reserves and no more.*

As such loans enter the circular flow and become deposits elsewhere; they create new excess reserves and further lending capacity. As a consequence,

- *The entire banking system can increase the volume of loans by the amount of excess reserves multiplied by the money multiplier.*

By keeping track of excess reserves, then, we can gauge the lending capacity of any bank or, with the aid of the money multiplier, the entire banking system.

The table summarizes the entire money multiplier process. In this case, we assume that all banks are initially "loaned up"—that is, without any excess reserves. The money multiplier process begins when someone deposits $100 in cash into a transactions account at Bank *A*. If the required reserve ratio is 20 percent, this initial deposit creates $80 of excess reserves at Bank *A* while adding $100 to total transactions deposits.

If Bank *A* uses its newly acquired excess reserves to make a loan that ultimately ends up in Bank *B*, two things happen: Bank *B* acquires $64 in excess reserves (0.80 × $80), and total transactions deposits increase by another $80.

The money multiplier process continues with a series of loans and deposits. When the 26th loan is made (by Bank *Z*), total loans grow by only $0.30 and transactions deposits by an equal amount. Should the process continue further, the *cumulative* change in loans will ultimately equal $400, that is, the money multiplier times initial excess reserves. The money supply will increase by the same amount.

Banks and the Circular Flow

The bookkeeping details of bank deposits and loans are rarely exciting and often confusing. But they do demonstrate convincingly that banks can create money. In that capacity, *banks perform two essential functions for the macro economy:*

1. Banks transfer money from savers to spenders by lending funds (reserves) held on deposit.

2. The banking system creates additional money by making loans in excess of total reserves.

In performing these two functions, banks change the size of the money supply, that is, the amount of purchasing power available for buying goods and services. Market participants may respond to these changes in the money supply by altering their spending behavior and shifting the aggregate demand curve.

The figure shows a simplified perspective on the role of banks in the circular flow. As before, income flows from product markets through business firms to factor markets and returns to consumers in the form of disposable income. Consumers spend most of their income but also save (don't spend) some of it. The leakage represented by consumer saving is a potential source of stabilization problems, particularly unemployment. If additional spending by business firms, foreigners, or governments doesn't compensate for consumer saving at full employment, a recessionary GDP gap will emerge, creating unemployment. Our interest here is in the role the banking system can play in encouraging such additional spending.

Suppose for the moment that *all* consumer saving was deposited in piggy banks rather than banks and that no one used checks. Under these circumstances, banks couldn't transfer money from savers to spenders by holding deposits and making loans.

In reality, a substantial portion of consumer saving *is* deposited in banks. These and other bank deposits can be used as the basis of loans, thereby returning purchasing power to the circular flow. In fact, the primary economic function of banks isn't to store money but to transfer purchasing power from savers to spenders. They do so by lending money to businesses for new plant and equipment, to consumers for new homes or cars, and to government entities that desire greater purchasing power. Moreover, because the banking system can make *multiple* loans from available reserves, banks don't have to receive all consumer saving in order to carry out their function. On the contrary, *the banking system can create any desired level of money supply if allowed to expand or reduce loan activity at will.*

A simple deposit or withdrawal will not create money. However, it can theoretically change the money supply:

$$\textbf{Maximum change in the money supply} = \frac{1}{\textbf{rrr}} \times \textbf{change in money supply}$$

In our example, given a money multiplier of 5, a deposit of $100 can theoretically change the money supply by $500. Money creation can only occur if the deposit is used by the bank as a loan or investment.

There are three major constraints on the deposit creation of the banking system.

1. **Deposits:** The first constraint is the willingness of consumers and businesses to continue using and accepting checks rather than cash in the marketplace. If people preferred to hold cash rather than checkbooks, banks wouldn't be able to acquire or maintain the reserves that are the foundation of bank lending activity.

2. **Borrowers:** The second constraint on deposit creation is the willingness of consumers, businesses, and governments to borrow the money that banks make available. The chain of events we've observed in deposit creation depends on the willingness of Auto USA to borrow $80, of Hammon's Hardware to borrow $64, and so on. If no one wanted to borrow any money, deposit creation would never begin. By the same reasoning, if all excess reserves aren't borrowed (lent), deposit creation won't live up to its theoretical potential.

3. **Regulation:** The third major constraint on deposit creation is the Federal Reserve System. As we've observed, the Fed may limit deposit creation by imposing

$$M^S = \frac{1}{rr} \times \textbf{original deposit}$$

Endnotes

[1]The reserves themselves may be held in the form of cash in the bank's vault but are usually held as credits with one of the regional Federal Reserve banks.

[2]Because of the Fed's assumed minimum reserve requirement (20 percent), National Bank can now lend only $80 rather than $100, as before.

[3]In actuality, banks rarely "go" anywhere; such interbank reserve movements are handled by bank clearinghouses and regional Federal Reserve banks. The effect is the same, however. The nature and use of bank reserves are discussed more fully in the next chapter.

[4]The money multiplier $(\frac{1}{r})$ is the sum of the infinite geometric progression

$$1 + (1-r) + (1-r)^2 \div (1-r)^3 + (1-r)^\infty$$

Reference

Federal Reserve Bank (2008, March 27). *Federal Reserve Statistical Release* H.6 Money Stock Measures.

The Bitcoin Paradox That Undid Mt. Gox

By Ezra Galston

Late Monday night, the main exchange for the bitcoin virtual currency, the Tokyo-based Mt. Gox, shut its site, ceased all trading, and entered de facto bankruptcy. This followed months of delayed withdrawas, building consumer frustration, and a leaked document suggesting a gap between assets and liabilities of up to $350 million

Many bitcoin watchers—who also tend to be advocates—were stunned, but I wasn't. A few days before the shutdown, I had written an article for Comdesk, the leading online bitcoin news platform, called "Why Mt. Gox May be Headed for Bankruptcy." I used historical indicators from my experience in the online poker world to explain why Mt. Gox fit a pattern of virtual-wallet bankruptcies—namely, fund seizures, poor payment processors and technical accounting incongruities.

The Mt. Gox failure sparked many headlines, but the exchange's problems are hardly unique, and will likely cause other bitcoin exchanges to fail. Foremost among these—the same struggles encountered by online poker operators for a decade—are gray-marker payment processors, the potential for additional government seizures because of unclear regulatory environments, and the lack of ring-fencing around customer deposits.

These problems represent bitcoin's current paradox. Bitcoin is attempting to disrupt a regulatory framework and financial system that it must also depend on for its stability and growth.

Bitcoin's "blockchain" public ledger records every bitcoin transaction that has ever occurred, effectively defying the need for public auditing. In this respect bitcoin is supragovernmental, relying on technology and transparency to minimize dependency on government. Yet, at least for now, more government involvement is needed to prevent further failures of bitcoin exchanges.

Why? Because without a regulatory framework, credible payment processors—such as PayPal, Dwolla or Square—cannot service bitcoin exchanges. And because payment processor-disappear into the night. This puts enormous pressure on balance sheets and tempts operators to "borrow" from customer deposits.

Further, seizures from operator bank accounts—such as the $5 million seized from Mt. Gox last year in the wake of a federal investigation of the online Silk Road marketplace—will continue if the Justice

Department has cause to believe that transactions are being used for illicit purposes. How other governments will react to operator bank accounts in their locales is anyone's guess—and a big unknown. But operators of exchanges are expected to reimburse these seizures, no matter the costs.

Mt. Gox's largest failure was a technical one, with an alleged shortfall in bitcoins caused by improper accounting and oversight of reserves. Real-time digital signature verification can solve this problem, by-passing the need for traditional auditors. But implementation of such cutting-edge technology will need to be fully stress-tested. Meanwhile, exchanges would need to depend on either regulators or outside auditors to ensure that their digital signatures are accurate and not susceptible to manipulation.

This matters because the same leaked document that showed Mt. Gox to have lost 750,000 bitcoins also shows Mt. Gox to be holding only 40% of its flat liabilities—a loss of $32 million. These flat deposits were likely not ring-fenced from operating accounts and may have been misappropriated.

For bitcon investors, the good news is that risk and reward are correlated and big profits will be available for those willing to engage in a nascent, risky environment. Similarly, early professional online poker players who gambled with unlicensed, off-shore operators reaped big rewards from less talented players before the market matured. Also similar to Mt. Gox, hundreds of thousands of players lost their account balances over multiple bankruptcies when poker operators were found to have misappropriated customer deposits.

In the near term, the bitcoin community must embrace external regulation to ensure that credible vendors may participate in payment processing. A "BitLicense," proposed by the New York State Department of Financial Services, is a good start, but transmitter laws that differ by state may leave payment processors just as hesitant.

In the long run, Bitcoin's decentralization may well become strong enough to self-regulate and develop autonomously. But until then, community leaders should work closely with regulators rather than reject their efforts to develop essential safeguards.

Definitions

1. Money

2. Medium of exchange

3. Liquidity

4. Unit of account

5. Store of value

6. Double coincidence of wants

7. Transaction cost

8. Fiat money

9. Commodity money

10. Transaction demand

11. Speculative demand

12. Precautionary demand

13. Currency

14. Demand deposits

15. Deposit creation

16. Reserve ratio

17. Excess reserves

18. Money Multiplier

Multiple Choice

1. Money is
    a. an indicator of the scarcity of wants.
    b. anything that the government classifies as a trade commodity.
    c. anything that sellers accept in exchange for goods and services.
    d. a form of credit.
    e. a form of barter.

2. Liquidity refers to
    a. the ability of an asset to be easily converted into money.
    b. the difference between real and nominal money values.
    c. the ability of money to be a store of value.
    d. the availability of credit as form of money.
    e. the ability of a precious metal to be converted into spendable bank notes.

3. Exchanging one good for another without the use of money constitutes
    a. liquidity.
    b. token change.
    c. deferred payment.
    d. barter.
    e. Greshman's law.

4. A commodity would NOT likely be classified as money if it is
    a. portable.
    b. divisible.
    c. perishable.
    d. homogeneous in nature.
    e. predictable in value.

5. Credit constitutes
    a. money used as a standard of deferred payment.
    b. savings made available to borrowers.
    c. fiduciary currency.
    d. a form of liquid asset.
    e. bank loans converted into commodity money.

6. In Israel, many apartment leases quote rents in U.S. dollars, not in Israeli shekels. The explanation for this situation is that
    a. the shekel is not accepted as a medium of exchange.
    b. the rate of inflation in Israel has been very high and variable.
    c. many landlords in Israel are U.S. citizens.
    d. the shekel is not issued in convenient denominations.

7. Currency held outside banks + demand deposits + travelers checks + other checkable deposits is classified as:
   a. M1
   b. M2
   c. M3
   d. L

8. Which of the following institutions would not be considered a financial intermediary?
   a. auto insurance companies
   b. life insurance companies
   c. commercial banks
   d. pension funds

9. The central bank of the United States is known as the
   a. Federal Reserve System.
   b. Federal Deposit Insurance Corporation.
   c. Department of the Treasury.
   d. Federal Savings and Loan Insurance Corporation.

10. The international medium of exchange function of money is dominated by
    a. the currency of the importing nation.
    b. the currency of the exporting nation.
    c. the currencies of developing countries.
    d. the currencies of industrial countries.
    e. the European currency unit.

True/False

Directions: For the following statements, indicate whether the statement is true or false. If the statement is false, make the necessary change(s) in order for it to be a true statement.

1. In economics, when we talk about money, we are referring to a person's wealth.

2. The ease with which money is easily converted to goods and services is defined as a unit of account.

3. If money was eliminated from the economy, people would most likely turn to bartering before establishing a new type of money.

4. While bartering makes indirect transactions possible, money makes the more difficult, direct transactions possible.

5. The gold standard adopted by the United States is an example of fiat money.

6. The three types of demand for money discussed in this chapter are disposable, speculative, and precautionary demand.

7. Money supply is determined by the U.S. Congress, and regulated by the Federal Reserve.

8. *M1* includes currency plus traveler's checks, savings deposits, demand deposits, OCDs, and credit union share draft accounts.

9. *M3* includes *M2* plus large time deposits, repurchase agreements, Eurodollars, and institution-only money market mutual fund balances.

10. With a large reserve requirement, more money can be created by banks in the economy.

Short Answer/Essay Questions

1. Describe the functions of money.

2. What is fiat money? What is commodity money?

3. Who controls the money supply, and how?

4. What are the three functions of money? Which of the functions do the following items satisfy? Which do they not satisfy?
    a. A credit card

    b. A painting by Rembrandt

    c. A subway token

5. Explain how credit cards and debit cards affect the money supply in the economy.

6. Assume a required reserve ratio of 10 percent. A check for $80,000 is drawn on an account in Bank One and deposited in a demand deposit in Bank Two.

   a. How much have the excess reserves of Bank Two increased?

   b. How much in the form of new loans is Bank Two now able to extend to borrowers?

   c. By how much have reserves of Bank One decreased?

   d. By how much have excess reserves of Bank One decreased?

   e. The money supply has increased by how much?

7. If the required reserve ratio is 10 percent, what will be the maximum change in the money supply in each of the following situations?

   a. Ms. Cruz deposits in Bank Two a check drawn on Bank Three?

   b. Ms. Cruz buys a $5000 U.S. government bond from the Fed by drawing on her checking account.

   c. Ms. Cruz sells a $10,000 U.S. government bond to the Fed and deposits the $10,000 in Bank Three?

   d. Ms. Cruz finds $2,000 in coins and paper currency buried in her backyard and deposits that money in her checking account.

The Federal Reserve and Monetary Policy

Aaron Kohr/ Shutterstock.com

OBJECTIVES

1. To explain the role of the Federal Reserve in the U.S. monetary and financial system.
2. To describe the historical background in the creation of the Federal Reserve.
3. To describe the major functions of the Federal Reserve.
4. To explain the different tools/instruments of monetary policy.
5. To describe the reasons and implications of the current financial crisis.

The Central Bank of the United States

Every country has a **central bank**, a monetary authority that is in charge of monetary policy. The central bank is also responsible for monitoring and supervising banks and other financial intermediaries to assure that they function soundly.

In Japan, it is the Bank of Japan, in Germany the central bank is the Bundesbank, and in England it is the Bank of England. In England, the central bank is under the direct control of the government and, as such, is an instrument of government policy. In others, the central bank is a quasi-independent organization that carries out its own economic policies free from government intervention. In the United States, as mentioned in the previous chapter, the central bank is the Federal Reserve (Poole, 1992).

History of the Federal Reserve

In many nations, centralized control of the banking system goes back several centuries (Federal Bank of Atlanta, 1984). But in the United States, it is a relatively recent development. Because the founding fathers felt that a central bank would put too much power into too few hands, no provision was made for one in the Constitution. This led to many problems during the 1800s, when the money supply consisted primarily of notes issued by individual banks. Unless the bank was nearby, there was no way of knowing if a bank note was worth much more than the paper it was printed on. As a consequence, there were frequent runs on banks, which forced them either to call in their loans or close. By the early 1900s, and especially after the bank panic of 1907, it became clear that the country needed a central authority to regulate the banking system. Thus, in 1913 the Congress passed the Federal Reserve Act, which established the Federal Reserve Bank as the nation's central monetary authority.

The Federal Reserve comprises its headquarters in Washington DC and 12 regional branches located in major metropolitan areas around the country. Together they carry on a number of different housekeeping functions for the nation's 12,400 commercial banks, including acting as a clearinghouse for checks. The Federal Reserve Bank of New York is by far the largest branch, mostly because many of the nation's largest banks are located there. This is why they are called "money center" banks.

According to a Federal Reserve Bank publication "membership in the Federal Reserve System is voluntary, except for national banks, which are required by law to be members; state-chartered banks are admitted upon application if they meet certain requirements. Member banks subscribe to Federal Reserve Bank stock in the amount of 6 percent of their own capital and surplus. At the end of the year, the member banks receive a cumulative dividend of 6 percent of their paid-in stock.

The member banks do not, however, have the other rights and privileges normally associated with stock ownership." The Federal Reserve System is self-sustaining and is not dependent upon appropriations by the Federal Government. Income is derived primarily from interest on U.S. government securities that the Fed has acquired through open-market operations, one of the tools of monetary policy. While not operated for profit, the Federal Reserve Banks pay their own way, and turn over all earnings over and above the amount required to maintain a surplus equal to their paid-in capital to the Treasury of the United States.

The Nature of the Federal Reserve

The Fed is administered by a board of governors consisting of seven members, one of whom is the chairperson. The chairperson is appointed for a four-year term, renewable at the discretion of the U.S. president. The other six members are appointed by the president (with the consent of the Congress) for 14-year terms but are not eligible for reappointment. This means that the Fed has considerable independence, but it is not totally immune to political influence. For example, all members of the Federal Reserve Board during 1992 were appointed by Republican presidents.

The Federal Reserve Bank performs five major functions:

1. It serves as a **clearinghouse** for the collection of checks for its member banks, and, since 1980, for all banks in the country. This is a monumental task involving some 52 billion checks a year. Checks are cleared through an electronic transfer system, which debits and credits different banks' accounts. The checks are then returned to the issuing banks, where, in most cases, they end up in an envelope with your monthly bank statement.

2. It holds member banks' reserves on deposit as required by law. In 1990 it held some $40 billion in deposits, representing about half of the commercial bank reserves in the United States. Banks hold the rest as vault cash.

3. It performs a **supervisory** and regulatory function in the sense that it examines banks periodically to ensure that they are conforming to regulations and maintaining financial stability.

4. It acts as the **fiscal agent** for the federal government, that is, as the government's bank. Tax receipts, for example, are deposited with the Fed, and the Fed acts as agent for issuing government bonds.

5. Finally, and most importantly, the Fed controls and manages the nation's money supply. This is done through the operations of the Federal Open Market Committee.

Tools of Monetary Policy

The reason the Federal Reserve Bank is so powerful is that it has number of policy tools at its disposal with which it can influence economic activity. It can, for example, affect banks' ability to make loans and create money. In doing so, the Fed influences the level of interest rates, which affects almost everyone's purchasing and investment decisions.

The first tool of monetary policy is the **open-market operation**. Open-market operations are the purchases and sales of government bonds conducted by the Federal Open Market Committee (FOMC). Open-market operations are the policy instrument that the Fed uses most often. In fact, the Fed conducts open-market operations in New York bond markets almost every weekday. The FOMC can increase or decrease the amount of reserves available to banks—and therefore, the supply of money—by buying or selling U.S. Treasury bonds on the open bond market.

The Federal Reserve's open-market operations are easier to understand if you first think about a private individual buying or selling a federal bond in the financial markets. What happens if you decide to buy a Treasury bond? First, you go to a bank or directly to a bond dealer. You purchase the bond—let's say a $1,000 Series E Treasury bond—and pay for it with a check. When the check clears and the transaction is complete, your checking account balance is reduced by $1,000 and the bond dealer's account is increased by the same amount. But the net effect on the money supply is a wash—zero.

Now, let's suppose that the Federal Reserve Bank does the same thing. Where does the Fed go to buy a government bond? To the same place you did, a bond dealer. The Fed then writes a check to the dealer, who deposits it in his checking account. At that point, however, something magical happens. The bond dealer's account is increased by the amount of the purchase (which is often in the millions of dollars), so the dealer's bank has considerably more reserves to loan out than it did before. But nothing changes in anyone else's account, or in any other bank's reserves. Why? Because the Federal Reserve issued the check and there is no other account to charge it against.

When the check clears the bond dealer's bank, it is then returned to the Fed, and the Fed, in essence, simply files it away. As a result, bank reserves are increased by the amount of the Fed's bond purchase, the process of multiple expansion of deposits begins, and the money supply is increased accordingly. But there's more. When bank reserves are increased, banks have more funds available to loan. When the supply of anything is increased, its price falls. Since interest is the price of loanable funds, the eventual effect of the Fed increasing the money supply through open-market operations is to lower interest rates. This is reflected first in the federal funds rate because banks with excess reserves are now eager to lend them to other banks, and the competition forces rates down. The effect of the increase in the money supply shows up later in other interest rates, such as the **prime rate** (the rate banks charge their most creditworthy customers), other business loan rates, and mortgage rates.

Depending on its perceptions of the economic climate the FOMC can, of course, reverse this process and sell bonds in the open market. If the Federal Reserve sells bonds (or anything, for that matter), it receives a check from the bond dealer and clears it. This has the effect of reducing reserves at the dealer's bank, reducing the money supply (as the money creation process works in reverse), and raising interest rates due to the short supply of money.

The second policy the Fed can use to influence the economy is called the **discount rate**. The discount rate is the interest rate that the Fed charges when it makes loans to banks. Banks borrow from the Fed when they find themselves with too few reserves to meet reserve requirements. The lower the discount rate, the cheaper it is to borrow reserves. Hence, a reduction in the discount rate raises the monetary base and the money supply.

More often, when faced with short-term reserve deficiencies banks borrow from each other, usually on an "overnight" basis. The interest rate on such loans is called the **federal funds rate** (even though the federal government is not involved at all in the process). Because the availability of excess reserves to loan in the federal funds market is an important factor in banks' ability to extend credit, the federal funds rate is a much more useful indicator of Federal Reserve activities in the money market than is the discount rate. The Fed does use the discount rate to indicate its intentions, however, and changes it with some frequency. Also, it is important to note that the discount rate sets a floor below which interest rates will never fall because banks always have the option of borrowing from the Fed "discount window."

The third policy is called the **reserve requirement**. Reserve requirements are Fed regulations that impose on banks a minimum reserve–deposit ratio. An increase in reserve requirements raises the reserve–deposit ratio and thus lowers the money multiplier and the money supply. Changes in reserve requirements are the least frequently used of the Fed's three policy instruments.

A change in the amount of reserves banks are required to hold significantly affects their ability to extend loans and create new deposits. If the reserve requirement is 10 percent, then a new deposit in a bank can (theoretically) generate 10 times the amount of the deposit in new money as it shuffles around the banking system. If the reserve requirement is lowered to 5 percent, then the new deposit can expand 20 times. Consequently, adjusting reserve requirements can be a powerful influence on economic activity. Of course, such adjustments, especially when reserve requirements are increased, can be a rather traumatic experience for banks. Increased reserve requirements not only limit a bank's ability to generate new loans, but may require it to call in some existing loans, which can create problems for borrowers, to put it mildly. Such actions are not popular with banks and generate little enthusiasm in the business community. The reserve requirement has been changed just twice, once in the 1970s and once in 1983. In 1990, however, the reserve requirement for large commercial long-term deposits was eliminated, freeing up some $14 billion in new credit. Then, in 1992, the reserve requirement for checking account deposits was reduced to 10 percent.

The Fed in Action

As we've discussed, the Fed acts as a lender of last resort to commercial banks. This was seen in March 2008 when Bear Stearns, the world's fifth-largest investment bank, basically ran out of liquidity. J. P. Morgan, another investment bank stepped in and made an initial offer of $236 million to acquire Bear Stearns, whereas the Federal Reserve was initially going to bail out Bear Stearns in the amount of $30 billion. The end result was that J. P. Morgan paid $1 billion to acquire Bear Stearns, and the Fed paid the $29 billion difference. Why did the Fed step in and not let the market handle this situation? The Fed's unusual intervention was motivated by a concern that a rapid and disorderly failure of Bear Stearns would wreak havoc on the markets in which the firm is an intermediary, particularly the huge and important securities-repurchase, or "repo" market (Sidel, Berman, & Kelly, 2008).

Bear Stearns risked defaulting on these repo loans. If that happened, other securities dealers would find their access to repo loans restricted. The pledged securities behind those loans could be dumped in a fire sale, deepening the plunge in securities prices.

Theory to Application
Bank Failures and the Money Supply in the 1930s

Between August 1929 and March 1933 the money supply fell 28 percent (Mankiw, 2007). Some economists believe this large decline in the money supply was the primary cause of the Great Depression. Why was it that the money supply fell so dramatically?

The three variables that determine the money supply—the monetary base, the reserve–deposit ratio, and the currency–deposit ratio—are shown in Table 13.1 for 1929 and 1933. You can see that the fall in the money supply cannot be attributed to a fall in the monetary base: in fact, the monetary base rose 18 percent over this period. Instead, the money supply fell because the money multiplier fell 38 percent. The money multiplier fell because the currency–deposit and reserve–deposit ratios both rose substantially.

Table 13.1 The Money Supply and Its Determinants: 1929 and 1933

	August 1929	March 1933
Money Supply	26.5	19.0
Currency	3.9	5.5
Demand deposits	22.6	13.5
Monetary Base	7.1	8.4
Curreny	3.9	5.5
Reserves	3.2	2.9
Money Multiplier	3.7	2.3
Reserve-deposit ratio	0.14	0.21
Currency-deposit ratio	0.17	0.41

Source: Adapted from Milton Friedman and Anna Schwartz, *A Monetary History of the United States, 1867–1960* (Princeton, N.J.: Princeton University Press, 1963), Appendix A.

Most economists attribute the fall in the money multiplier to the large number of bank failures in the early 1930s. From 1930 to 1933, more than 9,000 banks suspended operations, often defaulting on their depositors. The bank failures caused the money supply to fall by altering the behavior of both depositors and bankers.

Bank failures raised the currency–deposit ratio by reducing public confidence in the banking system. People feared that bank failures would continue, and they began to view currency as a more desirable form of money than demand deposits. When they withdrew their deposits, they drained the banks of reserves. The process of money creation reversed itself as banks responded to lower reserves by reducing their outstanding balance of loans.

The fourth policy the Fed can use to influence the economy is called **moral suasion**. This involves persuading banks to implement the Federal Reserve's policy. For example, if the Fed wants to sell bonds to the public in order to limit money supply, they can simply ask banking institutions to buy the bonds. In this way, they can limit the amount of money circulating in the public.

The U.S. Financial Crisis of 2008

The recent financial crisis in the United States has impacted the nation and the global economy, in a way not seen in many decades. As of this writing, the nation's GDP growth rate has decline over 6 percent and the unemployment rate has gone up to over 9 percent. This recession has been ongoing for almost 17 months, which is over the classic definition of what a recession is. The question that we need to ask is what causes this recent crisis? How has the government address this problem? What is the role of the monetary policy in addressing these problems? What kind of innovations were implemented in order to alleviate this problem?

In the early part of 2008, there were big banking/insurance institutions that made headlines that triggered this crisis. When Bear Stearns and Lehman Brothers filed for bankruptcy, it started the whole series of events that lead to this mayhem of financial fiascoes. Let us examine carefully the reason behind the fall of these two institutions. Bear Stearns and Lehman Brothers are big investment banking institutions that provides capital for businesses. They are not the usual commercial banks that we see in the corner street as their main purpose is merely provide capital to the business sectors. Other services that they provide includes financial products such as credit default swaps (CDS) and other derivatives that are use in order to manage risk more efficiently. These investment houses buy all mortgages and package them into a collateralized debt obligations (CDOs) and eventually sell them in the global financial markets. These CDOs are assumed to be safe because they are backed up by mortgages and real estate properties. The process of packaging these mortgage loans into a collateralized debt obligation is called *securitization*. However, some of these mortgages are considered "subprime" mortgages. Subprime mortgage are mortgage that are given to unqualified borrowers. Some of these mortgages turned out to be bad loans because the borrowers defaulted. As these banks realized the effects of these bad loans in their financial statements, investors' confidence dropped significantly. These financial products are insured by another institution called AIG (American Insurance Group). AIG is a global insurance company that insures global financial products. As the value of their financial products decline, the value of the AIG's credit rating decreases, too. Huge amount of losses were incurred by AIG as the financial crisis unfolds.

As these events unfolded, the negative ripple effect in the economy began to roll out. Businesses began to shrink, consumer confidence fell, and the whole economy declined. The government has introduced new forms of monetary instruments to reduce the effects of an economic meltdown. The Federal Reserve lowered the interest rate to almost as low as zero to ease up the credit market.

The Federal Reserve introduced new instruments while this economic crisis unfolded. These new instruments include the following:

1. **Term Asset Lending Facility (TALF):** The purpose of TALF is to extend credit to consumers through student loans, auto loans, and small businesses. Its main objective is to give capital to banks in order to unthaw the credit market.

2. **Term Securities Lending Facility (TSLF):** This was recently introduced by the Federal Reserve to promote liquidity in the

financing markets for Treasury and other collateral. It allows the dealer with a trading relationship with the Federal Reserve (so-called primary dealers), to bid a fee to borrow a certain quantity of Treasury securities from the Fed to 28 days, while agreeing to provide securities as collateral. Dealers can then use the borrowed securities as collateral to obtain cash in the private market.

3. **Term Auction Facility (TAF):** This was a temporary program instituted by the Federal Reserve to alleviate the pressures of short-term funding as a result of the credit crunch that occurred in 2008. The credit crunch resulted from the increasing spread between the rate for overnight loans and the interbank rates. Under this program, the Fed auctions collateralized loans on a short-term basis to depository institutions that are generally in sound financial conditions. This program was also instituted by the Bank of England, Bank of Canada, the European Central Bank, and the Swiss National Bank.

In more recent news, the Secretary of the Treasury Timothy Geithner proposed a public-private investment program to deal with the toxic assets within the financial institutions. The new public-private investment program will set up funds to provide a market for the legacy loans and securities that currently burden the financial system. The program will purchase real estate–related loans from banks and securities from the broader markets. Banks will have the ability to sell pools of loans to dedicated funds, and investors will compete to have the ability to participate in those funds and take advantage of the financing provided by the government. The funds established under this program will have three essential design features. First, they will use government resources in the form of capital from the Treasury and financing from the FDIC and Federal Reserve to mobilize capital from private investors. Second, the public-private investment program will ensure that private-sector participants share the risks alongside the taxpayer, and that the taxpayer shares in the profits from these investments. Third, private-sector purchasers will establish the value of the loans and securities purchased under the program that will protect the government from overpaying for these assets. The impact of this program remains to be seen as it gets implemented in the future.

The Future of Financial Regulation

Because banks can offer their customers government-insured deposits and can borrow from the Federal Reserve, they have access to funds regardless of their level of risk. While other creditors would deny funds to a high-risk bank, insured depositors care little about the level of risk of their bank since they are protected from loss. Absent active supervision, loans from the Federal Reserve might also provide funds to high-risk banks. In certain circumstances, banks have a strongly perverse incentive to take excessive risk with taxpayer-guaranteed funds. This incentive results from the oft-discussed "moral-hazard" problem related to deposit insurance. Depositors are protected from loss by government-provided insurance. As a result they ignore bank riskiness when choosing which banks hold deposits. Banks, in turn, undertake riskier behavior when deciding which banks to hold their deposits. Banks, in turn, undertake riskier investments than they would if there no deposit insurance because they know there is no depositor-imposed penalty for doing so (Pellerin, Walter, & Wescott, 2009).

With the current financial crisis that is happening around the world, a call for an overhaul of the financial regulation became more evident. The purpose of this new proposed regulation is to avoid any form of systemic risk. Systemic risk is the risk involved in a failing financial institution that can possibly lead to a banking or financial systemwide problem. If the government failed to intervene to protect the liability holders of large, troubled institution, the financial difficulties of that institution might spread more widely. Intervention is more likely to flow to financial than to nonfinancial firms because of the interconnectedness of financial firms. For example, the list of creditors of a large financial institution typically includes other large financial institutions. Therefore, the failure of one financial institution may well lead to problems at others, or at least a reduction in lending by the institutions which are exposed to the failed institution. An instance of this occurred when Lehman Brothers' September 2008 bankruptcy led to large withdrawals from mutual funds, especially from those with significant holdings of Lehman commercial paper.

Reduced lending by firms directly exposed to a failed firm can produce problems for other financial firms. Financial firms' balance sheets often contain significant maturity mismatches—long-term assets funded by short-term liabilities. As a result, firms that normally borrow from an institution that reduced lending because of its exposure to a failed firm will be forced to seek other sources of funding to continue to fund its long-term assets. If many firms are exposed to the failed firm, then the supply of funds will decline, interest rates will rise, and sales of assets at fire-sale prices may result. Reduced lending by other institutions will tend to exacerbate weak economic conditions that often accompany the failure of a large financial institution. In such circumstances, policymakers are highly likely to provide financial aid to a large troubled institution known as "too-big-too fail (TBTF)." Because of this tendency, supervisors have reason to monitor the risk taking of large financial institutions (Pellerin, Walter, & Wescott, 2009).

References

Federal Bank of Atlanta. (1984, December). *Structure of the Federal Reserve*.

Mankiw, N. G. (2007). *Macroeconomics* (6th ed.). New York: Worth Publishers, 517.

Pellerin, S. R., Walter, J. R., & Wescott, P. (2009, May). The consolidation of financial market regulation: Pros, cons, and implications for the United States. The Federal Reserve Banks of Richmond.

Poole, J. C. (1992). *The ABC's of money and banking*. Winchester, VA: The Durrell Institute of Monetary Science, Shenandoah University.

Sidel, R., Berman, D. K., & Kelly, K. J. P. (2008, March 17). Morgan rescues bear Stearns. *The Wall Street Journal*, 1, A12.

'Sterilized' Bond Buying! is an Option for the Fed

By Jon Hilsenrath

Federal Reserve Officials are considering a new type of bond-buying program designed to subdue worries about future inflation if they decide to take new steps to boost the economy in the months ahead.

Under the new approach, the Fed would print new money to buy long-term mortgage or Treasury bonds but effectively tie up that money by borrowing it back for short periods at low rates. The aim of such an approach would be relieve anxieties that money printing could fuel inflation later, a fear widely expressed by critics of the Fed's previous efforts to aid the recovery.

Fed officials are set to meet next week and have signaled they are unlikely to launch new programs at that meeting. Moreover, it is far from certain the Fed will launch another program later on. If growth or inflation pick up much, officials seem unlikely to launch a bond-buying program because the economy might not need the extra help or because doing more could spur higher inflation. But if growth disappoints or inflation slows substantially, Fed officials might at some point deride to act again.

The Fed's approach to a bond-buying program matters a lot to many investors. More money printing could push commodities and stock prices up, or send the dollar lower, if it sparks a perception among investors that inflation is moving higher, said Michael Feroli, an economist with J.P. Morgan Chase. (The Fed news was cited as a reason stocks rose Wednesday.) However, if the Fed chooses a course aimed at restraining inflation expectations, the impact on those markets might be more muted.

Fed officials have used different types of bond-buying programs since 2008. In each case, the aim has been to drive down long-term interest rates to spur investment and spending by businesses and households. In case they decide to act again, they are exploring three approaches, according to people familiar with the matter. Those approaches are:

- First, they could use the method they used from 2008 into 2011, in which the Fed effectively printed money and used it to purchase Treasury securities and mortgage debt. The Fed already has acquired more than $2.3 trillion worth of securities in several rounds of purchases using this approach, widely known as quantitative easing, or QE.

Heard on the Street Long road when central banks unwind.

- Second, the Fed could reprise a program launched last year in which it is selling short-term Treasury securities and using the proceeds to buy long-term bonds. This $400 billion program, known as Operation Twist, allows the Fed to buy bonds without creating new money.

- Third, in the new approach, the Fed could print money to buy long-term bonds, but restrict how investors and banks use that money by using new market tools they have designed to better manage cash sloshing around in the financial system. This is known as "sterilized" QE.

The Fed's objectives under any of these program would be to reduce the holdings of long-term securities in the hands of investors and banks. The Fed believes that reducing the amount of long-term bonds in the hands of investors drives down long-term interest rates, encourages more risk-taking, and thus spurs spending and investment by households and businesses.

The differences between the three approaches involve when the money comes from and where it ends up. The Fed hasn't literally printed more money, but it has electronically credited the accounts of banks and investors with new money when it purchased their bonds under quantitative easing. The Fed has pumped more than $1.6 trillion in new money into the financial system this way and also has rejiggered its existing holdings, as part of its bond-buying efforts.

Many Fed officials believe the bank reserves it has devised as part of this money creation aren't an inflation threat. But they are acutely aware of a popular perception, also held by a few inside the Fed itself, that the money the Fed has created could cause an inflation problem down the road.

An approach that limits the amount of new money flowing into the system, through another Operation Twist or a sterilized operation, could help them manage that perception.

Under the third approach, the Fed would create new money as it buys long-term bonds. But then it would effectively lock up the money rather than letting it loose in the broader economy. The Fed would do this by borrowing the money back from investors for short periods—say, 28 days—in exchange for a low interest rate it would pay investors.

Transactions like those under the third scenario are called "reverse repos."

Definitions

1. Central Bank

2. Clearing house

3. Supervisory function

4. Fiscal agent

5. Open market operation

6. Prime rate

7. Federal funds rate

8. Reserve requirement

9. Moral suasion

10. Discount rate

Multiple Choice

1. The transactions demand for money is most closely related to the function of money as
   a. a unit of account.
   b. a medium of exchange.
   c. a store of purchasing power.
   d. a hedge against inflation.
   e. a standard of deferred payment.

2. The desire to keep assets in cash to take advantage of favorable changes in the value of noncash assets is called the
   a. speculative demand for money.
   b. wealth demand for money.
   c. risk interest in money.
   d. precautionary demand for money.
   e. transactions demand for money.

3. If interest rates increase
   a. the quantity of money demanded will increase.
   b. the quantity of money demanded will not change.
   c. the money demand function will shift to the right.
   d. the quantity of money demanded will decrease.
   e. the opportunity cost of holding bonds.

4. The interest rates represent
   a. the opportunity cost of holding money.
   b. the market demand for bonds.
   c. the index of creditworthiness for investors.
   d. the transactions demand for money.
   e. the opportunity cost of holding bonds.

5. Bank of Sun City has $800 million in deposits. The required reserve ratio is 20 percent. Bank of Sun city must keep _____ in reserves
   a. $70 million
   b. $700 million
   c. $140 million
   d. $160 million

6. Bank A has $100 million in reserves. Bank A is meeting its reserve requirement and has no excess reserves. The required reserve ratio is 20 percent. Bank A's demand deposit are:
   a. $120 million
   b. $200 million
   c. $500 million
   d. $600 million

7. The difference between a bank's total reserves and its required reserve is its
   a. excess reserves.
   b. required reserve ratio.
   c. profit margin.
   d. net worth.

8. In the United States, monetary policy is formally set by the
   a. Federal Open Market Committee.
   b. Council of Economic Advisors.
   c. Department of the Treasury.
   d. Office of Management and Budget.

9. Which of the following activities is not one of the responsibilities of the Federal Reserve?
   a. Clearing interbank payments
   b. Regulating the banking system
   c. Managing exchange rates
   d. Administering the federal tax code

10. Which of the following is not used by the Federal Reserve to change the money supply?
    a. The federal tax code
    b. The required reserve ratio
    c. The discount rate
    d. Open market operations

Resources

Principles of Macroeconomics Case & Fair

Economics Boyles/Melvin

True/False

Directions: For the following statements, indicate whether the statement is true or false. If the statement is false, make the necessary change(s) in order for it to be a true statement.

1. Money supply is controlled by local banks (lenders) and bank customers (borrowers).

2. Monetary policy in the United States is controlled by the Congress.

3. The different types of money supply include currency, M_1, M_2, and M_3.

4. The reserve ratio is defined as the amount of money banks can lend to customers and is set by the federal government.

5. The main functions of the regional Federal Reserve banks are to manage check clearing and to supervise banking and financial activities in the district.

6. The chairperson of the Federal Reserve reports to the President of the United States and the Congress.

7. The main tool to control money supply used by the Fed is setting and changing the reserve ratio.

8. The discount rate is the rate set by the Federal Reserve when lending money to other banks.

9. Moral suasion is the attempt to get local banks to adopt Federal Reserve policies.

10. According to information presented in this chapter, most economists believe passive Fed policies in the 1930s were the main cause of the major decrease in the money supply.

Chapter 14

International Trade

Anyka/Shutterstock.com

OBJECTIVES

1. To explain the basis of international trade.
2. To describe the law of absolute advantage.
3. To explain the law of comparative advantage.
4. To define the meaning of tariff.
5. To understand the reasons why tariffs are imposed.
6. To discuss the different types of tariffs.
7. To explain the economic implication of an import quota.

Chances are at least some of the clothing you're wearing right now bears a "Made in China" label. Software programmers in India probably wrote or debugged parts of the computer software you'll use for your studies this semester. If you ate a banana as a before-class snack, it probably came from Central America (if you are in the United States) or from Africa or the Caribbean (if you are in the European Union). And even if you think you drive a domestically produced car, at least some of the car's components almost certainly were produced in far-off locations. So you already have lots of day-to-day experience with **international trade**, even if you have never studied it. International trade has a big effect on your everyday life—probably bigger than you realize. International trade provides you with a wider variety of goods and services plus lower prices for those products than you could possibly enjoy without it. It also makes you interdependent in complex ways with clothing workers in China, programmers in India, banana growers in Ecuador, Cameroon, and St. Lucia, and automobile producers from Mexico to the Philippines.

Understanding international trade—what it is, how it works, why we do it, and how policymakers treat it—is absolutely essential to understanding today's world economy. Discussions of new degrees and even new types of international economic interdependence fill the news, and rapidly expanding international trade is one important reason. The fact that no nation is an economic island has never been more obvious. Citizens of many countries feel increasingly affected by external economic events over which they, and sometimes their national policymakers, exert less-than-total control. Many of the major economic stories that occupy newspaper headlines are stories about trade-related interdependence, its ramifications, and policymakers' and citizens' attempts to come to terms with it.

International trade is one of the most important topics in economics. The world is getting smaller over time because of technology. Goods and services can easily be shipped from one end of the globe to another any time of day. The percentage of exports and imports for the United States has been constantly increasing relative to GDP. In this chapter we will see the importance of international trade to the United States and to the world in general.

Why International Trade?

There are many reasons why international trade exists. One major reason is that different countries have different productive capabilities and resources. Different factor endowments can lead to different products and specialization of goods and services. For example, Saudi Arabia has an abundant amount of oil but scarce food resources. Saudi Arabia can export oil because they have an abundance of it, while they have to import food.

If international trade exists between two countries, then everyone benefits from this transaction. The reason is that international trade can lead to specialization that can make production more efficient (cost effective). Thus, both countries can produce more of the product in which they are specializing, causing an increase in overall global production. International trade can be looked at as international microeconomics; as you will see through your studies of international trade, many of the topics covered in microeconomics (such as the production possibilities curve and budget constraints) are also used to analyze international trade.

Theories of International Trade

Theory of Absolute Advantage

The theory of **absolute advantage** was formulated by Adam Smith in his book *The Wealth of Nations* (1776). According to this theory, countries should trade goods where they have an absolute lower cost or absolute higher production.

	Wheat (per bushel)	Wine (per gallon)
United States	100	50
France	50	40

In this model, we assume there are only two countries—the United States and France—producing both wheat and wine. The United States produces 100 bushels of wheat and 50 gallons of wine. France produces 50 bushels of wheat and 40 gallons of wine. Using the concept of absolute advantage, the United States has an absolute advantage in producing both wheat and wine because it can produce more of both wheat and wine. France, on the other hand, has an **absolute disadvantage** in producing both wheat and wine.

As you can see, there is no basis for trade in this example because the United States can produce more of both commodities in absolute terms. In the 19th century, economist David Ricardo formulated another theory of international trade, known as comparative advantage.

Theory of Comparative Advantage

The theory of *comparative advantage* refers to the ability of a country to produce a good at a lower opportunity cost, compared to the opportunity cost of other goods, than other countries with whom they trade.

Based on our previous example, instead of taking the production in absolute terms, we can take the relative cost of producing the commodity in each country. For example, we can ask ourselves, how much does it cost to produce a bushel of wheat in the United States? Because we do not have any prices (just output), we simply express it in terms of how much wine are we giving up to produce more wheat. Thus, we simply take the ratio of the production of wine relative to the production of wheat, which is 50/100, or ½, gallon of wine to produce a bushel of wheat. In France, on the other hand, it cost 40/50, or 4/5, gallon of wine to produce a bushel of wheat. Therefore, it is much more expensive to produce a bushel of wheat in France than in the United States.

One implication of this theory is that countries can specialize in producing the commodity where they have a comparative advantage. In our example, the United States has a comparative advantage in producing wheat, while France has a comparative advantage in producing wine. Therefore, the United States can specialize in producing wheat, France can specialize in wine production, and both countries can trade, leading to a greater amount of consumption of both goods as opposed to the countries producing those goods in **autarky** (the case of self-sufficiency, or no trade).

Tariffs

A **tariff** is a tax imposed on a good as it crosses a national boundary. Historically, tariffs were the most commonly used type of trade restriction; in recent years, however, use of tariffs has declined, and use of other trade restrictions has increased. Average tariff levels have fallen both in the United States and abroad, largely as a result of international negotiations conducted under the General Agreement on Tariffs and Trade (GATT), now called the World Trade Organization (WTO), a forum created for international negotiation of trade issues.

Why Would a Country Impose a Tariff?

A country might impose a tariff for any of four reasons. First, a tariff, like any tax, discourages consumption of a particular good. Placing a tariff on an imported good makes that good more costly to consumers. For example, during the OPEC oil price increases of the 1970s, many policymakers proposed a tariff on oil imports; proponents argued that the United States needed to reduce its consumption of oil, particularly foreign oil, and that a tariff presented one possible incentive.

A second reason for imposing a tariff, like any tax, is to generate government revenue. Developed countries rarely impose tariffs specifically to raise revenue because those countries have the infrastructure necessary to administer other taxes, such as personal and corporate income taxes. Many developing countries, however, still use tariffs to raise a significant share of the revenue needed to finance their governments' activities. Administration of an income tax requires a well-developed and effective bureaucracy, as well as a literate and settled population; countries lacking one or more of these requisites find it easier to administer tariffs by patrolling ports and national borders.

A third reason for imposing import tariffs is to discourage imports to eliminate a balance-of-trade deficit (that is, a situation in which payments to foreigners for imports exceed receipts from foreigners for exports; we'll discuss this more in the next chapter). A country designing a tariff to reduce a trade deficit would apply the tariff to all imports, or at least to a broad range of goods, rather than to a single good or a narrow range of goods. This motive involves tariffs as a tool of *macroeconomic* rather than *microeconomic* policy, so we won't focus on this motive here. However, tariffs aren't an effective method of reducing a balance-of-trade deficit, and proper use of other macroeconomic policy tools makes tariffs for balance-of-trade purposes unnecessary.

The fourth and most common purpose of tariffs is as a **protectionist policy**—a way to protect or insulate a domestic industry from competition by foreign producers of the same good. A protective tariff allows domestic producers to both capture a larger share of the domestic market and charge a higher price than would otherwise be possible.

Countries impose many more tariffs on imports than on exports, especially developed countries that don't use tariffs as a major source of government revenue. In fact, the U.S. Constitution makes export taxes illegal in the United States.

Tariffs are imposed in order to protect cottage industries so they can develop and eventually compete in the world market. However, problems arise if the industries that a country is protecting are industries for which the country has no comparative advantage. It is worthwhile protecting local industries if there is a comparative advantage in producing these particular commodities. Otherwise, it is not.

Another purpose for tariffs is to stop the lowering of the standard of living. For example, in the United States jobs are being transferred to Mexico because labor is cheaper in Mexico. In parts of the country where the industry is the sole employer, people may have a rather difficult time looking finding a new job. Tariffs can prevent these jobs from moving south of the border.

For proponents advocating free trade (meaning no tariffs), the main argument is that the market is more efficient when taxes are not imposed. Any kind of tax is considered a distortion to the market. An imposition of a tariff results in a temporary increase in price of the commodity. This increase in price is artificial and not brought by market forces. In this scenario, both the producer and the consumer assume the burden of the tax. An increase in price leads the producer to use its domestic resources to produce a much more expensive domestic product. An increase in price leads to a decrease in consumption for the consumer.

Theory to Application
Making Cheap Medicine Expensive

The Anopheles mosquito carries the protozoan parasite that causes malaria. Experts estimate that between 1 million and 2 million Africans, mostly children, die of malaria each year. In fact, 90 percent of world-wide deaths from malaria occur in sub-Saharan Africa. No effective malaria vaccine exists; most treatments work only in the short run and have serious side effects. Insecticide-treated bed nets provide one of the few effective precautions against contracting malaria. Studies conducted in Africa conclude that bed net use can reduce childhood malaria deaths by almost one-third. Bed nets sell in world markets for about $2.50, so surely everyone in malaria-prone areas uses nets. Right?

Wrong. Governments tariffed imported bed nets, raising their price to a level out of reach of many residents of Africa's poorest countries. Fourteen sub-Saharan governments tariffed bed nets at rates of 30 percent or higher, up to Senegal's 65 percent tariff, even though there were no domestic bed net producers to protect. The World Trade Organization has pressured governments to lower their tariffs on bed nets in an effort to control the spread of malaria (*The Economist*, 1998).

Types of Tariffs

There are three types of tariffs: ad-valorem tariffs, specific tariffs, and compound tariffs.

1. **Ad-Valorem tariffs** ("according to value") charge a specified percentage of the value for each unit imported of the tariffed good. For example, the United States imposes a tariff of 2.4 percent of a dog leash's value.

2. **Specific tariffs** charge a specified amount for each unit imported of the tariffed good. For example, the United States charges a tariff of $0.68 per live goat.

3. **Compound tariffs** combine a specific and ad valorem tariff on the same good.[1] This is the most common kind of tariff. It is almost similar to a sales tax; for example, a tariff of $100 per ton of steel plus 50 percent of its value.

Economic Implication of Tariffs

Tariffs are imposed by a third-party sector that reduces the efficiency of the market. Price distortions such as tariffs can be detrimental to the local as well as the world market. The model below can explain why this is the case.

Assume we start with an initial equilibrium at P_e and Q_e. If we designate P_w as the world price, we can see that the potential amount of excess demand ($Q^d - Q^s$) can be imported from the cheaper-producing country. But, with the introduction of the price with tariff (P_t), the gain in efficiency is lowered as a result of a higher price and lower amount of imports. The only sector that benefits from the tariff is the government sector with a gain of □ABCD. Inefficiencies in the market can be seen from the two triangles ΔE and ΔF. These triangles are deadweight losses attributable to inefficiency in both the producer

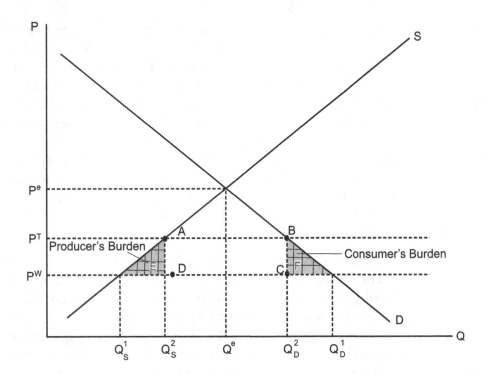

and consumers. The producer's side can be described as inefficient because it costs them a lot more to produce the commodity. From the consumer's side, there is inefficiency because the consumer is paying a higher price and buying a lower quantity of the commodity.

Theory to Application

China, Tariffs, and the WTO

China, one of the fastest-growing parties to trade, wanted to join the World Trade Organization, and began trying to gain entry in 1986. China had helped found the GATT (predecessor to the WTO) in 1947, but the Taiwan-based government had withdrawn in 1950 after the Communists took power on the mainland. In 1986, China applied to resume membership. GATT members ruled that membership couldn't be resumed, but that China could negotiate for accession as a new member. The negotiations proved long (15 years) and acrimonious, in part because of the nonmarket-based nature of China's economy. China wanted to complete accession before January 1, 1995, so it could be a founding member of the WTO, which took effect on that date; but negotiators failed to make the deadline. The results of the Uruguay Round enhanced China's incentive to achieve membership. Member countries agreed to phase out by 2005 the Agreement on Textiles and Clothing, which severely restricted China's textile and apparel exports, but the change would apply only to trade with WTO members.[2]

WTO members claimed that Chinese tariffs were too high, too variable across products, and too opaque for China to become a member. Chinese tariffs rose between 1987 and 1992. The government cut tariffs on more than 3,000 products in 1992, but only to an average rate of about 36 percent. Then Beijing raised tariffs in early 1995 on a list of goods bought primarily by foreigners. Chinese tariff reforms in 1996, shortly after formal WTO accession talks began, lowered average tariff rates from 36 percent to 23 percent, but the new rates remained above those of most members and even most developing countries. Some sectors, such as cars, still carried tariffs of 100 percent or more. And the tariff schedule's opacity remained. For example, the new system required wheat importers, up to "a certain level" of imports, to pay tariffs of 1 percent to 35 percent, while imports above "a certain level" had to pay tariffs of up to 180 percent. But the law failed to disclose the "certain level" (*The Economist*, 1996).

Late in 1997, China made additional concessions to try to win WTO membership. The government reduced its weighted-average tariff from 23 percent to 17 percent by cutting rates on more than 5,000 items, and promised to lower tariffs on all industrial goods to an average of no more than 10 percent by 2005. WTO accession negotiations between China and the United States continued erratically through 1999, and in November of that year the two countries announced successful completion of their bilateral negotiations.[3] China would reduce its tariffs to an average of 9.4 percent overall and to 7.1 percent on U.S. priority products. Auto tariffs, then at 80 to 100 percent, would fall to 25 percent by 2006; tariffs on telecom equipment would end; and agricultural tariffs would be cut from 31.5 percent to 14.5 percent. When the entire package of accession talks finally ended successfully in late 2001, China had promised to cut its tariffs on many products by 2004. By 2010, Chinese bound tariff rates will average 8.9 percent for industrial goods and 14.5 percent for farm products. Chinese consumers will enjoy significant increases in their consumer surplus from the approximately 80 percent drop in tariffs from levels existing in 1986.

Quotas

The simplest and most direct form of nontariff trade barrier is the import quota, a direct restriction on the quantity of a good imported during a specified period. Countries impose quotas for the same reasons they impose import tariffs. As in the case of tariffs, we'll focus on the protection issue: Quotas can protect a domestic industry from foreign competition. Developed countries (e.g., Japan, the United States, and the members of the European Union) have used import quotas primarily to protect agricultural producers. Developing countries, on the other hand, have used quotas on imported manufactured goods to try to stimulate growth of their manufacturing sectors.

There are two types of quotas: import quotas and tariff quotas. An **import quota** puts a limit on the amount or value that can be imported into a country. For example, an import quota could be initiated allowing only 500,000 tons of beef to come into the country in any given year. After that, no more beef may come in until the next quota period.

A **tariff quota**, on the other hand, puts a low tariff, or no tariff, upon goods imported into the country up to a certain amount. After that quota is reached, a higher tariff goes into effect. Tariffs provide revenues, while quotas benefit only those import licenses.

An **embargo** is a unique form of quota where no units of a particular commodity can be imported or, in some cases, exported. For example, the United States placed an export embargo on wheat to Russia in 1981.

A country can choose to place general restrictions on goods imported into or exported from the country in a variety of ways—for example, sanitary regulations, administrative protection, milling regulations, and marks of origin. These practices, in essence, restrict the amount of trade with a given country. The U.S. commercial history shows wide swings between extremely high protective tariffs, such as those used in the 1930s, to the relatively low tariffs in the 1960s and 1970s. In general, vested self-interest groups have lobbied for tariffs, which, though harmful to the country as a whole, can benefit some workers in the protected industries.

The imposition of a quota tends to lower the supply, quantity demanded, and ultimately the price of the importing country, thereby improving its terms of trade. A quota has no limits to its price effect: in contrast, a tariff does have limits to the price effect. Ordinarily, with a tariff, a government gets the price differential; with a quota, the importer gets the price differential. With the imposition of a quota, the availability of the goods demanded is reduced, resulting in a higher price being paid by the consumer. The difference between the competitive price and the higher price is received by the importer.

Theory to Application
Cotton Pits Farmer versus Farmer

For decades, markets for agricultural products in the industrial economies have been among the most highly protected in the world. Successive rounds of GATT/WTO talks either neglected agricultural protection or risked failure by attempting to address it. Uruguay Round, which took the latter course, finally made modest progress by requiring countries to replace many agricultural import quotas with tariffs. In 2002, a massive new U.S. farm bill halted several years of slow progress in reducing the support that distorts agricultural markets. That bill increased subsidies to U.S. farmers by approximately $7.5 billion.

U.S. cotton farmers received much of the subsidy amount. Approximately 25,000 U.S. farmers, with an average net worth of $800,000, raise cotton. Approximately half of their income comes from government subsidies. These subsidies transform the United States, one of the highest-cost cotton producers, into the world's largest cotton exporter and pushes down the world price of cotton. In 2001, even before the 2002 farm bill made the subsidy program still more generous,

U.S. cotton farmers received subsidy payments of approximately $3.4 billion on a 9.74 billion pound crop. With the new farm bill, farmers are now guaranteed approximately $0.70 per pound; when the market price falls below that level, government checks make up the difference (Thurow & Kilman, 2002). The checks allow farmers to plow their 10,000-acre cotton plantations in $125,000 air-conditioned tractors and use $300,000 mechanical pickers to harvest their crop. Other big cotton subsidizers include Spain and Greece, through the EU's Common Agricultural Policy, and China, the world's biggest producer.

Cotton farming in other parts of the world is very different. Ten million rural residents grow cotton in west and central Africa. Estimates suggest they could earn $250 million more per year if the United States stopped its cotton subsidies. Most of the African farmers plant, fertilize, and pick their cotton by hand, perhaps using an aging tractor to plow. In Mali, where per-capita income is $840 per year, cotton farmers received $0.11 per pound for their 2002 crop from the state-owned cotton company (remember, U.S. farmers are guaranteed $0.70 per pound). Other important African producers include Benin, Burkina Faso, and Chad, with annual per-capita incomes in 2002 of $1,020, $1,010, and $1,000 respectively.

In 2003, as part of the preliminary talks for the Doha round of WTO trade negotiations, African cotton producers asked their industrial-country fellow members to agree to a timetable to eliminate their cotton subsidies and, in the meantime, to pay compensation of $250 million per year to the African countries harmed by the subsidies. The talks collapsed over an impasse between the EU, which refused a demand by the United States and many developing countries to negotiate to eliminate all agricultural export subsidies, and developing countries, who refused to talk about issues of interest to the EU without progress on agriculture.

While African cotton producers complained about the damage they suffered from subsidies and asked for compensation, Brazil filed a WTO complaint against the United States. The 2002 complaint alleged that U.S. cotton subsidies distorted international trade in cotton, encouraged excess U.S. production, and pushed down the world price. A study by one economist found that without the subsidies U.S. cotton exports would have fallen by 41 percent between 1999 and 2001 and that the world price of cotton would have been 12.6 percent higher. In early 2004, the WTO issued a preliminary ruling in favor of Brazil. The United States announced its intention to appeal the ruling.

References

Alden, E. (2004, May 21). Cotton report frays the tempers of U.S. farmers, *Financial Times*.

Thurow, R., & Kilman, S. (2002, June 26). In U.S., cotton farmers thrive: In Africa, they fight to survive, *The Wall Street Journal.*

Under new laws (1996, April 13). *The Economist,* 62.

Endnotes

[1]Examples can be found in the U.S. *Harmonized Tariff Schedule,* http://www.usitc.gov/taffairs.htm.

[2]A World Bank study predicted a 375 percent increase in Chinese textile and apparel exports in the first 10 years after WTO entry (see China textiles braced for WTO pain as well as gain, *Financial Times,* August 16, 2001).

[3]Countries negotiating accession to the WTO must reach agreement with all member countries; bilateral negotiations with the United States and the European Union typically take the longest and determine the final outcome.

The Trouble with Outsourcing

Outsourcing is sometimes more hassle than it is worth

Schumpeter

When Ford's River Rouge Plant was completed in 1928 it boasted everything it needed to turn raw materials into finished cars: 100,000 workers. 16m square feet of factory floor, 100 miles of railway track and its own docks and furnaces. Today it is still Ford's largest plant, but only a shadow of its former glory. Most of the parts are made by sub-contractors and merely fitted together by the plant's 6,000 workers. The local steel mill is run by a Russian company, Severstal.

Outsourcing has transformed global business. Over the past few decades companies have contracted out everything from mopping the floors to spotting the flaws in their internet security. TPI, a company that specialises in the sector, estimates that $100 billion-worth of new contracts are signed every year. Oxford Economics reckons that in Britain, one of the world's most mature economies, 10% of workers toil away in "outsourced" jobs and companies spend $200 billion a year on outsourcing. Even war is being outsourced: America employs more contract workers in Afghanistan than regular troops.

Can the outsourcing boom go on indefinitely? And is the practice as useful as its advocates claim, or is the popular suspicion that it leads to cut corners and dismal service correct? There are signs that outsourcing often goes wrong, and that companies are rethinking their approach to it.

The Latest TPI quarterly index of outsourcing (which measures commercial contracts of $25m or more) suggests that the total value of such contracts for the second quarter of 2011 fell by 18% compared with the second quarter of 2010. Dismal figures in the Americas (ie, mostly the United States) dragged down the average: the value of contracts there was 50% lower in the second quarter of 2011 than in the first half of 2010. This is partly explained by America's gloomy economy, but even more by the maturity of the market: TPI suspects that much of what can sensibly be outsourced already has been.

Miles Robinson of Mayer Brown, a law firm, notes that there has also been an uptick in legal disputes over outsourcing. In one case EDS, an IT company, had to pay BSkyB, a media company, £318m ($469m) in damages. The two firms spent an estimated £70m on legal fees and were tied up in court for five months. Such nightmares are worse in India, where the courts move with Dickensian speed, or in China, where the legal system is patchy. And since many disputes stay out of court, the well of discontent with outsourcing is surely deeper than the legal record shows.

Some of the worst business disasters of recent years have been caused or aggravated by outsourcing. Eight years ago Boeing, America's biggest aeroplane-maker, decided to follow the example of car firms and hire contractors to do most of the grunt work on its new 787 Dreamliner. The result was a nightmare. Some of the parts did not fit together. Some of the dozens of sub-contractors failed to deliver their components on time, despite having sub-contracted their work to sub-sub-contractors. Boeing had to take over some of the sub-contractors to prevent them from collapsing. If the Dreamliner starts rolling off the production line towards the end of this year, as Boeing promises, it will be billions over budget and three years behind schedule.

Outsourcing can go wrong in a colourful variety of ways. Sometimes companies squeeze their contractors so hard that they are forced to cut corners. (This is a big problem in the car industry, where a handful of global firms can bully the 80,000 parts-makers.) Sometimes vendors overpromise in order to win a contract and then fail to deliver. Sometimes both parties write sloppy contracts. And some companies undermine their overall strategies with injudicious outsourcing. Service companies, for example, contract out customer complaints to foreign call centres and then wonder why their customers hate them.

When outsourcing goes wrong, it is the devil to put right. When companies outsource a job, they typically eliminate the department that used to do it. They become entwined with their contractors, handing over sensitive material and inviting contractors to work alongside their own staff. Extricating themselves from this tangle can be tough. It is much easier to close a department than to rebuild it. Sacking a contractor can mean that factories grind to a halt, bills languish unpaid and chaos mounts.

So far and no further

None of this means that companies are going to re-embrace the River Rouge model any time soon. Some companies, such as Boeing, are bringing more work back in-house, in the jargon. But the business logic behind outsourcing remains compelling, so long as it is done right. Many tasks are peripheral to a firm's core business and can be done better and more cheaply by specialists. Cleaning is an obvious example; many back-office jobs also fit the bill. Outsourcing firms offer labor arbitrage, using cheap Indians to enter data rather than expensive Swedes. They can offer economies of scale, too. TPI points out that, for all the problems in America, outsourcing is continuing to grow in emerging markets and, more surprisingly, in Europe, where Germany and France are late converts to the idea.

Companies are rethinking outsourcing, rather than jettisoning it. They are dumping huge long-term deals in favour of smaller, less rigid ones. The annualised value of "mega-relationships" worth $100m or more a year fell by 62% this year compared with last. Companies are forming relationships with several outsourcers, rather than putting all their eggs in few baskets. They are signing shorter contracts, too. But still, they need to think harder about what is their core business, and what is peripheral, And above all, newspaper editors need to say no to the temptation to outsource business columns to cheaper, hungrier writers.

Definitions

1. International trade

When one nation makes a transaction involving goods and services with another nation.

2. Absolute advantage

One nation can produce a certain good with higher productivity (or fewer inputs)

3. Absolute disadvantage

A nation that produces a certain good with lower productivity when compared to another nation.

4. Comparative advantage

When a nation has either the largest productivity advantage in producing a certain good or service, the smallest productivity disadvantage in producing a certain good or service.

5. Autarky

An economy that is self sufficient and does not take part in internation trade, or severely limits trade with the outside world.

6. Tariff

A tax on imported goods.

7. Protective tariffs

A tariff imposed to protect domestic firms from import competition.

8. Protectionist policy

A policy designed to protect domestic industries by placing restrictions on foreign competition.

9. Ad-valorem tariff

A tariff expressed as a fixed percentage of the value of the imported product.

10. Specific tariff

A tariff specified as an amount of currency per unit of the good.

11. Compound tariff

A tariff that combines both a specific and ad-valorem tariff.

12. Infant industry argument

The argument that tariffs should be used to protect infant industries in hope that they can develop and eventually compete on world market.

13. Import quota

A legal limit on the amount of a good that can be imported.

14. Tariff quota

No tariff or a lower tariff for an imported good for a certain amount.

15. Embargo

Forbids the importing of one or more commodities with a particular nation.

Multiple Choice

1. If baseballs are cheap in Zanesville and expensive in Fairport, the law of one price says:
   a. baseball must be more popular in Fairport.
   b. there will be a tendency for baseballs to flow from Fairport to Zanesville.
   c. there will be a tendency for baseballs to flow from Fairport to Zanesville, equalizing the prices.
   d. the price will rise in Zanesville and fall in Fairport.
   e. both b and d are correct.

2. Trade among countries differs from trade within countries because of
   a. shipping costs.
   b. prejudice.
   c. national sovereignty.
   d. monopoly.
   e. all of the above.

3. If there were no national sovereignty, which of the following barriers to international trade would still exist?
   a. Language
   b. Different currencies
   c. Shipping costs
   d. Tariffs
   e. All of the above

4. When trade occurs between two countries
   a. one country gains and the other loses.
   b. both parties gain.
   c. both parties lose.
   d. labor gains and capital loses.
   e. large countries usually gain, while small countries lose.

5. A difference between a tariff and a quota is that
   a. tarrifs generate revenue to the government, whereas quotas do not.
   b. tariffs restrict quantity, whereas quotas restrict price.
   c. tariffs benefit producers, whereas quotas benefit consumers.
   d. all of the above are true.
   e. only a and b are true.

6. International trade occurs because of
   a. specialization in production.
   b. specialization in consumption.
   c. effective government trade policies.
   d. manufacturing efficiencies for goods and delivery efficiencies for services.
   e. the inability of any single country to achieve economic self-sufficiency.

7. A country will specialize in the production of those goods for which its
   a. product quality is higher than that of other countries.
   b. degree of subsidization is more than that of other countries.
   c. opportunity costs of production are lower than opportunity costs in other countries.
   d. opportunity costs of production are higher than opportunity costs in other countries.
   e. opportunity costs of production are equal at the margin with opportunity costs in other countries.

8. Nations trade what they produce in excess of their own consumption to
   a. generate jobs for the domestic economy.
   b. earn "good will" from the world bank.
   c. prevent chronic surpluses from driving down domestic prices.
   d. acquire other things they want to consume.
   e. reduce the size of their foreign trade deficit.

9. The most heavily traded good in the world is
   a. gold.
   b. crude petroleum.
   c. gas, natural, and manufactured.
   d. refined petroleum products.
   e. telecommunications.

10. Because countries differ in their comparative advantages, they will tend to
   a. import goods in universally short supply.
   b. import goods of high quality and export goods of low quality.
   c. import and export goods from their most important industries.
   d. import and export different goods.
   e. import goods with relatively low opportunity costs and export goods with relatively high opportunity costs.

True/False

Directions: For the following statements, indicate whether the statement is true or false. If the statement is false, make the necessary change(s) in order for it to be a true statement.

1. Everyone benefits from international trade because trade leads to specialization and increased efficiency in production.

2. The ability to produce a good at a lower cost relative to other goods compared to another country is defined as absolute advantage.

3. Having an absolute advantage is neither necessary nor sufficient for a country to export goods.

4. The ability to produce a good at a lower cost, in terms of real resources, than another country is defined as comparative advantage.

5. With perfect competition and undistorted markets, countries tend to export goods for which they have a comparative advantage.

6. Tariffs encourage the consumption of imported goods.

7. The three types of tariffs discussed in this chapter include Ricardian, ad-valorem, and specific tariffs.

8. Quotas are like tariffs in that they protect a domestic industry from foreign competition.

9. With a quota, the government gets the price differential whereas with a tariff, the importer gets the price differential.

10. An embargo is a type of tariff imposed by a government.

Short Answer/Essay Questions

1. What are the home countries of these firms or the firms that produce these products?

    a. Nestlé   _____

    b. Shell   _____

    c. Lipton Tea   _____

    d. Baskin-Robbins   _____

    e. TV Guide   _____

    f. Bumble Bee Tuna   _____

    g. Sony   _____

    h. Adidas   _____

    i. Bayer Aspirin   _____

    j. Michelin Tires   _____

    k. Nike   _____

    l. Hardee's   _____

    m. Levi Strauss   _____

    n. Vaseline   _____

    o. Friskies   _____

2. In the *Theory to Application* article "Cotton Pits Farmer Versus Farmer," you learn about the protection of agriculture in industrialized economies versus developing ones. Assuming that you are a major authority at the WTO, what types of changes, if any, would you impose on member nations concerning agricultural protection (i.e., subsidies, tariffs, quotas, etc.).

Chapter 15

International Finance

Oia-ola/Shutterstock.com

OBJECTIVES

1. To explain the meaning of balance of payments.
2. To describe the different elements of a balance of payment.
3. To explain the importance of foreign exchange markets.
4. To discuss the different factors affecting the exchange rate.
5. To describe the different exchange rate systems and their implication to a given economy.

In the last chapter we dealt with international trade in goods and services. Now we turn to trade in financial assets. Such trade may be related to the financing of goods and services, and it may also be related to investors altering their portfolios, multinational firms transferring assets from one subsidiary to another, governments buying and selling different currencies to change exchange rates, or a myriad of daily events taking place.

This chapter will provide an overview of what is sometimes called "international monetary economics" or "international finance." In either case, we are addressing the financial monetary issues related to international transactions.

A lot of you may know that different countries have different monetary currencies. You might also wonder why, for example, the U.S. dollar is stronger than a Philippine peso. Or why there is a fluctuating value for the U.S. dollar relative to the Japanese Yen. The purpose of this chapter is to look at some macroeconomic issues of international finance. We will take a look at how exports and imports play a major role in determining the value of our currency relative to other currencies.

Balance of Payments

Our study of international finance begins with the **balance of payments**. Here, we learn how nations record transactions with the rest of the world. Terms like *trade surplus* and *trade deficit* have become newsworthy as public interest grows in knowing whether we sell more than we buy from the rest of the world . As we will learn, a country with a **trade surplus** exports more goods than it imports, and a country with a **trade deficit** imports more than it exports. The figures below illustrate the U.S. trade balance from 1990 to 2007 as well as economic growth over that same period. The numbers on the left side of the graph show the value of the trade deficit (which corresponds with the blue "trade balance" line) and the numbers on the right correspond with the percentage of economic growth (represented by the red "economic growth" line).

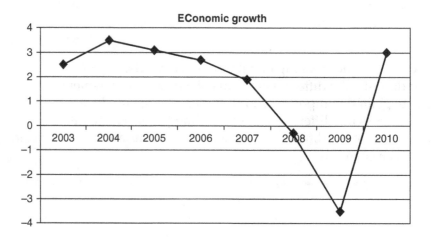

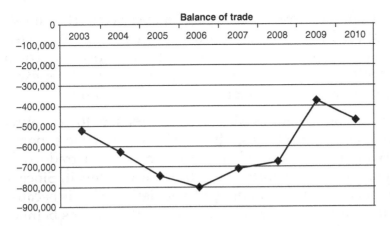

The balance of payment accounts (BOP) is a summary record of a country's economic transactions with foreign residents and governments over a year. There are two components of the BOP: the current account and the capital account. The **current account** is that part of the balance of payments recording a nation's exports and imports of goods and services and transfer payments. The **capital** account is the part of the balance of payments that records international borrowing, lending, and investment (basically, financial assets). The structure of the BOP account is as follows:

Current Account

1. Exports of Goods
2. *Minus* Imported Goods
3. *Equals* Balance of Trade (add rows 1 and 2)
4. *Plus* Exports of Services
5. *Minus* Imports of Services
6. *Equals* Balance of Services (add rows 4 and 5)
7. Balance of Goods and Services (add rows 3 and 6)
8. *Plus* Net Unilateral Transfer
9. *Equals Current Account Balance* (add rows 7 and 8)

Capital Account

1. U.S. Capital Going Abroad
2. *Minus* Foreign Capital Coming into the United States
3. *Equals Capital Account Balance* (add rows 1 and 2)
4. *Plus* Current Account Balance (row 9 from above)
   Equals Net International Investment

In any of these transactions, there will be two major flows of funds. One flow is a **debit**—any transactions that either supply the nation's currency or create a demand for foreign currency in the foreign exchange market, for example, Americans buying Japanese cars. They must first buy Japanese yen by supplying U.S. dollars. The other flow is a **credit**—any transactions that either supply a foreign currency or create a demand for the nation's currency in the foreign exchange market; for example, Japanese consumers buying American computers (exports).

The current accountincludes all payments related to the purchase and sale of goods and services. These primarily include exports and imports. When exports exceed imports, we call it a trade surplus. When imports exceed exports, we call it a trade deficit. Since 1975, the United States has been running a trade deficit. That is because we tend to import more than we export. One of the reasons behind this phenomenon is the fact that the U.S. dollar is strong relative to other currencies. Another component of the current account is the net unilateral transfer, for example, remittances to foreign countries, or the U.S. government giving foreign aid. These are usually a one-way money payment. Table 15-1 shows the top 10 and bottom10 current accounts in the world (out of 164 countries), as reported by *The CIA World Factbook*.

Table 15-1

Rank	Country	Current account balance	Date of Information
1	China	$280,600,000,000	2011 est.
2	Saudi Arabia	$151,400,000,000	2011 est.
3	Germany	$149,300,000,000	2011 est.
4	Japan	$122,800,000,000	2011 est.
5	Russia	$90,510,000,000	2011 est.
6	Switzerland	$76,700,000,000	2011 est.
7	Qatar	$76,370,000,000	2011 est.
8	Netherlands	$64,100,000,000	2011 est.
9	Norway	$63,500,000,000	2011 est.
10	Kuwait	$61,720,000,000	2011 est.
182	Australia	(−30,700,000,000)	2011 est.
183	European Union	(−32,720,000,000)	2011 est.
184	Canada	(−52,600,000,000)	2011 est.
185	Spain	(−60,900,000,000)	2011 est.
186	India	(−62,960,000,000)	2011 est.
187	Brazil	(−63,470,000,000)	2011 est.
188	United Kingdom	(−66,600,000,000)	2011 est.
189	Turkey	(−71,940,000,000)	2011 est.
190	France	(−74,300,000,000)	2011 est.
191	Italy	(−77,800,000,000)	2011 est.
192	United States	(−599,900,000,000)	2011 est.

Source: CIA World Factbook

The capital account, on the other hand, includes all payments related to the purchase and sale of assets and to borrowing and lending activities. An *outflow* of U.S. capital may be in the form of American purchase of foreign assets, whereas an *inflow* of foreign capital can be in the form of foreign purchases of U.S. assets and foreign loans to Americans. An example of this is when Germans choose to purchase U.S. treasury bills. The government possesses *official reserves* balances in the form of foreign currencies, gold, and its reserve position in the IMF and special drawing rights (SDR). Countries with deficits in the current account and capital accounts can draw on their reserves.

The balance of payments records all transactions between residents of the United States and residents of the rest of the world. Anything that creates a debit item in the U.S. balance of payments creates a supply of dollars (and a demand for foreign currency). When we import a German car or invest in German stocks—both debits in balance of payments accounting—we must first acquire euros in the foreign exchange market. Likewise, anything that creates a credit item in the U.S. balance of payments, such as the sale of domestic wheat or U.S. Treasury bonds, generates a demand for dollars (and a supply of foreign currency).

A country that incurs a current account deficit—such as the United States—is consuming more of the world's output than it is producing. Its imports are a debit in its current account, creating a supply of its own currency. Such a country must pay for its extra current consumption (its excess of imports) by giving foreigners financial claims on its future output (stocks, bonds, bank deposits, and so on). The resulting foreign capital inflows are credit items in the balance of payments and represent a demand for dollars. Current account and capital account balances must offset each other exactly (assuming that everything is measured correctly). In sum, neither an excess supply nor an excess demand for dollars exists.

The capital account does not passively respond to the current account, as the above implies. Myriad individuals make separate decisions about importing, exporting, and investing abroad, and each of these decisions affects the balance of payments independently. If at any time the collective intentions are not consistent with equilibrium in the accounts, attempts to enact these plans will cause the real exchange rate to change. The exchange rate adjustment in turn forces people to reevaluate their plans in such a way as to pull the current and capital accounts into balance. (Other economic variables, like interest rates, might also shift and contribute to the process.)

Theory to Application

The World's Largest Debtor

On September 16, 1985, the U.S. Commerce Department announced that the United States was a debtor nation for the first time since World War I. The magnitude of the current account deficit for 1985 and 1986 made the United States the largest international debtor in the world, with debts exceeding those of the developing country debtors such as Brazil and Mexico.

It is interesting to note that the United States reached its all-time high as net creditor in 1982, with net international investment of $147 billion. The rapid fall from 1982 to 1985 followed more than 60 years as a net creditor. In the 1950s and 1960s, U.S. foreign direct investment led the push for the net creditor improvement. In the 1970s, U.S. bank lending abroad increased the net creditor position.

Prior to the emergence of the United States as the major financial power in the world, Britain was the world's great creditor nation. In the nineteenth century and early twentieth century, England financed much of world trade and permitted access to British markets for debtor nations to earn the foreign exchange needed to service the debt. The rise of protectionist sentiment in the 1920s and 1930s led to barriers to trade that made it difficult for international debtors to repay their debts. The drop in world trade during the 1930s marked the end of Britain's dominance as an international lender. After World War II, the United States emerged as the dominant financial leader. How did the United States turn from a net creditor to a net debtor in the course of three years?

The U.S. story is recorded in the massive current account deficits and corresponding financial account surpluses of the early 1980s. To consume more at home than is produced (this is what you do when you run a current account deficit), the United States had to borrow from abroad. In the U.S. case, borrowing was at such a high level that the record net creditor position of 1982 was eliminated in just three years.

Behind the accounting record of the balance of payments lays the economic cause of the change. The world debt crisis of the 1980s caused a reduction in U.S. foreign lending as banks sought to lower their exposure to default risk. Record U.S. federal budget deficits made lending at home more attractive to U.S. banks as the deficits contributed to relatively high returns on U.S. loans. These same high returns, along with the perception of the United States as a "safe haven" for investment, made U.S. securities more attractive to foreign lenders.

There is nothing wrong with being a net debtor as long as the borrowed funds contribute to a more productive economy. Considering the magnitude of federal government borrowing in the 1980s, without the large inflow of foreign funds, U.S. interest rates would have been higher and investment would probably have been lower. If the borrowing has allowed a higher growth rate, then future generations, who share the burden of repaying the debt, will also enjoy a higher standard of living.

In the early 1980s, an appreciating dollar and high interest rates signaled the incentive for foreign investment in the United States. The large current account deficits and financial account surpluses have continued since then. If foreign portfolios reach a point where dollar-denominated assets are no longer desired, then the dollar will tend to depreciate, and interest rates will tend to fall. A falling financial account surplus will be matched by a falling current account deficit. Ultimately, conditions could change so that the United States once again becomes a net lender, and the title of "world's largest debtor" will fall to another.

Foreign Exchange Markets

Each day, more than $2.4 trillion worth of foreign exchange changes hands around the globe, an amount that far exceeds the daily value of world trade. This makes the foreign exchange market the world's largest financial market. The following table lists the percentages of trading volume involving a currency on one side of a transaction. Approximately 90 percent of these transactions involve U.S. dollars, but not all involve U.S. citizens. Monies are traded in the foreign exchange market, a global market whose electronic communications link traders around the world. The price of one money in terms of another is called the **exchange rate**. Relatively small changes in the prices at which these trades occur can have immediate and profound effects on economic events, ranging from family vacations to corporate profits. Large changes can shake governments, as recently demonstrated in Southeast Asia. Yet, despite the importance of exchange rates, most people find their behavior unfathomable.

Use of Currencies on One Side of the Transaction as a Percentage of Total Foreign-Exchange Market Volume

Currency	Percentage Share
U.S. Dollar	89
Euro	37
Japanese yen	20
British pound	17
Swiss franc	6
Australian dollar	6
Canadian dollar	4

Economists often view the nominal exchange rate (the foreign currency price of a dollar typically quoted in the *Wall Street Journal*) as the product of the real exchange rate and a component reflecting the difference between domestic and foreign inflation. Unlike their nominal counterparts, real exchange rates are not directly observable, but economists estimate them because of their influence on international competitiveness. This dichotomy between a real exchange rate and an inflation differential has proved useful for understanding the complex connections between economic fundamentals and nominal exchange rates, and especially for appreciating the role of monetary policy in determining exchange rates.

An exchange rate is the relative price of one nation's money versus another's. Say, for example, that €1.57 (euros) exchange for one U.S. dollar. If the Federal Reserve creates excessive amounts of dollars (more than people currently wish to hold) at a faster pace than the European Central Bank (ECB) issues excessive amounts of euros, the value of the dollar will fall relative to the euro.

The **spot rate** is the current actual exchange rate of a given currency. For example, the spot rate for the U.S. dollar relative to the euro in the example above is €1.57. The spot rate of a given currency changes every minute depending on the market for a given currency. For business purposes, a more commonly used type of exchange rate is the *forward market rate*. This is the exchange rate that can be locked in for a future time. For example, a U.S. importer of German cars would like to import German cars next month. The importer may have some expectation that the value of the euro will appreciate in the next couple of weeks. In order to hedge against any fluctuations in the exchange rate market, the importer can buy the euro at the forward market. The rate that he will be charged is called the forward rate. In theory, the forward rate is the sum of the spot rate plus the interest rate spread between the two countries involved.

For example, an investor is speculating that the value of the euro will appreciate. The current spot price is $0.40 per euro. In 3 months, the anticipated spot priced of the euro will be $0.50. The investor can purchase euros at today's spot rate of $0.40 and deposit them in a bank to earn interest. In 3 months, the investor can sell the euros at the prevailing spot price of $0.50 per euro. The investor profits $0.10 per euro. However, if the assumption is wrong and the spot price of the euro falls, the investor incurs a loss, reselling the euros at a price lower than the purchase price.

Another type of exchange rate that is used in business is the **cross rate**. Cross rate is the exchange rate between two countries viewed from a third country. Most currency speculators use this in a typical arbitrage currency market. An arbitrage market is a market where currencies are bought where the price is low and sold where the price is high simultaneously. One reason why there is a disparity between the buying and the selling price can be accounted for the fact that the demand for certain currencies is different in various regions of the world. For example, the demand for the U.S. dollar may be strong in Asia while it is weak in Europe. Currency traders can take advantage of the difference in the prices for each market. Caution should be taken in trading in this type of market because price differential can be volatile.

Ignoring the difficulties associated with expectations and perceptions of monetary policy, the dynamics underlying the dollar's depreciation might proceed as follows: Faster money growth creates inflationary pressure in the United States, causing people to shift their purchases away from U.S. goods toward the now relatively less expensive German goods. To acquire German goods, however, people must first convert their dollars to euros. The increased demand for euros (and the greater supply of dollars) will bid up the value of the mark relative to the dollar in the foreign exchange market—that is, the dollar will depreciate against the euro. Holding other things constant, this dollar depreciation will continue as long as the U.S. inflation rate exceeds the German inflation rate, and will tend to match the inflation differential between the two countries. If, for example, Germany's inflation rate is 2 percent per year and the U.S. inflation rate is 3 percent per year, the dollar will depreciate 1 percent per year against the euro, other things being equal.

The explanation above contains two important implications for monetary policy. First, because monetary policy ultimately determines only the domestic inflation rate, a central bank that wants to engineer a depreciation of its currency must create more money than its trading partners and thereby generate a higher inflation rate. Second, because any resulting exchange rate depreciation will ultimately offset the inflation differential, a monetary-induced depreciation cannot secure a competitive trade advantage. The real exchange rate will remain unaffected in the long term. Any trading gains from engineering dollar depreciation are purely transitory, lasting only until prices fully adjust.

Economists refer to the relationship linking exchange-rate movements and inflation rates across countries as relative purchasing power parity (PPP). Recent estimates suggest that once disturbed, PPP takes an average of 8 years to become reestablished. One interpretation of this finding is that goods prices adjust slowly in comparison to monetary shocks, implying that monetary policy maybe able to affect the real exchange rate in the interim. A second interpretation is that nonmonetary events, such as productivity shocks or changes in preferences for domestic versus foreign goods, are important determinants of exchange rate movements. The latter perspective draws attention to the determination of real exchange rates.

Factors Affecting the Exchange Rate

In order to understand how different factors will affect the exchange rate, we will use a supply and demand analysis. Why would another country demand the U.S. dollar? Suppose that someone from another country wants to purchase a stock of a U.S. company, he will then need to exchange his currency for U.S. dollars, so he can purchase U.S. stock. Now, suppose that an American wants to invest stock in a company abroad; she will supply U.S. dollars in the foreign exchange market, so she can attain foreign currency to purchase that foreign stock. The exchange rate is then determined at the equilibrium of the foreign exchange rate where supply equals demand. We will now examine the three facts that affect the foreign exchange rate, which are (a) relative inflation rates, (b) **relative interest rates,** and (c) relative income rates.

Relative Inflation Rates

Changes in relative inflation rates can affect international trade activity, which influences the demand and supply for currencies, and therefore influences exchange rates. The sudden swings in U.S. inflation could cause an increase in U.S. demand for British goods, and therefore also cause an increase in the U.S. demand for British pounds. In addition, the jump in U.S. inflation should decrease the British desire for U.S. goods and therefore reduce the supply of pounds for sale.

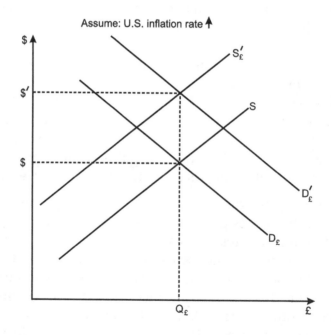

Relative Interest Rates

Assume that U.S. interest rates rise where British interest rates remain constant. In this case, U.S. corporations will likely reduce the demand for pounds, since the U.S. rates are now more attractive relative to British rates, and there is less desire for British bank deposits. This means that U.S. corporations and households will invest more money domestically. Since U.S. rates will now look more attractive to British corporations with excess cash, the supply of pounds for sale by British corporations should increase as they establish more deposits in the United States. British corporations and households will reduce their investment at home to invest more in the United States.

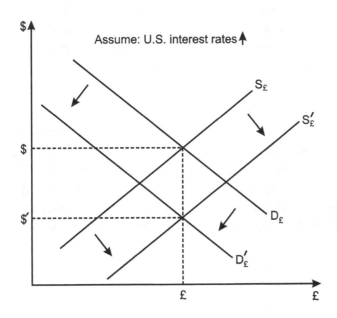

Relative Income Levels

An increase in U.S. income would increase the demand for British goods, assuming British income is constant.

Other factors affecting foreign exchange rates include government controls such as imposition of foreign exchange barriers, trade barriers, and intervening in foreign exchange markets. Expectations play a major role, too. Foreign exchange markets react to any news that may have future effect. For example, news of a potential surge in the U.S. inflation rate may cause currency to sell pounds, anticipating a future decrease in the dollar value.

Exchange Rate Systems

Fixed Exchange Rate

In fixed exchange rates, exchange rates are held constant or allowed to fluctuate only within very narrow boundaries. If an exchange rate begins to move too much, governments can intervene to maintain it within the boundaries. From 1944–1971, exchange rates were typically fixed according to a system planned at the Bretton Woods Agreement. The managerial duties of a multinational corporation (MNC) are less difficult with a fixed exchange rate. However, there is still the risk that the government will alter the value of a specific currency.

Freely Floating Exchange Rate

With a freely floating exchange rate, exchange rate values are determined by market forces without intervention by various governments. Under such a system, MNCs need to devote substantial resources to measuring and managing exposure to exchange rates. One advantage of this exchange rate system is that U.S. inflation would have a greater impact on inflation in other countries within a fixed exchange rate system than it would in a floating exchange rate system. U.S. inflation can be translated into appreciation of British pounds, but the actual price of the goods as measured in British pounds is constant.

Managed Floating Exchange Rate

Here exchange rates are allowed to fluctuate on a daily basis, yet the government does intervene to prevent currencies from moving too much. For example, during the economic crisis of 1997, Malaysia introduced the managed float in order to stabilize the value of its currency, the Malaysian Ringgit. In this way, the currency does affect the real output of the economy significantly, especially during an economic crisis.

Theory to Application

The Chinese Currency Controversy

From 1995 to 2005 the Chinese currency, the yuan, was pegged to the dollar at an exchange rate of 8.28 yuan per U.S. dollar. In other words, the Chinese central bank stood ready to buy and sell yuan at this price. This policy of fixing the exchange rate was combined with a policy of restricting international capital flows. Chinese citizens were not allowed to convert their savings into dollars or euros and invest abroad.

Many observers believed that by the early 2000s, the yuan was significantly undervalued. They suggested that if the yuan were allowed to float, it would increase in value relative to the dollar. The evidence in favor of this hypothesis was that to maintain the fixed exchange rate, China was accumulating large dollar reserves. That is, the Chinese central bank had to supply yuan and demand dollars in foreign-exchange markets to keep the yuan at the pegged level. If this intervention in the currency market ceased, the yuan would rise in value compared to the dollar.

The pegged yuan became a contentious political issue in the United States. U.S. producers that competed against Chinese imports complained that the undervalued yuan made Chinese goods cheaper, putting U.S. producers at a disadvantage. (Of course, U.S. consumers benefited from inexpensive imports, but in the politics of international trade, producers usually shout louder than consumers.) In response to these concerns, President Bush called on China to let its currency float.

Charles Schumer, senator from New York, proposed a more drastic step—a tariff of 27.5 percent on Chinese imports until China adjusted the value of its currency.

In July 2005 China announced that it would move in the direction of a floating exchange rate. Under the new policy, it would still intervene in foreign-exchange markets to prevent large and sudden movements in the exchange rate, but it would permit gradual changes. Moreover, it would judge the value of the yuan not just relative to the dollar but relative to a broad basket of currencies. Five months later, the exchange rate had moved to 8.08 yuan per dollar—a 2.4 percent appreciation of the yuan, far smaller than the 20 to 30 percent that Senator Schumer and other China critics were looking for.

Was the yuan really undervalued by such a large amount? To answer this question, we must first ask, compared to what? The critics of Chinese policy may well have been correct that the yuan would have appreciated substantially if the Chinese had stopped intervening in foreign-exchange markets while keeping their other policies the same. But a movement to a fully floating exchange rate could well have been coupled with a movement toward free capital mobility. If so, the currency implications could have been very different, as many Chinese citizens might have tried to move some of their savings abroad. While the central bank would no longer have been demanding dollars to fix the exchange rate, private investors would have been demanding dollars to add U.S. assets to their portfolios. In this case, the change in policy could well have caused the yuan to depreciate rather than appreciate.

The Concept of the Euro: Current Trends in International Finance

On January 1, 1999, eleven European countries took a daring plunge. They agreed to replace their national currencies with a new currency, the euro, and to transfer fundamental powers from their individual central banks to a newly created central bank. Few symbols of national sovereignty are as powerful as coins and banknotes, and never before has a sizable country not had its own currency. Relinquishing its currency is clearly an enormous political and constitutional decision for any nation. History, therefore, changed radically with the launch of the euro. Furthermore, there are no precedents for the new central bank arrangements. A group of European countries with no histories of monetary sovereignty and long-standing central banks are now part of a system managed by a common, but independent, European Central Bank that is not accountable to any government or decision-making body. This central bank has the sole power to issue the common currency, the euro, and to control the area's monetary policy.

Why participate in the new arrangement? The answer is that monetary union involves the pooling of national sovereignty to promote economic and political integration in Europe. From an economic viewpoint, the creation of a single currency has long been seen as necessary for establishing a truly integrated, single European market. From a political viewpoint, the euro was considered a step toward the development of social and foreign policies at the European level by accelerating and consolidating the construction of supranational institutions and policies.

Economics Focus
Beefed-Up Burgernomics

A gourmet version of the Big Mac index suggests that the yuan is not that undervalued

The Big Mac index celebrates its 25th birthday this year. Invented by *The Economist* in 1986 as a lighthearted guide to whether currencies are at their "correct" level, it was never intended as a precise gauge of currency misalignment, merely a tool to make exchange-rate theory more digestible. Yet the Big Mac index has become a global standard, included in several economic textbooks and the subject of at least 20 academic studies. American politicians have even cited the index in their demands for a big appreciation of the Chinese yuan. With so many people taking the hamburger standard so seriously, it may be time to beef it up.

Burgernomics is based on the theory of purchasing-power parity (PPP), the notion that in the long run exchange rates should move towards the rate that would equalise the prices of an identical basket of goods and services (in this case, a burger) in any two countries. The average price of a Big Mac in America is $4.07; in China it is only $2.27 at market exchange rates, 44% cheaper. In other words, the raw Big Mac index suggests that the yuan is undervalued by 44% against the dollar. In contrast, the currencies of Switzerland and Norway appear to be overvalued by around 100%. The euro (based on a weighted average of prices in member countries) is overvalued by 21% against the dollar; sterling is slightly undervalued; the Japanese yen seems to be spot-on. For the first time, we have included India in our survey. McDonald's does not sell Big Macs there, so we have taken the price of a Maharaja Mac, made with chicken instead of beef. Meat accounts for less than 10% of a burger's total cost, so this is unlikely to distort results hugely. It indicates that the rupee is 53% undervalued.

Ketchup growth

Some find burgernomics hard to swallow. Burgers cannot easily be traded across borders, and prices are distorted by big differences in the cost of non-traded local inputs such as rent and workers' wages. The Big Mac index suggests that most emerging-market currencies are significantly undervalued, for instance (Brazil and Argentina are the big exceptions). But you would expect average prices to be cheaper in poor countries than in rich ones because labour costs are lower. This is the basis of the so-called "Balassa-Samuelson effect". Rich countries have much higher productivity and hence higher wages in the traded-goods sector than poor countries do. Because firms compete for workers, this also pushes up wages in non-tradable goods and services, where rich countries' productivity advantage is smaller. So average prices are cheaper in poor countries. The top chart shows a strong positive relationship between the dollar price of a Big Mac and GDP per person.

China's average income is only one-tenth of that in America so economic theory would suggest that its exchange rate should be below its long-run PPP (i.e., the rate that would leave a burger costing the same in the two countries). PPP signals where exchange rates should be heading in the long run, as China gets richer, but it says little about today's equilibrium rate. However, the relationship between prices and GDP per person can perhaps be used to estimate the current fair value of a currency. The top chart shows the "line of best fit" between Big Mac prices and GDP per person for 48 countries. The difference between the price predicted by the red line for each country, given its income per head, and its actual price offers a better guide to currency under- and overvaluation than the PPP-based "raw" index.

This alternative recipe, with its adjustment for GDP per person, indicates that the Brazilian real is still badly overcooked, at more than 100% too dear (see lower chart). The euro is 36% overvalued against the dollar, and our beefed-up index also throws useful light on the uncompetitiveness of some economies within the euro area. Comparing burger prices in member countries, the adjusted Big Mac index shows that the "exchange rates" of Italy, Spain, Greece and Portugal are all significantly overvalued relative to that of Germany. As for China, the yuan is close to its fair value against the greenback on the adjusted measure, although both are undervalued against many other currencies.

Super-size jubilee

In trade-weighted terms our calculations suggest that the yuan is a modest 7% undervalued, hardly grounds for a trade war. That is less than previous estimates of a 20–25% undervaluation, based on models that calculate the appreciation in the yuan needed to reduce China's current-account surplus to a manageable level of, say, 3% of GDP. Even this surplus-based method now points to a smaller yuan undervaluation than it used to because China's surplus has shrunk. Several private-sector economists forecast that it could drop below 4% of GDP this year, down from nearly 11% in 2007. As its productivity rises over time China must continue to allow its real exchange rate to rise (either through currency appreciation or through inflation), but our new burger barometer suggests that the yuan is not hugely undervalued today.

A quarter of a century after its first grilling, burgernomics is still far from perfect, but if adjusted for GDP per person it becomes tastier. All the more reason to keep putting our money where our mouth is.

The Chinese Renminbi: What's Real, What's Not

Patrick Higgins and Owen F. Humpage

On July 21, China devalued its currency—the renminbi—2.1 percent to 8.11 per dollar and revised its procedures for exchange-rate management. The new operating method—supposedly similar to Singapore's—provides China with a more flexible, but less transparent, mechanism for its exchange-market interventions. Since the revaluation, however, the renminbi has not changed much, suggesting that this move might not immediately herald a series of renminbi appreciations.

Many claim that China scores an unfair trade advantage against the United States because it keeps the renminbi at an artificially attractive rate relative to the dollar. If China revalued its currency or allowed it to float freely in the foreign-exchange market, so the argument goes, its competitive edge would dull, and our trade deficit with China—$180 billion in the twelve months ending May 2005, a full 26 percent of the total U.S. trade deficit in goods—would shrink.

To be sure, China is not a free-market economy; it maintains a network of trade restraints, financial controls, corporate subsidies, state-run enterprises, and state-directed investments that enhance its ability to compete in global markets. These practices are problematic and the legitimate targets of criticism by anyone whom they harm. But complaints about the peg giving China a huge trade advantage against the United States seem overstated.

This *Economic Commentary* argues that revaluing the renminbi or introducing more exchange-rate flexibility will, at best, affect China's trade competitiveness only temporarily and will, in the process, divert focus from the real problem: China's command economy. To keep the renminbi at its current level, China creates an artificial demand for renminbi through substantial restraints on financial outflows and, to a lesser degree, on imports. As these restraints weaken while trade continues to expand, China will find the nominal peg increasingly difficult to maintain. To understand why these restraints matter more than the peg, we must first distinguish between the nominal and the real renminbi exchange rate.

What's Real?

Between mid-1995 and the recent devaluation, China maintained the exchange value of the renminbi at approximately 8.3 per dollar. This pegged value and the recent 8.1 renminbi-dollar exchange rate tell us nothing about China's competitiveness relative to the United States because they ignore price patterns in the two countries. If the renminbi cost of goods in China were rising faster than the dollar price of the same goods in the United States, any initial trade gain associated with a fixed exchange rate would soon erode away. The real renminbi-dollar exchange rate adjusts the peg value for U.S. and Chinese inflation differentials, thereby providing a clearer picture of China's competitive position. All else constant, a real appreciation of the dollar relative to the renminbi places the United States at a competitive disadvantage vis-a-vis China, while a real depreciation has the opposite effect.

On a real basis, the dollar appreciated only 2.6 percent against the renminbi between June 1995 and May 2005; such a small movement cannot confer much of a trade advantage on China. The real exchange rate has, however, undergone some large swings over the past decade. Between June 1995 and October 1997, the dollar depreciated 11.4 percent against the renminbi on a real basis because China's inflation rate exceeded the U.S. inflation rate. Between October 1997 and October 2003, however, China's inflation rate dipped below the U.S. inflation rate, causing the dollar to appreciate 17.2 percent on a real basis against the renminbi. Since October 2003, China's inflation rate has generally exceeded ours, and the dollar has again depreciated 1.1 percent against the renminbi in real terms. The recent revaluation moves the real renminbi-dollar exchange rate approximately back to its mid-1995 level.

Critics might complain that our calculations are flawed because we do not correct for China having set the initial renminbi-dollar exchange rate at an artificially favorable level. Many contend that the initial peg undervalued the renminbi, and if China had originally pegged its currency to the dollar at a lower, more reasonable value, say, 7.3 to 1 instead of 8.3 to 1—that is, had substantially revalued the renminbi—our simple calculations might show an entirely different outcome, one more consistent with their allegations.

To claim that China undervalued its peg and continues to do so, analysts must somehow divine the long-run "equilibrium" value of the renminbi-dollar exchange rate. This often involves a number of rather arbitrary judgments and assumptions about the underlying economic model. Typically, the calculations involve comparing relative inflation patterns in China and the United States, possibly with some allowance for productivity trends in both countries, and estimating a "sustainable" configuration for Chinese balance-of-payments relationships.

Determining an equilibrium exchange rate for a developed, market-based, financially mature country is challenging, but doing so for a developing country like China, which is undergoing serious structural change, is next to impossible. Since it embarked on an economic liberalization program in 1978, China has been inching away from a system of state-directed economic activity, where prices and exchange rates had virtually no role in resource allocation, to a more market-friendly model. What might constitute an equilibrium under one economic structure need not hold under another. Consequently, the continuing fundamental and structural changes that China has undertaken must make any calculation of an equilibrium renminbi-dollar exchange rate highly suspect. As the International Monetary Fund recently noted, "… it is difficult to arrive at any firm and robust conclusions about the equilibrium level of the renminbi using existing techniques." Underscoring the point, recent estimates of the renminbi's undervaluation are rather imprecise, ranging at least from 5 to 40 percent. Five years ago, however, many thought that the renminbi was overvalued.

Even if China undervalues the renminbi with the intention of making products and investment opportunities in the country cheap, any trade advantage would erode as prices adjusted; furthermore, the greater the undervaluation, the faster any gain would dissipate. If China undervalues the renminbi, the local price of its goods will tend to rise as Chinese exports and investment opportunities attract worldwide demand. Moreover, to keep the renminbi stable relative to the dollar in the face of an overall balance-of-payments surplus, the People's Bank of China—the country's central bank—must buy dollars on the foreign-exchange market. China has indeed been doing so and, as a result, its official holdings of international reserves have risen dramatically. The process, however, expands China's money stock and can eventually cause inflation. This inflation-generating mechanism should prevent China from realizing a long-term trade advantage from undervaluing the renminbi. Empirical estimates suggest that any such advantage would disappear with a half-life of approximately four years.

This, however, has not happened, further suggesting that the renminbi might not have been so far out of line at 8.3 per dollar. Between 1995 and 1997, China's inflation rate fell, and between 1997 and 2003, China experienced two mild deflations. Overall, since 1997, China's inflation rate has almost always remained within 4 percentage points of the U.S. rate, and when the rates have diverged, China's has tended to return close to the U.S. inflation rate. Countries that keep their exchange rate pegged or very stable typically experience such a general correspondence between their inflation rates.

What's Not Real?

Of course, the People's Bank of China might attempt to offset the inflationary impact of its dollar gains, and thereby the appreciation of the real renminbi, by selling domestic assets from its portfolio or by increasing nonmonetary liabilities on its balance sheet. Such actions, called sterilization or sterilized intervention, will jeopardize the exchange-rate peg unless accompanied by restrictions on imports and controls on financial outflows.

The People's Bank generally did not sterilize the monetary consequences of its reserve purchases until relatively recently. Between the second quarter of 1995, when the peg began, and the third quarter of 2004, China's central bank acquired the equivalent of Rmb 4.6 trillion in foreign exchange—believed to be mostly dollars. This caused China's monetary base to expand 14 percent per year. Most of this money growth, however, has accommodated the increase in the demand for money that is associated with China's rapid economic growth. Chinese inflation has actually moderated since 1995.

Since mid-2002, however, the People's Bank of China has sterilized part—sometimes a substantial part—of the increase in its foreign exchange reserves, preventing them from raising its monetary base. In addition, the People's Bank has attempted to blunt the inflationary consequences of its dollar accumulation by increasing bank reserve requirements, which reduces the amount of bank loans that a given change in the monetary base can support, and by directly attempting to curb investment spending.

Most economists contend, however, that sterilized intervention will not work. If—as has been the case—maintaining a stable exchange rate requires the People's Bank to buy dollars with renminbi, the exchange rate cannot remain unchanged should the Bank then reabsorb these renminbi reserves through other operations. Instead, the Chinese government must promote stability by creating a persistent demand for these renminbi at the existing exchange rate. China does this primarily through artificial restraints on financial flows. In general, Chinese policies favor net inflows of foreign direct investment, encourage exports over imports, and—most importantly—discourage other types of private financial outflows, largely by limiting the amount of dollars that China's residents might hold and their ability to invest in foreign assets. Remove the restraints and corresponding policies, and the demand for renminbi will fall relative to the supply, and domestic prices will rise. The adjustment will drive the real renminbi exchange value and China's balance of payments to a new, market-determined equilibrium.

Conclusion

Arguing that China's exchange-rate policies undervalue the renminbi for a strategic trade advantage is a hard sell because, beyond the very short run, nominal exchange rates do not seem to matter much for trade. A more solid argument might be that China's network of restraints on private financial outflows and policies that promote net exports interfere with the natural adjustment of the real exchange rate.

As China's restraints continue to weaken, either out of compliance with its World Trade Organization commitments or the market's proclivity to scale such barriers, and as the country's international trade and investments grow, tightly managing the nominal exchange rate without increases in Chinese prices—and a real appreciation—will prove increasingly difficult. Sterilizing reserve gains will become useless. At that point, which may not be far off, increased exchange-rate flexibility will be necessary.

Definitions

1. Balance of payments

A summary record of a country's international economic transactions in a given period of time.

2. Debit

Any transactions that either supply the nation's currency or create a demand for foreign currency in the exchange market.

3. Credit

Any transactions that either supply a foreign currency or create a demand for the nation's currency in the foreign exchange market.

4. Current accounts

The broadest measure of the trade balance, looking at imports and exports of goods, services, investment income and unilateral transfers.

5. Capital accounts

That part of the balance of payments recording a nation's outflow and inflow of financial securities.

6. Trade deficit

When imports exceed exports.

7. Exchange rate

The rate at which a country makes exchanges in world markets.

8. Relative interest rates

When interest rates increase in one nation while remaining constant in another nation.

9. Fixed exchange rate

An exchange rate set by the central bank's willingness to buy and sell the domestic currency for foreign currencies at a predetermined price.

10. Freely floating exchange rate

An exchange rate that the central bank allows to change in response to changing economic conditions and economic policies.

Multiple Choice

1. Exchange rate policy is an important element of
   a. macroeconomic policy.
   b. microeconomic policy.
   c. military strategic policy.
   d. foreign diplomatic policy.
   e. domestic economic policy.

2. The link between two nations' monies is known as a(n)
   a. short interest rate.
   b. exchange rate.
   c. long interest rate.
   d. LIBOR rate.
   e. inflation rate.

3. Suppose that the price of an ounce of gold is $60 in the United States and 10 euros in Holland. Then the
   a. dollar is worth one-sixth the value of gold.
   b. dollar is worth six times the value of a euro.
   c. euro is worth six times the value of a dollar.
   d. U.S. economy must be six times larger than that of Holland.
   e. Dutch economy must be six times larger than the U.S. economy.

4. Suppose that a country's government keeps the exchange rate between two or more currencies constant over time. This policy is known as a(n)
   a. fixed exchange rate policy.
   b. floating exchange rate policy.
   c. managed floating exchange rate policy.
   d. laissez-faire exchange rate policy.
   e. interventionistic exchange rate policy.

5. The United States maintains an exchange rate that is
   a. pegged to the Special Drawing Right.
   b. a fixed rate.
   c. pegged to a composite of currencies.
   d. a managed floating exchange rate.
   e. subject to a cooperative arrangement with the European Monetary System.

6. An exchange rate policy that maintains a rate held constant over time, or pegged, is known as a
   a. fixed exchange rate policy.
   b. floating exchange rate policy.
   c. laissez-faire exchange rate policy.
   d. managed floating exchange rate policy.
   e. interventionistic exchange rate policy.

7. An exchange rate is the price of
   a. an identical good in each of two countries.
   b. one money in terms of another.
   c. national security.
   d. economic cooperation.
   e. one nation's economic production when compared with that of another.

8. Suppose that you have just returned to the United States from a summer vacation in England, where you exchanged American dollars for British pounds. Your economic actions
   a. increased the supply of British pounds in England.
   b. decreased the supply of British pounds in America.
   c. decreased the supply of American dollars in England.
   d. increased the demand for American dollars in America.
   e. increased the supply of American dollars in England.

9. In the absence of intervention, an increase in demand for a currency will cause a(n)
   a. depreciation of its exchange rate.
   b. devaluation of its currency.
   c. appreciation of its exchange rate.
   d. shift in the supply of currency.
   e. fixed exchange rate.

10. Any firm that lends money across international borders has to deal with the issue of
    a. balance of payments.
    b. foreign exchange risk.
    c. international banking regulation.
    d. comparative advantage.
    e. government regulation.

Short Answer/Essay Questions

Exchange Rates

1. A camera manufactured in the United States costs $100. Using the exchange rates listed in the table (see next page), what would the camera cost in each of the following countries (use Tuesday's quote):

    a. Argentina

    b. Brazil

    c. Canada

    d. Philippines

    e. Mexico

2. The U.S. dollar price of a Swedish krona changes from $1572 to $1730.
    a. Has the dollar depreciated or appreciated against the krona?

    b. Has the krona appreciated or depreciated against the dollar?

3. Suppose that 1 British pound = $2.4110 in New York, $1 = 3.997 Malaysian ringgit in Kuala Lumpur, and 1 Malaysian ringgit = 0.1088 British pound in London.

   a. By holding 1 British pound, how could you profit from these exchange rates?

4. In the Theory to Application article "The World's Largest Debtor," we learn how the United States went from the largest creditor in the world to the largest debtor. How do you feel this affects the U.S. economy compared to other countries (if at all)? What do you feel the United States should do (if anything) about holding this status? Does it make a significant difference? Explain your answer.

U.S. dollar foreign exchange rates in late New York trading

Country/Currency	—— Tues —— in U.S.$	per U.S.$	U.S.$ vs, YTD chg (%)
Americas			
Argentina peso*	.3167	3.1576	0.3
Brazil real	.5900	1.6949	−4.8
Canada dollar	.9862	1.0140	2.0
1–mas forward	.9857	1.0145	**2.1**
3–mas forward	.9846	1.0156	**2.3**
6–mas forward	.9829	1.0174	**2.4**
Chile peso	.002289	436.87	−12.3
Colombia peso	.0005529	1808.65	−10.4
Ecuador U.S. dollar	1	1	unch
Mexico peso*	.0946	10.5675	−3.2
Peru new sol	.3704	2.700	−9.9
Uruguay peso+	.05000	20.00	−7.2
Venezuela b.fuerte	.466287	2.1446	unch

Country/Currency	—— Tues —— in U.S.$	per U.S.$	U.S.$ vs, YTD chg (%)
Asia-Pacific			
Australian dollar	.9300	1.0756	−5.7
China yuan	.1428	7.0012	−4.1
Hong Kong dollar	.1284	7.7880	−0.1
India rupee	.02500	40.000	1.5
Indonesia rupiah	.0001087	9200	−2.0
Japan yen	.009749	102.57	−8.0
1–mos forward	.009767	102.39	−7.8
3–mos forward	.009795	102.09	−7.5
6–mos forward	.009835	101.68	−7.1
Malaysia ringgit§	.3136	3.1888	−3.6
New Zealand dollar	.7978	1.2534	−4.0
Pakistan rupee	.01585	63.092	2.3
Philippines peso	.0241	41.546	0.7
Singapore dollar	.7251	1.3791	−4.3
South Korea won	.0010245	976.09	4.3
Taiwan dollar	.03281	30.479	−6.0
Thailand bath	.03156	31.686	5.4
Vietnam dong	.00006208	16109	0.5

Country/Currency	—— Tues —— in U.S.$	per U.S.$	U.S.$ vs, YTD chg (%)
Europe			
Czech Rep. koruna**	.06266	15.959	−12.2
Denmark krone	.2106	4.7483	−7.0
Euro area euro	1.5708	.6366	−7.1
Hungary forint	.006177	161.89	−6.6
Norway krone	.1974	5.0659	−6.7
Poland zloty	.4544	2.2007	−10.8
Russia ruble#	.04244	23.563	−4.1
Slovak Rep koruna	.04830	20.704	−10.0
Sweden krona	.1677	5.9630	−7.8
Switzerland franc	.9857	1.0145	−10.5
1–mos forward	.9861	1.0141	−10.3
3–mos forward	.9859	1.0143	−10.0
6–mos forward	.9854	1.0148	−9.6
Turkey lira**	.7745	1.2912	10.6
UK pound	1.9689	.5079	0.9
1–mos forward	1.9646	.5090	1.1
3–mos forward	1.9554	.5114	1.4
6–mos forward	1.9421	.5149	1.7

Country/Currency	—— Tues —— in U.S.$	per U.S.$	U.S.$ vs, YTD chg (%)
Middle East/Africa			
Bahrain dinar	2.6521	.3771	0.3
Egypt pound*	.1835	5.4484	−1.5
Israel shekel	.2769	3.6114	−6.3
Jordan dinar	1.4112	.7086	unch
Kuwait dinar	3.7608	.2659	−2.7
Lebanon pound	.0006614	1511.94	unch
Saudi Arabia riyal	.2666	3.7509	unch
South Africa rand	.1285	7.7821	13.7
UAE dirham	.2723	3.6724	unch
SDR††	1.6349	.6117	−3.4

*Floating   † Financial   § Government rate   ‡ Russian Central Bank rate   ** Rebased as of Jan. 1, 2005
††Special Drawing Rights (SDR), from the International Monetary Fund; based on exchange rates for U.S., British, and Japanese currencies.
Note: Based on trading among banks of $1 million and more, as quoted at 4 p.m. ET by Reuters.

APPENDIX

A Math Review

This appendix presents the mathematical tools and the mathematical results used in this book.

Functions

A function, f, is a *rule* that assigns to each value of a variable *(x)*, called the *argument* of the function, one and only one value [*f(x)*], referred to as the *value of the function at x*. The *domain* of a function refers to the set of possible values of *x*; the *range* is the set of all possible values for *f(x)*. Functions are generally defined by algebraic formulas.

Functions are used informally in this book as a way of denoting how a variable depends on one or more other variables. In some cases, we look at how a variable *Y* moves with a variable *X*. This relation is written as:

$$Y + f(X)$$

$$(+)$$

A plus sign below *X* indicates a positive relation: an increase in *X* leads to an increase in *Y*. A minus sign below *X* indicates a negative relation: an increase in *X* leads to a decrease in *Y*.

In some cases, we allow the variable *Y* to depend on more than one variable. For example, we allow *Y* to depend on *X* and *Z*:

$$Y + f(X, Z)$$

$$(+, -)$$

The signs indicate that an increase in *X* leads to an increase in *Y*, and that an increase in *Z* leads to a decrease in *Y*.

An example of such a function is the investment function:

$$I = I(Y, i)$$

$$(+, -)$$

This equation says that investment, *I*, increases with production, *Y*, and decreases with the interest rate, *i*.

In some cases, it is reasonable to assume that the relation between two or more variables is a linear relation. A given increase always leads to the same increase in *Y*. In that case, the function is given by:

$$Y = a + bX$$

This relation can be represented by a line giving *Y* for any value of *X*.

Graphs, Slopes, and Intercepts

In graphing a function such as $y = f(x)$, x is placed on the horizontal axis and is known as the *independent variable*; y is placed on the vertical axis and is called the dependent variable. The graph of a linear function is a straight line (see Figure A-1).

The parameter a gives the value of Y when X is equal to zero. It is called the intercept because it gives the value of Y when the line representing the relation "intercepts" (crosses) the vertical axis.

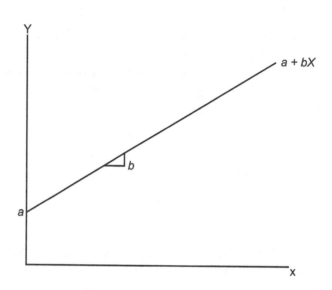

The parameter b tells us how much Y increases when X increases by one. It is called the slope because it is equal to the slope of the line representing the relation. The *slope* of a line measures the change in y (Δy) divided by a change in x (Δx). The slope indicates the steepness and direction of a line. The greater the absolute value of the slope, the steeper the line. A positively sloped line moves up from left to right; a negatively sloped line moves down. The slope of a horizontal line, for which $\Delta y = 0$, is zero. The slope of a vertical line, for which $\Delta x = 0$, is undefined (i.e., does not exist because division by zero is impossible). The *y intercept* is the point where the graph crosses the y axis; it occurs when $x = 0$. The *x intercept* is the point where the line intersects the x axis; it occurs when $y = 0$.

A simple linear relation is the relation $Y = X$, which is represented by a 45-degree line with a slope of one. Another example of a linear relation is the consumption function equation:

$$C = Ca + bY_D$$

where C is consumption, and Y_D is disposable income. Ca tells us what consumption would be if disposable income was zero. b tells us how much consumption increases when income increases by one unit; b is called the marginal propensity to consume.

Income Determination Models

Income determination models generally express the equilibrium level of income in a four-sector economy as:

$$Y = C + I + G + (X - M)$$

where Y = income, C = consumption, I = investment, G = government expenditures, X = exports, and M = imports. By substituting the information supplied in the problem, it is an easy matter to solve for the equilibrium level of income. *Aggregating* (summing) the variables on the right allows the equation to be graphed in two-dimensional space.

Example. Assume a simple two-sector economy where $Y = C + I$, $C = Ca + bY$, and $I = Ia$. Assume further that $Ca = 85$, $b = 0.9$, and $Ia = 55$. The equilibrium level of income can be calculated in terms of: (1) the general parameters, and (2) the specific values assigned to these parameters.

1. The *equilibrium equation* is:

$$Y = C + I$$

   Substituting for C and I,

$$Y = Ca + bY + Ia$$

   Solving for Y,

$$Y - bY = Ca + Ia$$

$$Y(1 - b) = Ca + Ia$$

$$Y = \frac{Ca + Ia}{1 - b}$$

   The solution in this form is called the reduced form. The reduced form (or solution equation) expresses the endogenous variable (in this instance, Y) as an explicit function of the exogenous variables (Ca, Ia) and the parameter b.

2. The specific equilibrium level of income can be calculated by substituting the numerical values for the parameters in either the original equation (a) or the reduced form (b):

   a)
$$Y = Ca + bY + Ia = 85 + 0.9Y + 55$$

$$Y - 0.9Y = 140$$

$$0.1Y = 140$$

$$Y = 1400$$

   b)
$$Y = \frac{Ca + Ia}{1 - b} = \frac{85 + 55}{1 - 0.9}$$

$$Y = 1400$$

The term $(1/1 - b)$ is called the *autonomous expenditure multiplier* in economics. It measures the multiple effect each dollar of autonomous spending has on the equilibrium income. Since $b = $ MPC in the income determination model, the multiplier $= (1/1 - $ MPC$)$.

Note: Decimals may be converted to fractions for ease in working with the income determination model. For example, $0.1 = (1/10)$, $0.9 = (9/10)$, $0.5 = (1/2)$, $0.2 = (1/5)$, and so on.

SYMBOLS USED IN THIS BOOK

Symbol	Term	Introduced in Chapter
$()^d$	Superscript^d means demanded	
$()^e$	Superscript^e means expected	
$()_t$	Subscript$_t$ means time period/year t	7
AC	Average cost	4
AP	Average product	4
AR	Average revenue	5
ATC	Average total cost	4
AVC	Average variable cost	4
C	Consumption, Cost	6, 4
CCA	Capital consumption allowance	6
CPI	Consumer price index	7
^ep	Price elasticity of demand	3
G	Government spending	6
GDP	Gross domestic product	6
g, g_y	Growth rate of output	6
I	Fixed investment	6
IBT	Indirect business taxes	6
K	Capital stock	4
L	Labor force	1
$LRAC$	Long-run average total cost	4
M	Imports	6
MC	Marginal cost	4
MP	Marginal product	4
MR	Marginal revenue	5
NDP	Net domestic product	6
NY	National income	6
P_c	Price ceiling	3

GLOSSARY

Absolute Advantage—one nation can produce a certain good with higher productivity (or fewer inputs).

Absolute Disadvantage—a nation that produces a certain good with lower productivity when compared to another nation.

Ad-valorem Tariff—a tariff expressed as a fixed percentage of the value of the imported product.

Aggregate Demand (AD)—the total quantity of output demanded at alternative price levels in a given time period.

Aggregate Supply (AS)—the total quantity of output producers are willing and able to supply at alternative price levels in a given time period.

Aggregate Supply Shocks—the supply curve shifts as a result of an unexpected change in the price of a commodity.

Autarky—an economy that is self-sufficient and does not take part in international trade, or severely limits trade with the outside world.

Automatic Stabilizers—the property of taxes and certain government spending that they help stimulate aggregate demand when the economy is declining and hold down aggregate demand as the economy is expanding.

Autonomous Consumption—the portion of consumption that does not change with income.

Autonomous Investment—the portion of investment that is unaffected by changes with income.

Average Cost—Total cost divided by output; a common measure of cost per unit.

Average Fixed Cost—total fixed cost divided by total output.

Average Product (AP)—output divided by input.

Average Propensity to Consume (APC)—the ratio of consumption to income.

Average Propensity to Save (APS)—the ratio of saving to income.

Balance of Payments—a summary record of a country's international economic transactions in a given period of time.

Barrier to Entry—factors that prevent new firms from entering a market.

Budget Deficit—a shortfall of receipts from government expenditure.

Budget Surplus—an excess of receipts over expenditure.

Business Cycle—the rise and fall of the economy from troughs of recessions to peaks in periods of growth and back again.

Capital Account—that part of the balance of payments recording a nation's outflow and inflow of financial securities.

Capital—the stock of equipment and structures used in production; also can refer to the funds to finance the accumulation of equipment and structures.

Central Bank—the institution responsible for the conduct of monetary policy, such as the Federal Reserve in the United States.

Ceteris Paribus—in economic analysis, holding all other factors constant so that the only factor.

Change in Demand—a shift in the demand curve.

Change in Quantity Demanded—movement along the demand curve in response to a change in price.

Civilian Noninstitutionalized Population (CNIP)—people who are participating in the labor force by either working or actively seeking a job.

Classical Aggregate Supply—vertical supply curve; real output is unaffected by changes in prices.

Clearinghouse—the Federal Reserve Bank clears checks for its member banks by debiting and crediting them to different bank accounts.

Coase Theorem—the assumption that private parties can resolve an externality problem on their own through bargaining where government role is limited.

Commodity Money—money that is intrinsically useful and would be valued even if it did not serve as money being studied is allowed to change.

Comparative Advantage—when a nation has either the largest productivity advantage in producing a certain good or service, compared to other nations, or if it has no area productivity advantage, the smallest productivity disadvantage in producing a certain good or service.

Competitive Markets—a situation in which there are many individuals or firms, so that the actions of any one of them do not influence market prices.

Compound Tariff—a tariff that combines both a specific and ad-valorem tariff; it is expressed as a fixed percentage of the value of the imported product plus an amount of currency per unit of the good.

Concave from the Origin—the production possibility curve is concaved because of the law of increasing opportunity cost.

Constant Returns of scale—when a larger firm produces at the same average cost of production of a smaller firm.

Consumption Function—a relationship showing the determinants of consumption, for example, a relationship between consumption and disposable income.

Consumption—goods and services purchased by consumers.

Cost-benefit analysis—a procedure that compares the costs and benefits that is used for making a decision.

Cost-Push Inflation—inflation resulting from shocks to aggregate supply.

Credit—any transactions that either supply a foreign currency or create a demand for the nation's currency in the foreign exchange market.

Cross Rate—in foreign exchange, the price of one currency in terms of another currency in the market of a third country; for example, the exchange rate between Japanese yen and euros would be considered a cross rate in the U.S. market.

Crowding Out Effect—the reduction in investment that results when expansionary fiscal policy raises the interest rate—the market price at which resources are transferred between the present and the future; the return to saving and the cost of borrowing.

Currency—the sum of outstanding paper money and coins.

Current Account—the broadest measure of the trade balance, looking at imports and exports of goods, services, investment income, and unilateral transfers.

Cyclical Unemployment—the unemployment associated with short-run economic fluctuations; the deviation of the unemployment rate from the natural rate.

Debit—any transactions that either supply the nation's currency or create a demand for foreign currency in the exchange market.

Deflation—a decrease in the overall level of prices.

Demand Deposits—assets that are held in banks and can be used on demand to make transactions, such as checking accounts.

Demand-Pull Inflation—inflation resulting from shocks to aggregate demand.

Demand—the relationship between market price and the quantity demanded; it is a line, not a single quantity.

Deposit Creation—process where banks transforms reserves into more money in the money supply.

Depreciation—the reduction in the capital stock that occurs over time because of aging and use; can also be a fall in the value of a currency relative to other currencies in the market for foreign exchange.

Depression—a very severe recession.

Diminishing Marginal Returns—hypothesis that the cost associated with producing one more unit of a good rises as more of that good is produced.

Discount Rate—the interest rate that the Fed charges when it makes loans to banks.

Discouraged Worker—individuals who have left the labor force because they believe that there is little hope of finding a job.

Discretionary Fiscal Spending—those elements of the federal budget not determined by past legislative or executive commitments.

Diseconomies of Scale—when a larger firm produces at a higher average cost of production than a smaller firm.

Disposable Income—income remaining after the payment of taxes.

Double Coincidence of Wants—a situation in which two individuals each have precisely the good that the other wants.

Double Counting—when the same good is counted twice in GDP.

Econometrics—the application of mathematics and statistics to the study of economic and financial data.

Economic Growth—an increase in output or real GDP; an expansion of production possibilities.

Economic Profit—the amount of revenue remaining for the owners of a firm after all of the factors of production have been compensated.

Economics—the study of the allocation of scarce resources among alternative final uses.

Economies of Scale—when a larger firm can produce at a lower average cost of production than a smaller firm, at least up to some level of output.

Economies of Scope—when a firm reduces its unit cost by producing a multiple goods and services.

Efficiency—when a market operates without wasted effort; that is, no excess quantity supplied and no excess quantity demanded at the prevailing price.

Elasticity—the percentage change in a variable caused by a one percent change in another variable.

Embargo—forbids the importing of one or more commodities with a particular nation.

Entrepreneurship—the assembling of resources to produce new or improved products or technologies.

Equilibrium—a state of balance between opposing forces, such as the balance of supply and demand in a market.

Excess Reserves—total reserves minus required reserves.

Exchange Rate—the rate at which a country makes exchanges in world markets.

Expenditure Approach—$GDP = C + I + G + (X - M)$ where C is gross private domestic consumption, I is gross private domestic investment, G is gross public consumption and investment, and X is net exports (exports–imports).

Export—goods and services sold to other countries.

Factors of Production—an input used to produce goods and services; for example, capital or labor.

Federal Funds Rate—the interest rate for interbank reserve loans.

Federal Reserve—the central bank of the United States.

Fiat Money—money that is not intrinsically useful and is valued only because it is used as money.

Final Good—A good that requires no further processing or transformation to be ready for use by consumers, investors, or government.

Firm—any organization that turns input into outputs.

Fiscal Agent—the Federal Reserve Bank takes fiscal responsibilities for the federal government.

Fiscal Policy—the government's choice regarding levels of spending and taxation.

Fixed Exchange Rate—an exchange rate that is set by the central bank's willingness to buy and sell the domestic currency for foreign currencies at a predetermined price.

Floating Exchange Rate—an exchange rate that the central bank allows to change in response to changing economic conditions and economic policies.

Flow Variable—a variable measured as a quantity per unit of time.

Frictional Unemployment—the unemployment that results because it takes time for workers to search for the jobs that best suit their skills and tastes.

Government Expenditure—goods and services bought by the government.

Government-purchases Multiplier—the change in aggregate income resulting from a $1.00 change in government purchases.

Gross Domestic Product (GDP)—the total income earned domestically, including the income earned by foreign-owned factors of production; the total expenditure on domestically produced goods.

Hyperinflation—extremely high inflation.

Import Quota—a legal limit on the amount of a good that can be imported.

Imports—goods and services bought from other countries.

Income Approach—the approach to calculating GDP that involves measuring the income generated to all of the participants in the economy.

Income Effect—the part of the change in quantity demanded that is caused by a change in real income.

Induced Consumption—the portion of consumption that changes with income.

Infant Industry Argument—the argument that tariffs should be used to protect infant industries in hope that they can develop and eventually compete on the world market.

Inflation Rate—the annual percentage rate of increase in the average price level.

Inflation—an increase in the overall level of prices.

Inflationary Gap—the amount by which equilibrium income/output exceeds full employment income/output.

Interest Rate Effect—an increase in interest rates decreases GDP by reducing investments.

Intermediate Good—goods or services purchased for use as input in the production of final goods or services.

International Trade Effect—appreciation of the dollar relative to other currencies reduces net exports by making domestic goods more expensive to foreigners, which reduces GDP.

International Trade—when one nation makes a transaction involving goods and services with another nation.

Investment Multiplier—one divided by marginal propensity to save.

Investment—goods purchased by individuals and firms to add to their stock of capital.

Keynesian Aggregate Supply—horizontal supply curve; a decrease in demand will decrease real output.

Keynesian Cross—a simple model of income determination, based on the idea in Keynes's *General Theory*, which shows how changes in spending can have a multiplied effect on aggregate income.

Labor Force Participation Rate—the percentage of the adult population in the labor force.

Labor Force—those in the population who have a job or are looking for a job.

Law of Demand—ceteris paribus, when the price of a commodity increases, the quantity demanded decreases.

Law of Supply—ceteris paribus, when the price of a commodity increases, the quantity supplied increases.

Liquidity Trap—the portion of the money demand curve that is horizontal; people are willing to hold unlimited amounts of money at some (low) interest rate.

Liquidity—readily convertible into the medium of exchange; easily used to make transactions.

Long Run—the period of time in which a firm may consider all of its inputs to be variable in making its decisions.

Lump-sum Taxes—taxes that do not change when income changes.

M_1, M_2, M_3—various measures of the stock of money; where larger numbers signify a broader definition of money.

Macroeconomics—the aggregated to-down view of the economy, focused on such issues as unemployment, inflation, economic growth, and the balance of trade.

Mandatory Fiscal Spending—spending authorized by permanent law rather than annual appropriations such as Social Security, Medicare, and Medicaid.

Marginal Product—the additional output that can be produced by adding one more unit of a particular input while holding all other inputs constant.

Marginal Propensity to Consume (MPC)—the increase in consumption resulting from a $1.00 increase in disposable income.

Market Equilibrium—occurs when supply equals demand; this is where the market clears.

Market Failure—a situation that occurs when markets become inefficient as a result of participants pursuing their own self-interest.

Maximize Resources—using resources efficiently where one good cannot be produced without giving up the other good.

Medium of Exchange—the item widely accepted in transactions for goods and services; one of the functions of money.

Microeconomics—the study of individual markets, firms, and decision makers.

Monetary Base—the sum of currency and bank reserves.

Monetary Policy—the central bank's choice regarding the supply of money.

Money Multiplier—the increase in the money supply resulting from a $1.00 increase in the monetary base.

Money Supply—the total stock of money in the economy; currency held by the public plus money in accounts in banks.

Money—the stock of assets used for transactions.

Monopoly—when a single seller has all or most of the sales in a given market.

Moral Suasion—a Federal Reserve policy that is used to pursue banks to implement its policies, such as asking them to purchase bonds to reduce the money in circulation.

Municipal Bond—a bond that issued by a local government.

Mutual Interdependence—firms consider the behavior of their competitors when making decisions.

NAIRU—Nonaccelerating inflation rate of unemployment.

National Income Accounting—the accounting system that measures GDP and many other related statistics.

Natural Rate of Unemployment—the steady-state rate of unemployment; the rate of unemployment toward which the economy gravitates in the long run.

Negative Externalities—cost incurred by a third party not participating in the market.

Negative Relationship—a relationship that exists when an increase in X causes a decrease in Y.

Net Domestic Product—gross domestic product minus depreciation.

Net Exports—exports minus imports.

Nonexcludable Goods—impossible to prevent people from benefiting from a commodity, including those who did not pay for it.

Nonrival Goods—one person's consumption of a good does not prevent consumption of the good by others.

Normative Economics—the branch of economics that incorporates value judgments (that is, normative judgments) about what the economy ought to be like or what particular policy actions ought to be recommended to achieve a desirable goal.

Oligopoly—a market with few firms, but more than one.

Open Market Operations—the purchase or sale of government bonds by the central bank for the purpose of increasing or decreasing the money supply.

Opportunity Cost—the cost of a good as measured by the alternative uses that are forgone by producing the good.

Output—the total value of all of the goods and services produced in an economy.

Peak—when real income reaches its highest.

Personal Consumption—goods and services that are consumed by households for domestic use.

Personal disposable income—personal income minus personal income tax.

Positive Economics—the branch of economics that concerns the description and explanation of economic phenomena.

Positive Externalities—benefit incurred by a third party not participating in the market.

Positive Relationship—a relationship that exists when an increase in X causes an increase in Y.

Precautionary Demand—money held for unexpected market transactions or for emergencies.

Price Ceiling—when government sets a price above which more cannot be charged.

Price Elasticity of Demand—the percentage change in quantity demanded divided by the percentage change in price.

Price Floor—when government sets a price below which less cannot be charged.

Price Level—the price of a good or service is what must be given in exchange for the good.

Price Taker—a firm or individual whose decisions regarding buying or selling have no effect on the prevailing market price of a good.

Prime Rate—the interest rate that banks charge their most creditworthy customers.

Private Goods—commodities that are rival and excludable.

Production Function—the mathematical relationship showing how the quantities of the factors of production determine the quantity of goods and services produced.

Production Incentive—when suppliers have an incentive to produce more if they know that the price of the commodity being sold is increasing.

Production Possibility Curves—a graph showing all the possible combinations of goods that can be produced with a fixed amount of resources.

Profit Incentive—as prices increase, suppliers are able to make more money on each unit of commodity that they produce and sell.

Profit—the income of firm owners; total revenue minus total cost.

Protectionist Policy—a policy designed to protect domestic industries by placing restrictions on foreign competition.

Protective Tariff—a tariff imposed to protect domestic firms from import competition.

Public Goods—commodities that are nonrival and nonexcludable.

Purchasing-Power Parity—the doctrine according to which goods must sell for the same price in every country, implying that the nominal exchange rate reflects differences in price levels.

Recession—a sustained period of falling real income.

Recessionary Gap—the amount by which equilibrium income/output falls short of full employment income/output.

Relative Interest Rates—when interest rates increase in one nation while interest rates remain constant in another nation, the nation in which interest rates increased in will become more attractive to the nation who's interest rates remain constant.

Rent—the cost of hiring a machine.

Reserve Ratio—bank reserves divided by total deposits.

Reserve Requirement—regulations imposed on banks by the central bank that specify a minimum reserve-deposit ratio.

Scarcity—not enough resources to meet demand.

Seasonal Unemployment—unemployment due to seasonal changes in employment or labor supply.

Short Run—the period of time in which a firm must consider some inputs to be fixed in making its decisions.

Shutdown Price—the price below which the firm will choose to produce no output in the short run; equal to minimum average variable cost.

Specific Tariff—a tariff specified as an amount of currency per unit of the good.

Speculative Demand—money held for speculative purposes, for later financial opportunities.

Spot Rate—exchange rate which applies to "on the spot" delivery of the currency.

Stagflation—a situation of falling output and rising prices; combination of stagnation and inflation.

Stock Variable—a variable measured as a quantity at a point in time; also shares of ownership in a corporation.

Store of Value—a way of transferring purchasing power from the present to the future; one of the functions of money.

Structural Unemployment—the unemployment resulting from wage rigidity and job rationing.

Substitution Effect—the part of the change in quantity demanded that is caused by substitution of one good for another.

Sunk Cost—expenditure that once made cannot be recovered.

Supervisory Function—the Federal Reserve Bank examines banks to make sure banks are complying with regulations and maintaining financial stability.

Supply—the relationship between market price and the quantity supplied; it is not a line, not a single quantity.

Tariff Quota—no tariff or a lower tariff for an imported good for a certain amount. There is a higher tariff for each quantity above the restricted amount.

Tariff—a tax on imported goods.

Tax Multiplier—the change in aggregate income resulting from a one-dollar change in taxes.

Theory of demand and supply—a model used to determine the price and quantity of a given commodity.

Trade Deficit—when imports exceed exports.

Trade Surplus—

Tradeoffs—occurs when one good must be given up to get another good.

Transaction Cost—the extra costs (beyond the price of the purchase) of conducting a transaction, whether those costs are money, time, or inconvenience.

Transaction Demand—money held for the purpose of making everyday market purchases.

Trough—when real income reaches its lowest.

Underemployment of Resources—using resources inefficiently where one good can be produced more without giving up the other good.

Underground Economy—economic transactions that are hidden in order to evade taxes or conceal illegal activity.

Unemployment Rate—the percentage of those in the labor force who do not have jobs.

Unit of Account—the measure in which prices and other accounting records are recorded; one of the functions of money.

Value Added—the value of a firm's output minus the value of the intermediate goods the firm purchased.

Wages—the cost of hiring a worker.

Wealth Effect—a change in consumer spending caused by a change in the value of owned assets.

X-inefficiency—occurs when firms waste resources where one good could be made more without making less of another usually a result of a lack of competition.

INDEX